LIBRARY/NEW ENGLAND INST. OF TECHNOLOGY

P9-CNE-560

BF 575 .B3 M34 2003

McDaniel, Patricia

Shrinking violets and Caspar
  Milquetoasts

DATE DUE

DEMCO 38-297

NEW ENGLAND INSTITUTE
OF TECHNOLOGY
LIBRARY

Shrinking Violets and Caspar Milquetoasts

The American Social Experience

SERIES

James Kirby Martin
GENERAL EDITOR

Paula S. Fass, Steven H. Mintz, Carl Prince, James W. Reed & Peter N. Stearns
EDITORS

Shrinking Violets and Caspar Milquetoasts

Shyness, Power, and Intimacy in the United States, 1950–1995

PATRICIA A. McDANIEL

NEW ENGLAND INSTITUTE
OF TECHNOLOGY
LIBRARY

NEW YORK UNIVERSITY PRESS
New York and London

1/04

#52386320

NEW YORK UNIVERSITY PRESS
New York and London
www.nyupress.org

© 2003 by New York University
All rights reserved.

Library of Congress Cataloging-in-Publication Data
McDaniel, Patricia (Patricia A.)
Shrinking violets and Caspar Milquetoasts :
shyness, power, and intimacy in the United States, 1950–1995 /
Patricia McDaniel.
p. cm. — (The American social experience series)
Includes bibliographical references and index.
ISBN 0–8147–5677–8 (alk. paper) — ISBN 0–8147–5678–6 (pbk. : alk. paper)
1. Bashfulness—History.   2. Bashfulness—Social aspects—United States.
I. Title.   II. Series.
BF575.B3M34 2003
155.2'32—dc21   2003011890

New York University Press books are printed on acid-free paper,
and their binding materials are chosen for strength and durability.

Manufactured in the United States of America

10 9 8 7 6 5 4 3 2 1

Contents

Acknowledgments

I owe a number of people a great deal of thanks for the intellectual and emotional support and assistance they offered me in the course of writing this book. Peter Stearns, whose work on the history of emotions informs my own, was an enthusiastic supporter of the dissertation on which the book is based. It was largely due to his efforts that the dissertation came to the attention of NYU Press. Others who were instrumental in the dissertation stage of the book include Jeanne Bowlan, Sue Rovi, Jennifer Fuld, Judith Gerson, Richard Williams, Sarah Rosenfield, Patricia Roos, Roberto Franzosi, Jerry and Carroll McDaniel, Mary and Arvin Parrent, and Catherine and Ferrell Rollins.

For friendship, food, fun, and intellectual stimulation during the process of transforming the dissertation into a book, I thank Melissa Green, Nina Mulia and Peter Varadi, Anne Lown, Kitty McDaniel, Francesca and Aedan Raynal, Michelle Boyle, and Tom and Tina Avila. For helpfully spotting a number of typos throughout the manuscript and for research assistance, my thanks to Brian Skinner.

I offer my biggest thanks to Katharine Jones. Her steady friendship, critical eye, good humor, and patient willingness to read and comment upon numerous drafts of the manuscript sustained me throughout the writing process.

CHAPTER ONE

Introduction

A shy maid does not make a pretty picture.

(Bryant 1960, 33)

Timorousness is little understood by women of today, and yet it is a most bewitching charm of womanhood. It can be described as an air of timid fearlessness, of self-conscious modesty and of pretty confusion.

(Andelin 1970, 152)

Timidity and unassertiveness are just as healthy for the average young female as is a thrice-daily dose of cyanide.

(Ellis 1979, 30)

Don't approach the boss like a timid, lukewarm Caspar Milquetoast.

(Simmons 1953, 89)

A clever secretary I know says that she is, among other things, . . . a doormat . . . to her boss.

(MacGibbon 1954, 47)

Successful people are rarely shy, and . . . your own success is the best proof that you have nothing to be shy about.

(Korda 1977, 120)

> Women often find men of the "quiet" type more lovable
> than those who brag.   (Albert 1957, 177)

> Don't wait for a man to notice you. Maybe he, too, is
> holding back out of shyness!"   (Grice 1985, 71)

> Most men are not shy, just not really, really interested if
> they don't approach you. It's hard to accept that, we
> know."   (Fein and Schneider 1995, 27)

The variety of opinions expressed in the quotations above neatly illustrates that attitudes toward shyness vary not only by context—that is, who is shy, and under what circumstances—but also over time. In other words, emotions such as shyness have a history.[1] An emotion that might be considered relatively unremarkable in one era can acquire great significance in another. Throughout most of the twentieth century shyness fell into the former camp: before the late 1970s, shyness was regarded at times with suspicion, but without a great deal of concentrated alarm. Then, in 1977, psychologist Philip G. Zimbardo published the first self-help book devoted entirely to shyness, its causes, consequences, and cures.[2] This marked the discovery of shyness as a serious and wide-ranging social problem in the United States, one that had previously escaped the attention of both the mental health community and the media. Since then, shyness has come under increased scrutiny, and the shy have been offered a dizzying assortment of remedies for their condition, including more self-help books, individual and group therapy sessions, and, recently, drugs such as Prozac, Zoloft, and Paxil.

This book explores why shyness became the object of such concern in the 1970s. Although I investigate attitudes toward shyness as far back as the Middle Ages, I focus my efforts on contrasting popular media representations of shyness in the 1950s with those in the 1970s and the contemporary era (1985–1995). I rely for evidence on a sample of popular self-help, etiquette, and advice books that devote some or all of their contents to the topic of shyness. These books provide a wide-angle view of representations of shyness, since they discuss it in relationship to courtship, marriage, friendship, business success, and psychological health. In addition, the profitability of the self-help genre suggests that self-help books constitute an important popular source of knowledge of the standards and norms that help shape how individuals define, interpret, and express shyness. Through a systematic examination of these texts' treatment of shyness—its causes, consequences, and suggested remedies—I aim to show how and why American cultural standards governing shyness have changed since the 1950s. In doing so, I explore the ideological implications of these standards, analyzing how they reproduce and maintain power differences between and among women and men. Perceived emotional differences between women and men, whites and blacks, have long served as rationales for gender and racial inequities, and shyness has played a prominent role in these rationalizations.

From Shyness to Social Phobia

Although this book focuses on popular media representations of shyness, it is also important to understand the mental health community's perspective on shyness. This perspective is sometimes reflected in self-help books written by "lay people"; in addition, mental health professionals occasionally author popular self-help books on shyness. Since the late 1970s, there has been a steady growth in the number of articles on shyness—its symptoms, causes, consequences, and possible cures—written by mental health professionals (fig. 1.1). There were four English-language articles on shyness published in medical or psychology journals between 1896 and 1970.[3] Between 1971 and 1980, however, 38 articles or books were published; during the period 1981 and 1990, this number leaped to 212. The figure for 1991–1995—106 articles or books—suggests that professional interest in shyness has declined somewhat, but when we add to them articles and books published on the topic of "social phobia," a new, clinical term for shyness, it is clear that this is not so: from 1991 to 1995, 337 articles or books on social phobia appeared (fig. 1.2). These numbers alone show that psychologists and other mental health professionals have grown increasingly interested in claiming

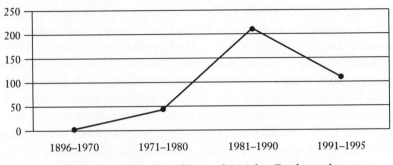

Figure 1.1. Number of Journal Articles, Books, and
Dissertations Indexed in PsycInfo on Shyness

shyness as an important mental health issue that is subject to their authority and intervention.

In staking their claim to shyness, psychologists began by creating a myriad of clinical terms to describe more precisely the emotion they were scrutinizing, as well as particular behaviors associated with it. These terms included reticence, social anxiety, communication avoidance, social phobia, communication apprehension, behavioral inhibition, nonassertiveness, social skills deficit, minimal dating behavior, behavioral inhibition to the unfamiliar, avoidant personality disorder, social communicative anxiety, dispositional speech anxiety, and unwillingness to communicate (Arkowitz 1977; Beatty and Beatty 1976; Buss 1984; Daly and Stafford 1984; Greist 1995; Kagan 1989; Kelly 1982; Leary 1983; McCroskey 1984; Phillips 1984; Plomin and Stocker 1989; Turner, Beidel, and Townsley 1990; Wender and Klein 1981).[4] As suggested by this proliferation of clinical terms, psychologists disagreed about what, exactly, shyness was; some claimed that shyness was a stable personality characteristic (Cheek and Watson 1989; Crozier 1979), while others saw it as a transient, situation-specific trait (Izard and Hyson 1986; Leary 1986). Still others argued that it was both (Asendorpf 1989; Buss 1984; McCroskey 1984; McCroskey and Beatty 1984). In spite of these disagreements, the terms they used to rename shyness shared a common theme: they had a more negative connotation than "shyness." Words like "anxiety," "phobia," and "disorder" implied a degree of deviance or abnormality, a condition that required treatment so that the afflicted could join the ranks of the "normal." Assigning a clinical label to shyness was an important part of the process of constructing shyness as deviant.

Next, psychologists attempted to identify symptoms of shyness, as well as its causes and consequences. A few argued that shyness was an inherited trait (Kagan 1989; Kagan, Reznick, and Snidman 1988), but most focused their energies on explaining the social conditions that fostered it, such as novel or formal situations, or poor parental socialization practices (Asendorpf 1986; Buss 1984; Buss 1986; Daly and Stafford 1984; Eastburg and Johnson 1990; Gilmartin 1985; McCroskey 1984). Symptoms of shyness included nervousness in social encounters, reluctance to engage in social interactions, failure to participate appropriately in social situations, fear of negative evaluation, slow speech patterns, silence, lack of eye contact, and blushing (Arkin, Lake, and Baumgardner 1986, 193; Buss 1980; Daly 1978; Izard and Hyson 1986, 149; Leary 1986; Leary and Schlenker 1981; Pilkonis 1977, 602–3). Psychologists reported that men and women were equally likely to be shy, except during adolescence, when girls reported higher levels of shyness than boys (Crozier 1986; Zimbardo 1986).

To differentiate the shy from the normal more precisely, psychologists developed a number of scales and survey questions to measure shyness both generally and in particular situations. These included the Shyness Survey, the Shyness Scale, MMPI-2 Social Introversion Scale, the Fear Survey Schedule, the Survey of Heterosexual Interactions, Eysenck Personality Questionnaire, the Social Reticence Scale, the Social Avoidance and Distress Scale, the Social Situations Questionnaire, the Interaction Anxiousness Scale, and the Beck Anxiety Inventory (Beck et al. 1988;

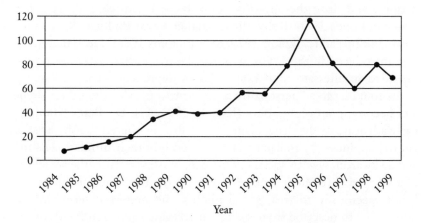

Year

Figure 1.2. Number of Journal Articles, Books, and
Dissertations Indexed in PsycInfo on Social Phobia

Cheek and Buss 1981; Glass and Arnkoff 1989; Jones and Russell 1982; Leary and Kowalski 1993; Seiber and Meyers 1992; Trower, Bryant, and Shaw 1978; Twentyman and McFall 1975; Zimbardo [1977] 1995). The proliferation and variety of these scales reinforced the notion that no instance of shyness was too insignificant to escape the notice and potential intervention of mental health professionals.

Psychologists were unanimous in their assessment that shyness had a largely negative impact on the person who experienced it and on those around her or him: Daly and Stafford (1984, 135–41) identified in the social psychological literature (published in the 1970s and early 1980s) over two hundred negative outcomes associated with shyness, including perceived unattractiveness and incompetence, low self-esteem, alienation, loneliness, conformity, and submission. They also noted that murderers, pedophiles, and child neglecters were more likely to be defined by others as "shy."[5] Other researchers linked shyness to bulimia and other health problems (such as Parkinson's disease) as well as to alcohol and drug abuse (Bell et al. 1995; Otto et al. 1992; Page 1990; Segal and Figley 1985).

Given these dire consequences, psychologists urged a variety of treatments for shyness: social skills training through role playing; systematic desensitization, a method of training the shy to become less sensitive to anxiety-eliciting stimuli by learning relaxation techniques; cognitive restructuring, a technique which taught the shy to replace the irrational thoughts that produce shyness with more reasonable, positive thoughts; rhetoritherapy, a method of improving speech performance in social situations; and drug therapy (Fremouw 1984; Friedrich and Goss 1984; Glass and Shea 1986; Kelly 1984; Kramer 1993; Phillips 1986; Phillips 1991; Phillips and Sokoloff 1979, 389; Pilkonis 1986). Drug therapy was first introduced in the 1990s, with the discovery that Prozac—originally intended to alleviate moderate levels of depression—caused some patients to undergo a "personality transformation," shedding their shyness and becoming more outgoing (Kramer 1993, 11). Dr. Peter Kramer, an early advocate of the drug, claimed that Prozac offered the shy a "shortcut to happiness" by replacing almost overnight their timidity, sensitivity and awkwardness with social confidence, brashness, and "the social skills of a salesman" (Kramer 1993, 26). Paxil is the new drug of choice, marketed specifically to treat social phobia, the preferred term since the mid-1990s to describe shyness. The marketing campaign for Paxil eases the worries of those who might fear the implications of manipulating their personalities through drug treatments. Through the slogan "imagine being allergic to people," Paxil's creators suggest that taking a drug for shyness is of no more consequence than taking a pill for an unpleasant physical ailment.

Mental health professionals advocated treatment for shy women as well as shy men; they did not see shyness as somehow more acceptable or appropriate for women. This was a break with a long-held assumption that shyness was a highly desirable feminine emotion, a laudable sign of modesty and chastity (see chapter 2). Since one of the goals of treatment was to make the shy more assertive, it is possible to regard mental health professionals' approach as particularly empowering for women. After all, assertiveness training was one of the cornerstones of the women's movement, a means of ensuring that women's voices were heard (Henley 1979). In the chapters that follow, I examine more closely this question regarding the liberatory impact of new shyness norms for women and men.

The emergence and plasticity of the term "social phobia"—also known as "social anxiety disorder"—provide a good example of how shyness has been transformed by psychologists from a potentially uncomfortable yet relatively "normal" experience into a pathological one (see Cottle 1999). The malady "social phobia" was first introduced into the psychological mainstream with its inclusion in the 1980 version of the Diagnostic and Statistical Manual of Mental Health Disorders (DSM), the manual mental health professionals use both to diagnose patients and to assure coverage by health insurers (Cottle 1999, 26). The 1980 definition of social phobia suggested that it was an extreme form of what many of us would label shyness: "a persistent, irrational fear of, and compelling desire to avoid, situations in which the individual may be exposed to scrutiny by others and fears that he or she may act in a way that will be humiliating or embarrassing" (American Psychiatric Association 1980, 228).[6] Based on this definition, researchers estimated that two to three percent of the population suffered from social phobia (Cottle 1999, 26). In 1987, after "additional analysis," the definition was altered so that social phobia now sounded like a less extreme form of shyness: "a persistent fear of one or more situations . . . in which the person is exposed to possible scrutiny by others and fears that he or she may do something or act in a way that will be humiliating or embarrassing" (American Psychiatric Association 1987, 243; Cottle 1999, 26). The new definition lost the term "irrational" to describe the type of fear experienced, as well as the terms "compelling desire to avoid" that defined the intensity of fear inspired by social situations. Thus, the DSM suggested that even a mild amount of shyness was unacceptable. This looser definition resulted in a revision of estimates of the numbers of Americans likely to be afflicted with the disorder at some point in their lives: 1 in 8, or thirteen percent (Cottle 1999, 27). After depression and alcoholism, social phobia now ranked as the third most common mental illness in the United States (Cottle 1999, 24).

The 1994 edition of the DSM made an effort to draw a boundary between "common shyness" and social phobia, urging clinicians not to mistake the former for the latter (American Psychiatric Association 1994, 416). Yet descriptions of common features of the disease suggested that there were no clear distinctions between the two. The manual identified social phobics as hypersensitive to criticism, negative evaluation, or rejection; nonassertive; lacking in self-esteem and social skills; and suffering from clammy hands, tremors, and blushing (413); these were the same qualities that psychologists had attributed to shyness in the previous decade. Thus, what psychologists had once considered "shyness" was now officially transformed into a mental disorder. This transformation served the interests of pharmaceutical companies by creating a large population of patients—both children and adults—in need of medication to control their "disease" (Cottle 1999, 28). By underwriting education and outreach campaigns for such groups as the Anxiety Disorders Association of America, pharmaceutical manufacturers made sure that this population was made aware of its need for treatment (Cottle 1999, 28). The transformation of shyness into a serious mental illness also fed and justified psychologists' interest in it, resulting in more research into the disorder (Cottle 1999, 28). More important, the medicalization of shyness made plain the ideal personality that individuals should strive for—outgoing, gregarious, assertive—and reduced tolerance for those who did not measure up to this ideal. Behavior that had once been acceptable was now considered a serious threat to mental health.

Defining Shyness

As the shifting meaning of "social phobia" illustrates, there is no one simple or authoritative definition of shyness. Definitions as well as perceptions of shyness alter over time. Changing perceptions of shyness are often easier to detect than changing definitions, as those who employ the term often fail to define it, assuming that others already possess a commonsense understanding of the term. This was certainly the case in the self-help and etiquette books that I examined for evidence of the emotional culture of shyness. As a result, I often relied on the authors' choice of particular synonyms, such as bashfulness, timidity, meekness, modesty, reticence, withdrawal, taciturnity, and inhibition to provide a sense of the meaning of shyness in a particular age.

As the variety of these synonyms suggest, self-help authors treated shyness as an emotion, a set of behaviors, and a personality trait. Their advice about shyness was aimed at those who suffered from feelings of shyness in particular situations and, as result, acted shy, as well as those who considered themselves to have a shy personality—that is, they felt and acted shy most of the time. Authors offered up "non-shy" feelings and behavior, such as extroversion, friendliness, gregariousness, and boldness, as a counterpoint to shy feelings and behavior; these, too, provided evidence of what shyness meant in a particular time period. Because of this contrast between shyness and other emotions and behaviors in my sources, in the pages that follow I discuss not just shyness, but behaviors and emotions that are considered to be the opposite of shyness. This provides a broad view of how shyness relates to other feelings and social behaviors that might be called for in social situations.

Although the point of this book is to highlight the variety of ways that shyness has been conceptualized and defined over time, it seems important to offer a tentative, "common sense" definition of "shyness," as it might be understood by twenty-first-century readers. Bearing in mind that this definition does not necessarily apply in all time periods, I loosely define "shyness" as feelings of fear or discomfort in social situations.

The Socially Constructed Nature of Emotions

From a social-constructionist perspective, emotions are social experiences, or processes, rather than visceral sensations that happen to our unwitting bodies.[7] Shyness and other emotions are learned in social relationships, experienced in connection to others, and interpreted in reference to one's relationship to others (Averill 1984, 25; Denzin 1984, 51–52; Hochschild 1979; Lynch 1990, 5; McCarthy 1989, 65; Perinbanayagam 1989, 76). While acknowledging that bodily sensations have some role to play in the meaning of emotion, social constructionists focus their attention on the social meanings of these sensations. According to Shott (1979, 1321–22), since the bodily sensations accompanying various emotions are often quite similar, bodily clues do not enable individuals to differentiate between different emotions: "What is required, in addition, is the belief that some emotion is the most appropriate explanation for a state of arousal." Thus, one experiences an emotion such as shyness when one interprets a social situation as warranting a feeling of shyness; the physiological sensation of blushing that may take place does not cause but rather offers proof of the feeling (Denzin 1983, 403; Shott 1979, 1321–22). Knowledge about whether or not a particular social situation calls for shyness or another emotion is supplied by a society's "emotional culture" or "emotionology," the historically variable cultural conventions and standards that govern the experience and expression of emotion (Gordon 1989, 115; Stearns and Stearns 1985, 813).[8]

At the heart of emotional cultures are feeling and display rules. Feeling rules are norms that establish standards regarding the proper extent, direction, and duration of emotion (Hochschild 1979, 564; see also Averill 1984, 31), while display rules set limits on the outward expression of behaviors associated with emotion (Ekman 1971, 225). For example, contemporary feeling rules dictate that a feeling of shyness (or "stage fright") is warranted when speaking in front of a group; display rules permit a response of nervous laughter or stuttering but prohibit a lapse into complete silence. In an effort to conform to feeling and display rules, individuals often engage in "emotion work" or "emotion management," conscious bodily, expressive, or cognitive techniques that aim to produce appropriate emotions or suppress inappropriate ones (Hochschild 1979, 561). The public speaker experiencing shyness might try to control or suppress the feeling by slowing her breathing, smiling, or by envisioning the members of the audience in their underwear.

People also perform emotion work for others.[9] In doing so, they do not simply help others to produce or suppress particular emotions. Emotion work in this context involves building self-esteem, understanding and managing emotions, and providing emotional support—in other words, "doing intimacy" (Duncombe and Marsden 1993, 221; James 1989). Women often do this work. Hochschild (1983, 165) explains that "especially in the American middle-class, women tend to manage feeling more because they depend on men for money, and one of the various ways of repaying their debt is to do extra emotion work—*especially emotion work that affirms, enhances, and celebrates the well-being and status of others*" (emphasis in original). Thus, in interpersonal relationships, women tend to smile and laugh more in efforts to build intimacy, and to act as "conversational cheerleaders" to sustain intimacy (Blumstein and Schwartz 1983; Cline and Spender 1987, 97–98; Hochschild 1983, 168). Various emotions are invoked or suppressed in performing emotion work to create and sustain intimacy, including shyness. As I show in the chapters that follow, prevailing emotion norms for women and men will influence how exactly shyness is managed in the course of performing emotion work.

Emotional cultures are conveyed through "language, rituals, art forms, and other publicly available symbolic vehicles of meaning" produced by a variety of individuals and institutions (Gordon 1989, 115). The popular-print media has played a particularly important role in producing and maintaining the emotional culture of shyness. Long before shyness was transformed into a matter of mental health, it was subject to rules of etiquette, politeness, and civility. In the West, this tradition dates to the Middle Ages, when moralists writing pedagogical and pastoral literature for and about aristocratic and peasant women urged them to display their "natural" shyness in the company of men (Casagrande 1992, 85, 100). In the twentieth- and twenty-first-century United States, authors of etiquette and self-help books have assumed responsibility for dispensing advice about the management and display of shyness in social situations. Until the 1970s, these self-help authors were usually "lay people"—nonpsychologists—who discussed shyness as just one of many issues related to success, character building, courtship, and personality improvement. In the late 1970s, lay people were joined by psychologists, who, for the first time, wrote a number of popular texts devoted entirely to shyness and its "cure."[10] These books, along with those written by lay people, provided ordinary members of society with commonsense knowledge of the cultural norms and conventions that governed the expression and display of shyness.

Ideology and Emotional Culture

Emotional cultures contain ideology—meaning constructed and conveyed by symbolic forms that serves to establish and sustain relations of power (Thompson 1990, 7).[11] Ideologies produce a "set of meanings that constitute the common sense of a society" (Fiske 1987, 6). This "common sense" provides a framework for making sense of relations of domination and subordination; it tells us who we are, what men and women are like, what is good, right, and just, and what is possible or impossible (Therborn 1980, 18; Williams 1977, 110). It is not "brainwashing" so much as "the tendency of public discourse to make some forms of experience readily available to consciousness while ignoring or suppressing others" (Lears 1985, 577). Ideology operates through five main practices: legitimation, the defense and justification of power relations as worthy of respect; dissimulation, practices which conceal or deny power relations; unification, the process of establishing a collective identity for individuals regardless of their differences; fragmentation, the process of dividing individuals who might otherwise collectively challenge a dominant power; and reification, the naturalization of power relations as ahistorical and permanent (Thompson 1990, 61–66). These practices may overlap, and some may, at different points in time, be more successful than others in helping to sustain relations of domination (Thompson 1990, 60–61).

The power relations most clearly implicated in the emotional culture of shyness are gender, race, and class relations, reproduced and maintained in those arenas in which individuals live out their daily emotional and physical lives—the home, the workplace, and the peer group (Thompson 1990, 9). As I show in chapter 2, shyness has traditionally been regarded as a "feminine" emotion, a sign of modesty and passivity and a justification for women's absence from positions of power. At the same time, the meanings associated with shyness have also been used to uphold racial and class hierarchies among women and men. In the antebellum South, for example, shyness was one of the many qualities thought to distinguish privileged white women from black women slaves. This emotional distinction helped to justify slaveholders' refusal to grant black women the protected status of "True Woman" (Jewell 1992, 36; Leslie 1988, 19; Morton 1988, 41; Mullings 1996, 112–13; Scott 1970, 16).

A form of shyness—"reserve"—has also played a role in supporting class hierarchies. In the eighteenth century, the middle classes rested their claim to social superiority on their ability to display a graceful reserve in public, in contrast to the "awkward stiffness" of the working classes. Throughout this book, I examine the ways in which the more contemporary emotional culture of shyness supports and justifies these kinds of unequal gender, class, and race relationships by naturalizing, defending, and concealing men's institutional power over women, dividing whites from blacks, and separating women and men into two dissimilar groups.

I also investigate how the emotional culture of shyness *challenges* relationships of power. Ideologies are constantly contested and disrupted, both in "articulate and concerted attacks, and . . . in the mundane symbolic exchanges of everyday life" (Thompson 1990, 68). To reduce their potential for disruption, ideologies often incorporate and modify or co-opt these critiques (Williams 1977, 112). The contemporary psychological perspective on shyness can be regarded as a challenge to gender ideologies. Psychologists urge both women and men to replace shyness with asserdiveness, behavior that challenges an important source of male power: men's monopoly on public speech. I explore this and other challenges to gender, race, and class ideologies, as well as the ways in which these ideologies minimize the subversive potential of such challenges.

Emotional Culture and Emotional Experience

While ideologies about emotion provide important insights into how emotions may be used to enforce hierarchical relationships, their significance is contingent upon the close correspondence between a society's emotional culture and the emotional experience of individuals. Some evidence for such a link can be found in Sommers's (1988, 28) study of young adults' evaluations of and experiences with both positive and negative emotions. They tended to experience more often those emotions that they valued more highly, and to experience more rarely those emotions that they valued less. This is not to suggest, however, that emotional cultures necessarily *cause* emotional experiences, since individuals are always capable of breaking feeling rules (Coulter 1989, 45). Instead, an emotional culture is a resource on which individuals can draw to determine the intelligibility, rationality, and appropriateness of emotional experience (Coulter 1989, 46). It is a "tool kit" of symbols, rituals, and commonsense worldviews that facilitates particular understandings and expressions of emotions (Swidler 1986, 277). This tool kit contains resources that individuals may choose to ignore; for example, an individual may be aware that shyness is prohibited or devalued, but may value the feeling of shyness nonetheless.

Moreover, some resources available now will only be widely used in the future—there may be a time lag between the availability of emotional symbols and rituals and their acceptance (Stearns and Stearns 1988, 7). The existence of "rule breakers" and time lags points to the importance of not mistaking emotional standards for emotional experience. Although I focus primarily on emotional standards in this book, where possible, I cite empirical evidence to show the impact of these standards— that is, how individuals actually behaved.

Why Emotional Cultures Change: The Historical Context of the 1950s, 1970s, 1980s, and 1990s

Like rules in general, the norms and conventions that govern emotion are subject to change. Economic changes and shifts in gender and sexual norms are particularly important in explaining shifts in the emotional culture of shyness.[12] The 1950s was generally a period of affluence for many Americans: until the end of the decade, unemployment was low, consumer spending was high, and industries expanded to meet the rising demand for durable goods (Jezer 1982, 120). At the same time, bureaucracies and the service sector were growing in size and importance. The white-collar workers employed by bureaucracies and service industries were required to handle people rather than things (Mills 1953, 65). Thus, friendliness, courtesy, and attentiveness to others were highly marketable qualities; indeed, according to Mills (1953, 187), this white-collar personality diffused throughout society, becoming the model for social interactions of all sorts. To the extent that an emotion such as shyness was considered to interfere with one's ability to effectively handle people, we would expect there to have been little tolerance for shyness in the 1950s' workplace.

The 1950s are usually characterized as a period of bland conformity to traditional gender and sexual practices and ideologies among middle-class whites. On the one hand, there is a great deal of evidence to support this characterization: the low average age of marriage,[13] the dramatic growth in the birth rate,[14] and the pervasive cultural promotion and endorsement of the domestic role for middle-class white women (Friedan 1963) and the breadwinner role for middle-class white men (Ehrenreich 1983, 14–26). On the other hand, some historians have suggested that despite the apparent hegemony of the domestic ideal, competing discourses were in play. For example, in her analysis of mass circulation magazines from the period, Meyerowitz (1994) found evidence to suggest that in addition to celebrating white women's domestic role, the popular media regarded with approval white women's work outside the home in paid and nonpaid public service work. The two competing visions of proper womanhood were frequently reconciled by using evidence of femininity and domesticity—such as traditional feminine appearance and motherhood—to legitimate white women's public achievements, thus reassuring readers that "conventional gender distinctions and heterosexuality remained intact even as women competed successfully in work, politics and sport" (Meyerowitz 1994, 234).

Similarly, Breines (1992) argued that part of the reason there was so much emphasis placed on white middle-class women's domesticity was precisely because the possibilities for change existed as they never had before. Indicators like white women's growing labor force participation,[15] prosperity, the expansion of higher education, and an increased emphasis on sexual pleasure for married women[16] held out the possibility for white women's autonomy and equality (Breines 1992, 11). It was anxiety over the liberating possibilities of these changes that helped account for the rather vocal defense of traditional (white middle-class) femininity (Breines 1992, 11).

A fear of homosexuality also underlay the 1950s defense of traditional white middle-class femininity. The congressional crusade launched in 1950 to purge Communist spies and "sexual perverts" from government employment incited a widespread fear of a "homosexual menace"—a fear bolstered by scientist Alfred Kinsey's startling revelations that homosexual activity was fairly common, particularly among white men[17] (D'Emilio 1983, 41; Kinsey 1953; Kinsey, Pomeroy, and Martin 1948). Armed with scientific "proof" of the pervasiveness of the problem, state and local governments as well as private employers participated in the witch hunts; all told, 20 percent of the labor force faced security investigations aimed at screening out homosexuals, and thousands were refused employment or fired on suspicion of being homosexual (D'Emilio 1983, 46). For both women and men, any deviation from prescribed gender practices called one's sexuality into question; for women in particular, the physical markers of clothing and hairstyle were regarded as the primary indicators of sexuality: women wearing men's clothes or sporting "mannish" haircuts were suspected of being lesbians (Nestle 1981; Penn 1993). Stereotypical feminine and masculine behavior offered proof of heterosexuality, thus reassuring an anxious public that changes in women's roles did not spell the end of heterosexuality and its attendant power relations (Blount 1996; Penn 1993). In this climate, we would expect shyness to offer additional proof of femininity, and thus be sanctioned for white women and prohibited for white men.

Black women were less able to live up to the 1950s' domestic ideology, since work outside the home was often essential to their own and their families' survival. Black men's high rates of unemployment and low wages meant that black women could not afford to confine their labor to the home.[18] Within their own communities, their work in the paid labor force was often highly valued and respected, as were the traits of assertiveness and strength that were assumed to be an integral component of this tradition of work (Jones 1985, 268–74; Meyerowitz 1994, 233). However, some black commentators began to question the value of these traits when the number of black households headed by women began to rise (Frazier 1948).[19] Thus, we would expect shyness for black women, too, to offer important proof of femininity, a sign that they respected black men's rightful position as head of the household.

Events of the 1960s, particularly the sexual revolution and the women's movement, resulted in dramatic changes in attitudes toward intimate heterosexual relationships and "proper" gender behaviors in the 1970s. Highlights of the sexual revolution included the introduction of the birth control pill into the consumer market in 1960; the decriminalization of all forms of private sexual contact between consenting adults in Illinois in 1962; the opening of the first singles bar in New York City in 1964; the abolition of curfews and visitor restrictions at some colleges at the end of the 1960s; nudity on stage and in mainstream movies; the growing visibility of pornography; more frequent portrayals of gay and lesbian life in the mass media; and the adoption of the nation's first no-fault divorce law in California in 1970 (D'Emilio 1983, 129; Mintz and Kellogg 1988, 208–9). For young women and men, both black and white, dating was no longer a means of garnering prestige, but simply another form of social contact (Modell 1989, 291). Dating also became less common among younger teenagers.[20] The rules governing sexual behavior while dating had changed as well: during the 1950s, premarital sex was likely to occur only among engaged couples; by the early 1970s, the majority of young people no longer valued sexual abstinence while dating, and sex came to be a "normal" part of even casual dating (Bell and Coughey 1980; Chafe 1995, 436–37; Modell 1989, 314). Given the traditional link between women's shyness and sexual modesty, it is likely that in the more sexually expressive 1970s, women's shyness would have been more stigmatized than before.

The women's movement also influenced Americans' changing conceptions of proper gender behaviors. Ending women's silence was the centerpiece of the movement: feminists made headlines by picketing the Miss America contest, storming meetings of professional associations to demand equal employment opportunities, calling a national strike, and sitting in at the editorial offices of *Ladies Home Journal* to force changes in the magazine's content and staff (Chafe 1972, 227; Echols 1989, 196). Consciousness-raising taught women to uncover the political nature of personal experiences of oppression, and assertiveness training gave women the tools to verbally demand and defend their rights (Echols 1989, 83; Henley 1979, 6). The impact of the movement was relatively profound, since even women who rejected feminists as too extreme were likely to support feminist positions on day-care centers, abortion, employment for women, and domestic equality (Chafe 1995, 434). In embracing feminist ideas regarding personal fulfillment, control over their bodies, and freedom from domestic responsibilities, these women rejected the 1950s ideal of the "happy homemaker." With so much emphasis on letting women's voices be heard, women's shyness might have been regarded as a sign of the oppressive past.

Men, too, were the objects of a "liberation" movement in the 1970s. Male liberationists argued that men as well as women had an interest in redefining gender roles. Society's expectation that men be the primary breadwinners resulted in dissatisfying, unequal relationships with women. The competitiveness of the workplace, coupled with homophobia and fear of intimacy also meant that men were starved of emotionally satisfying relationships with other men (Farrell 1974; Fasteau 1974, 6–19). In an effort to change these patterns, male liberationists actively supported women's bid for equality by establishing a men's support network for the National Organization of Women and voicing their support for feminist causes (Connell 1995, 207). They also organized consciousness-raising groups in an effort to learn to be more open, honest, and intimate with one another (Connell 1995, 207; Delaney 2000). In an environment that encouraged free and frank discussions between men, men's shyness might have been regarded as a mark of repression.

The growth of the psychology profession also played an important role in the emotional culture of shyness in the 1970s. In 1940, fewer than three hundred members of the American Psychological Association were clinical psychologists; by 1970, approximately twenty thousand psychiatrists were ministering to one million people on an outpatient basis, while ten thousand psychologists were providing some kind of counseling service (Herman 1995, 262). Much of this growth had to do with the gradual acceptance by the general public of the concept of using psychotherapy to cope with "normal" or everyday problems, rather than reserving it for the mentally ill (Herman 1995, 262). Thus, Americans grew accustomed not only to the authority of the psychological profession, but also to the notion that talking about one's feelings or emotions was essential to mental health. Both had implications for the emotional culture of shyness. The status of the profession ensured that psychological ideas increasingly shaped the emotional culture of shyness, while the link between communication and mental health may have increased concern about shyness, an emotion whose many symptoms included the failure to speak.

The 1980s and 1990s were marked by conflict between liberals and conservatives over the meaning and purpose of a variety of American institutions, including the family, law, politics, education, and the arts (Nolan 1996). Conservatives—often referred to as "the New Right"— saw themselves as challenging the counterculture of the 1960s, with its "situation-ethics morality in which the immediate concern about your personal needs outweighs any obligation to others" (Thomas 1995, 12). They considered abortion, sex education in schools, teenage sexuality, and gay rights to be incompatible with the traditional "family" values they held dear (Herman 1997, 137–69; Oden 1993, p. 1978). Many blamed feminists for encouraging women to enter the workforce, leading to a growing divorce rate,[21] and held the sexual revolution responsible for the spread of AIDS, teenage pregnancy, and sexually transmitted diseases (Bondi 1996, 380, 399; Mintz and Kellogg 1988, 234).

The political power of the New Right was made clear in the 1980 election. Ronald Reagan, a Republican sympathetic to the New Right's position on abortion, school prayer, and homosexuality, gained control of the presidency, while conservative legislators regained control of the Senate. They attempted to ban abortion, deny government benefits to homosexuals, prohibit the use of certain forms of contraceptives, and cut off funding for schools whose curriculum ignored or denied the existence of fundamental differences between the sexes (D'Emilio and Freedman 1988, 349).

The 1980s also featured a backlash against feminism in the mainstream media (Faludi 1991, 76). Newspapers and magazines offered women a distressing picture of the "gains" won by the women's movement: a "man shortage" for women who delayed marriage past their twenties; an "infertility epidemic" among women who postponed childbearing; and a plunge into near-poverty for women who took advantage of no-fault divorce laws (Faludi 1991, 3). Despite the fact that the studies on which these statements were based proved to be flawed, the retractions made few headlines, and the sentiment fostered by the original studies—that women's efforts to achieve equality with men were responsible for women's unhappiness—lingered throughout much of the 1980s (Bondi 1996, 398; Faludi 1991, 12).

Cultural conflicts between liberals and conservatives continued to flare up in the 1990s. The 1992 presidential campaign featured debates over family values,[22] the proper role of women in society,[23] and homosexuality.[24] With Democrat Bill Clinton's election to the presidency, these debates grew fiercer as he appointed a number of women to high-level positions within his administration, overturned the "gag rule" that had prohibited federally funded family planning centers from discussing abortion with clients, and worked to remove the ban on gays in the military (Woodard 1996, 134). His presidential style—emotional, empathetic, and physically demonstrative with men as well as women—was also evocative of 1970s' male liberationist ideas regarding the need for a more emotional form of masculinity. When conservative Republicans gained control of both houses of Congress in 1994, they did so, in part, by capitalizing on the challenge they posed to Clinton's "liberal" policies, summarized in the "Contract with America," a pledge to support conservative ideas signed by Republican congressional candidates (*Encyclopedia of Contemporary American Culture* 2001, 31). Given the "culture wars" of the 1980s and 1990s, we could expect a mix of "conservative" and "liberal" views of shyness in this time period. The "conservative" view would emphasize shyness as a highly appropriate, feminine emotion for women, and highly inappropriate for men; the "liberal" view would see women's and men's shyness as incompatible with modern, expansive ideas of femininity and masculinity.

Overview of the Book

In this book, I focus primarily on adult shyness, because I am interested in how adults, who are presumed to be fully functioning members of society, are expected to behave. Advice to parents of shy children was sometimes less illuminating about the emotional culture of shyness than advice to shy adults because children's shyness was often regarded as a relatively "normal" stage that the child would outgrow. However, I do discuss advice to parents of shy children where it is appropriate, highlighting consistencies as well as differences with advice to shy adults.

In chapter 2, I provide a broad overview of the history of shyness in the West from the Middle Ages to the early part of the twentieth century. Beginning in chapter 3, I turn my attention to the last half of the twentieth century, examining shyness standards in three interpersonal arenas: heterosexual relationships (chapters 3 and 4), the workplace (chapter 5), and platonic relationships (chapter 6). Due to limitations in the available evidence (see appendix A), the majority of my discussion is limited to white middle-class shyness norms. However, in chapter 4, I do examine African American shyness norms in the context of heterosexual relationships, a particularly important arena for understanding the highly charged debate surrounding the meaning of shyness for African American women and men.

In appendix A, I explain how I selected and analyzed the self-help, etiquette, and advice books, child-rearing manuals, and magazine articles that provided evidence of shyness norms. Appendix B lists reference information for each of these books and magazine articles, and is divided into three sections that correspond to the time periods in which each book or article was published (1950–1960, 1970–1980, or 1985–1995). The bibliography contains reference information for scholarly sources as well as popular sources that were not part of the sample of self-help books and magazine articles.

CHAPTER TWO

The Emotional Culture of Shyness from the Middle Ages to the Early Twentieth Century

> The dutie of the husband is, to deale with many men: and of the wives, to talke with fewe. The dutie of the husband is, to bee entermeddling: and of the wife to bee solitarie and withdrawne. The dutie of the man is, to bee skilfull in talke: and of the wife, to boast of silence.
>
> —Robert Cleaver,
> *A Godly Forme of Householde Government* (1598)

In order to appreciate the significance of the emotional culture of shyness in the last half of the twentieth century, it is important to understand the history that precedes it. In this chapter, I use existing historical research to piece together an outline of the shifting cultural norms and conventions governing shyness for Western women and men from medieval Europe to early twentieth century America. In doing so, I demonstrate the socially constructed nature of shyness and, more importantly, highlight the ideological content of shyness norms, that is, how they have often been used to support hierarchies of gender, class, and race. Given that historians have not focused a great deal of attention on shyness, I frequently had to "read for" this history of shyness in their discussions of behavior commonly linked to or contrasted with shyness, such as silence, timidity, and speech. What follows is therefore not an exhaustive or exclusive discussion of shyness, but rather a history of attitudes toward a range of behaviors and emotions that bear some relationship to shyness. A good portion of this history relies upon images of women and men as set down by authors of didactic literature (e.g., courtesy and etiquette books),[1] texts that construct, reproduce, and disseminate normative conceptions of appropriate behavior. Thus, in keeping with the rest of the book, my focus is on what the available sources suggest about prevailing attitudes toward shyness, not on women's and men's actual experience of it, although the two are ultimately linked (see chapter 1).

Medieval Codes of Conduct

In medieval (western) Europe,[2] shyness—defined as bashfulness, timidity, and fear of others—was regarded as a particularly female character trait, a consequence of women's instinctive, "animal" natures (Casagrande 1992, 88, 91). Male clerics and moralists encouraged women of all ranks to cultivate their inborn shyness, since it acted as a protective veil that guarded their virtue;[3] without it, a woman was no better "than one of those wild animals which grow accustomed to the company of men and become tame, letting themselves be petted and stroked" (Giles of Rome 1607, 342, cited in Casagrande 1992, 85). Women had to work at their bashfulness, however, since the same animal nature that made them shy was also thought to make them naturally inquisitive, talkative, and argumentative (Casagrande 1992, 98). Thus, they were repeatedly accused in sermons and treatises of abusing the gift of speech through their gossip and nagging (Casagrande 1992, 98; Hallissy 1993, 75–88; Schein 1994, 148). In addition to sowing domestic disharmony, this love of talk threatened women's chastity, since it signaled an easily corruptible interest in the outside world (Casagrande 1992, 99; Hallissy 1993, 62). To guard against the corrupting possibilities of speech, women were encouraged to emulate the Virgin Mary, a woman whose silence—the Bible revealed that she spoke no more than four times—was considered the ultimate sign of her purity and goodness (Hallissy 1993, 61). A woman's closed mouth signaled a lack of interest in the social world of men, and control of her sexual appetite.

Proper feminine shyness was not limited to silence, but also encompassed a woman's gestures and movements. Women were told to keep their bodies nearly immobile, in the manner characteristic of a frightened animal: "She should not laugh, but smile without showing her teeth; she should not look straight ahead, wide-eyed, but look down, with eyelids half-closed; she should not sob, wring her hands, or shake her head, but weep in silence" (Casagrande 1992, 95). When allowed or required to speak, she was instructed to follow the rule of *taciturnitas*: to speak only when necessary, in a quiet tone, and in moderation (Casagrande 1992, 100). She was to choose her words carefully, so that they complemented the mood of the speaker, expressing joy with the joyous, and seriousness with the serious; in other words, she was to be a "tuning fork," vibrating to the tune of others (Hallissy 1993, 63). She was not to communicate her own opinions or feelings, but only to reflect others' back to them, thus insuring that her speech would remain inoffensive and nonconfrontational.

Women's silence played such an important role in the medieval feminine ideal because it guaranteed male authority by ensuring that "nothing . . . ar[o]se as equivalent to his word" (Brooke-Rose 1986, 310; see also Laskaya 1995, 41). For aristocratic women, prohibitions on speech and movement also reflected their ultimate value as property that guaranteed the continuation of the male hierarchy. During the tenth century, western European noble families replaced "horizontal" lines of kinship that grouped together two or three generations of male and female blood relations with "vertical" lines of kinship organized in terms of the male line only.[4] Thus, ensuring proper paternity became very important to husbands: "The worst danger was that a wife might be made pregnant by a man other than her husband, and children of a blood different from that of the master might one day bear the name of his ancestors and succeed to their inheritance" (Duby 1983, 47). Since women were thought to be constitutionally disposed toward "the sin of the flesh," it was the husband's duty to exercise strict control over his wife's sexuality (Duby 1983, 47). This was made difficult by the fact that in aristocratic households, the wife faced many potential "temptations" in the sense that she regularly interacted with many men: she welcomed the guests, supervised the male servants, and ran the household (Duby 1983, 47). The family honor depended upon her conducting herself properly with these men. By idealizing shyness in women, men shifted some of the burden of policing women's sexual behavior to women themselves.

Attitudes toward male shyness in the middle ages were less definitive. Men were not considered to be shy by nature. However, characteristics associated with shyness, including submission and silence, were expected of most medieval men, since they were required to obey their superiors in the social hierarchy; in addition, Christian ideals stressed the spiritual value of meekness and humility (Laskaya 1995, 16, 25). But these ideals coexisted with the expectation that men command and control others, particularly their wives, through violence if necessary (Laskaya 1995, 26). The bold, heroic warrior was a consistent theme of medieval litera-ture, a man who fearlessly conquered and subdued others (Laskaya 1995, 15). Shyness, conceptualized as some degree of fear of others, would be at odds with this version of medieval masculinity.

Troubadours extolling the virtues of *fin amour,* or "courtly love," of-fered aristocratic women and men an alternative to ideals of masculinity and femininity based on brute force or Christian meekness and silent submission. The game of courtly love was played between a married no-blewoman and an unmarried knight of her household; in it, the knight attempted to win the heart of his chosen lady through noble acts, brav-ery, loyalty, and self-sacrifice (Duby 1992, 250). In certain courts, the knight's cultivation of wit and manners won more admiration than his skill at arms (Barber 1970, 88). Thus, aristocratic masculinity came to encompass a degree of verbal sophistication as a mark of status, a way for the knight to demonstrate his distance from his ruder fellows. Shyness, if ever there had been a place for it, was further removed from the ideal of aristocratic male behavior.

The lady he was hoping to impress was permitted to drop some of her reserve to engage in conversation with her knight; in fact, her ability to converse pleasantly and amiably was one of the ways she demonstrated that she was worthy of his love (Bornstein 1983, 38). Yet she was still cautioned against talking or laughing too loudly, or speaking too much (Bornstein 1983, 36, 41). A degree of silence remained a necessary aspect of her behavior. This slightly altered ideal of femininity was not created with the goal of undermining the husband's authority over his wife. In-stead, the values promoted by courtly love supported the political needs of the lord of the castle, who required self-sacrifice and faithfulness in his knights, the very same gifts that knights were encouraged to offer to their chosen ladies (Duby 1992, 261). Aristocratic women gained some benefit from the game of courtly love, since it idealized and exalted them (Bornstein 1983, 41), but it exacted a steep price, for it ultimately made women objects of sexual pleasure to be exchanged between men (symbolically if not literally). For precisely this reason, Christine de Pisan, a contemporary of the male poets who idealized courtly love, warned women against it, calling it *folle* (crazy) rather than *fin* (fine) *amour* (Bornstein 1983, 44).

Changing Renaissance Ideals

The flowering of court culture during the Renaissance brought with it a greater emphasis on more refined social skills for men at court in a variety of situations, not simply when wooing ladies. The hot-tempered, emotionally expressive medieval knight was transformed into the more "civilized" courtier (Curtin 1985, 398–99; see also Elias 1978, 201, 215–17). To be successful, the courtier had to combine skill at arms with grace, agreeableness, refinement, and, above all, conversational skill. Elegant speech was a mark of sophistication and civility, a way for male courtiers to win material rewards from a king or prince (Scaglione 1991, 256). For those gentlemen who were unsure of the new rules, courtesy books provided help: they offered detailed instructions on proper social behavior, including the art of conversation, for aspiring courtiers. Silence and timidity were generally frowned upon by authors of courtesy texts. Instead, they stressed that the gentleman must be both willing to speak—to "pay his share of the conversational bill"—and be adept at appearing comfortable and at ease when doing so (Anglo 1977, 41; Della Casa [1558] 1990, 22, 47).

Since conversation was best performed as a dialogue, men turned to women to share in verbal displays of wit and manners; however, old fears about the sexual significance of women's speech circumscribed their role.[5] Her reputation under constant threat, the lady at court was advised by authors of courtesy books to "defend herself through a calculated rhetoric of words and gestures" (Jones 1987, 43). Her rhetorical defense consisted of tempering affability with modesty: she had to be willing to engage with men in conversations on potentially scandalous topics such as love while firmly rejecting any overtly sexual language or behavior (Jones 1987, 45; Scaglione 1991, 410). Maintaining this delicate balance no doubt mitigated women's potential to disrupt the male-dominated court, for it ensured that they would ultimately curb their tongues to avoid the label "whore."

Women outside of court culture negotiated different demands. On the one hand, they could not successfully fulfill their economic duties to their families if they were too demure in the marketplace (Amussen 1988, 119). Yet if they took too much verbal license with their husbands or neighbors, they faced harsh censure. An aggressively outspoken woman was labeled a "scold," legally defined in England as "a troublesome and angry woman who, by her brawling and wrangling amongst her neighbours, doth break the public peace, and beget, cherish and increase public discord" (Thomas 1971, 528).[6] Along with women who beat or cuckolded their husbands, the scold was a stock figure in sermons and literature addressed to women (Amussen 1988, 103). All three female figures were perceived as dangerous because they threatened to disrupt, and possibly even invert, a hierarchical social order that depended upon women's submissiveness (Henderson and McManus 1985, 62; Jardine 1983, 106).

To minimize this danger, scolds were subject to a number of punishments, sometimes meted out by a mob of angry men. These included the cucking stool,[7] to which a woman was strapped and then dunked over her head in a river, stagnant pond, or cesspool; and the scold's bridle or "brank," an instrument that locked the woman's head inside an iron cage fitted with a two- to three-inch-long metal gag, sometimes studded with spikes, that depressed her tongue (Amussen 1988, 103; Barstow 1994, 28; Boose 1991, 205; Fletcher 1995, 273).[8] Both punishments involved a noisy public display, with the accused women carted through the town and subject to jeers; however, the woman wearing the scold's bridle suffered additional physical pain, as she was yanked through town by a chain affixed to the bridle, every jerk disturbing the gag and threatening to break her teeth, shatter her jawbone, or lacerate her tongue (Boose 1991, 205). If this form of torture was not sufficient to silence scolding women, they could always be sentenced to death, particularly if their scolding was perceived as evidence of a witch's curse (Macfarlane 1970, 159).

But despite these prohibitions, scolds were sometimes given license to play an important role in the community: that of its unofficial conscience (Davis 1975, 147). This role was considered appropriate for a woman, since self-restraint was not part of her nature, and because her status as a mother made it only natural that she defend the community against perceived injustices (Davis 1975, 150).[9] Thus, women were frequently central players in riots and tax revolts throughout western Europe. One such tax revolt in 1645 in Montpellier was led by a woman "who shouted for death for the tax-collectors who were taking the bread from their children's mouths" (Davis 1975, 146). Likewise, in England in 1693 a number of Northampton women went to market "with knives stuck in their girdles to force [the price of] corn at their own rates" (Thompson 1971, 115). Female assertiveness was acceptable provided that it was employed in the defense of the family or community, not in a challenge to men's authority over women.

Men's fear of the disruptive power of women's speech is evident in the era's moral and legal prescriptions against female gossip. Despite the fact that the term "gossip" suggests trivial, idle talk, men viewed it with suspicion, wary both of its potential for fomenting rebellion among women, who frequently relied on it as an outlet for aggression, and of its potential to expose secrets about family life and gender relations (Spacks 1985, 30; Tebbutt 1995, 23). By sharing their secrets and complaints, gossiping women formed bonds of solidarity with one another, bonds that may have led them to question male authority and wisdom (Spacks 1985, 46–47). Gossip also drew women away from their domestic chores, away from "the more privatized family life which was becoming a necessary feature of respectability" (Tebbutt 1995, 23). Thus, women and men were frequently reminded of the sexual implications of women's speech, of the link between women's talk and "whorish" behavior (Spacks 1985, 40). When moralizing failed to control women's tongues, men sometimes turned to more drastic measures: in England in 1547 a proclamation was issued forbidding women to "meet together to babble and talk" and ordering husbands to "keep their wives in their houses" (Wright 1935, 467). Idealizing shyness in women was a more subtle method of controlling women's gossip: by constructing speech as antithetical to proper femininity, women would be encouraged to avoid it.

The Rise of the Middle Class

The emerging middle class of the seventeenth century also viewed women's speech with suspicion, not simply because it symbolized women's sexuality, but, in a new twist, because it symbolized women's propensity to spend (Jones 1987, 55). Women who were loose with words were now considered loose both sexually and with their husbands' cash. In order for men to secure the purity of middle-class women's bodies and their other property, moralists recommended confining women to the home (George 1973, 157; Jones 1987, 52). Removed from the temptations of public life, the domestic middle-class woman served as a symbol of the distance that the middle class saw between itself and what it viewed as the decadent and immoral upper classes (Jones 1987, 52). Unlike the flirtatious woman of the courts, the bourgeois woman "avoydes a too neere conversation with man. . . . Her language is not copius but opposit, and she had rather suffer the reproach of being dull company, than have the title of Witty, with that of Bold and Wanton . . . she knowes silence in a woman is the most persuading oratory" (Castara 1640, 75, cited in George 1973, 161).

But conversation was important to middle-class men, since it was an important means of rising through the ranks. Middle-class men studiously read courtesy books and conversation manuals to learn how to converse wittily and learnedly, like "gentlemen" (Wright 1935, 130). Blunt speech was no longer good form—it was now necessary to use graceful language in order to succeed in all areas of life, from commerce to love. As the publishers of a handbook on the art of compliments put it, "hee that speakes best, speeds best, and shall be sure to be preferred before the plaine meaning man" (cited in Wright 1935, 136). Likewise, shyness, or "a foolish shamefastness" which caused a man to "hang down his head and blush at every light word" was regarded as incompatible with gentility (Cleland 1607, cited in Fletcher 1995, 334). With middle-class men embracing upper-class models of behavior, the expectation that men be articulate conversationalists was becoming the norm.

The Power of Women's Speech

Upper-class women held on to and expanded the tradition of their witty engagement in conversation through their participation in salons, rejecting silence as the ideal for women. Salons were first established in France at the beginning of the seventeenth century and were in some senses an extension of court society to the lower ranks of the upper classes.[10] They were a place where fashionable men and women mingled, where educated women had a chance to share their knowledge and men practiced the art of gallantry, "polite, civilized attention to the ladies" (Dulong 1993, 396). The important difference between salons and the court was that salons were run by women, and although men participated, women set the tone of the gathering (Lougee 1976, 5). Presiding over salons was considered a public role for women, and it was not without controversy. Those who defended women's participation in salons did so based on a new conception of womanhood. Where once woman's nonrational "animal" nature had made her predisposed toward sin, it now made her predisposed toward virtue:

> [A] revised epistemology which emphasized the value of human feelings made non-rational women the repository of sentiment. Alterations in social values denigrating heroic strength made weak woman into the representative of delicacy. And cosmologies celebrating love as the creative principle of the universe turned lustful woman into the purveyor of beneficent love. (Lougee 1976, 31)

With woman accorded such an important role in society, there could be no harm in her speech. As naturally virtuous, she had nothing to lose by conversing with and interacting with men. In fact, it was her duty to do so, in order to teach men her feminine virtues. Through her, men learned how to converse wittily, thus allowing them to participate in all the pleasures of society (Lougee 1976, 52). The most successful pupils earned the title "effeminate," "the highest commendation one can give him" (Saint-Gabriel 1655, 63, cited in Lougee 1976, 32).

While upper-class women were being given a remarkable opportunity to mold the behavior of men, men still had greater license to speak in arenas outside of salons. Even within the salons, women were still tied to an ideal of femininity that in many ways valorized shyness: the ideal woman may not have been silent, but she was delicate, sensitive, and sweet—all qualities associated with shyness. These qualities may have had the effect of blunting the potentially disruptive effect of women's speech in public. When women did disrupt the community with their public speech, they were ejected from it. In revolutionary France, meetings of women's political clubs and popular societies were banned by the French National Assembly after a number of public disturbances were caused by gatherings of revolutionary women. Legislators justified the ban by producing an elaborate defense of traditional femininity:

> We must say that this question is related essentially to morals, and without morals, no republic. Does the honesty of woman allow her to display herself in public and to struggle against men? to argue in full

view of a public about questions on which the salvation of the republic depends? In general, women are ill suited for elevated thoughts and serious meditations, and if, among ancient peoples, their natural timidity and modesty did not allow them to appear outside their families, then in the French Republic do you want them to be seen coming into the gallery to political assemblies as men do? abandoning both reserve—source of all the virtues of their sex—and care of their family? . . . We believe . . . that a woman should not leave her family to meddle in the affairs of government. . . . You will destroy these alleged popular societies of women which the aristocracy would want to set up to put [women] at odds with men, to divide the latter by forcing them to take sides in these quarrels, and to stir up disorder. (From the Debates of the National Convention, cited in Weber 1995, 302)

This statement draws on a number of recurring themes in the history of women and shyness. First, the legislators highlight the relationship between women's speech and their sexuality (which they label "honesty") to argue against a public role for women in the new government. To encourage women's compliance, they imply that the success of the revolution depends on their silence, their confinement to the home. Next, they remind women (some of whom seem to have temporarily forgotten) that regardless of their wish to take a public role, their well-established "natural" shyness prevents it. If they were to flout Nature's conventions, their speech would disrupt both the domestic and political arenas. Finally, the French legislators draw upon the image of an immoral aristocracy to defend their ban on women's public speech: women from the lower and middle classes should reject the example set by upper-class women and instead embrace silence as a symbol of republican virtue. In England, Mary Wollstonecraft's demands for equality inspired a similar defense of femininity by authors of conduct literature for the middle classes (Quinlan 1941, 143). Middle-class women were encouraged to limit their notions of power to the domestic sphere, where their influence would be felt through the "passive power of gentleness" (Davidoff and Hall 1987, 116).

Early American Conceptions of Shyness

Evidence of early American colonists' conceptions of shyness is limited to the related concepts of meekness and modesty. The colonists did not regard meekness as a particularly feminine or masculine trait; instead, it was "but a species of the general humility prescribed for both sexes" (Ryan 1975, 63; see also Ulrich 1979, 64). Men *and* women were expected to submit humbly to their superiors, to fate, to God, and to their social responsibilities—a style of obedience that was inculcated in childhood (Kamensky 1997, 24; Rotundo 1993, 13). In the hierarchically organized colonial society, submission was considered a virtue, since it enabled children and adults to fulfill their duties without complaint. Verbal modesty was key to fulfilling these duties, for all. Children were to be seen rather than heard, the virtuous woman "held her tongue demurely," and the godly man was a quiet man, a man who meditated before speaking, and whose words, when they did come, were moderate in quantity and in style (Kamensky 1998, 27–29). But at the same time, men were expected to know when to abandon submission and quietness in favor of assertiveness, for "the very duties that demanded submission to some people and to some social expectations required action against others" (Rotundo 1993, 14). Thus, men were expected to chastise subordinates when necessary, and lay claim to scarce resources on behalf of their families (Rotundo 1993, 14). Similarly, modesty and meekness could not interfere with a woman's ability to manage the household, a task that required frequent contact with neighbors of both sexes, in private homes and in public taverns (Ryan 1975, 76).

Yet despite this apparent equality in behavioral ideals, men had more opportunities for public speech—moderate though it might be—than women. Unlike girls, boys could look forward to an adulthood in which they were permitted to preach, vote, dissent, publish, contract, promise, swear oaths, sing psalms, and publicly profess faith (Kamensky 1998, 28). While these verbal privileges were not without their risks—men could be punished for overstepping the bounds of modest public speech and insulting their superiors—the usual punishment of a public apology was mild (Kamensky 1998, 32, 38). Women's verbal crimes, by contrast, were often punished with physical violence, even death. "Railing and scurrilous language" could land a woman in court, subject to fines or whipping (Cott 1972, 60). In keeping with English tradition, scolds were frequently accused of the capital crime of witchcraft (Karlsen 1987, 29).

Women's gossip, while less threatening than displays of female anger, was also viewed as a danger to community order and was discouraged in the European manner by the threat of gagging, ducking,[11] and cleft sticks "slipped over too-busy tongues" (Carson 1966, 55; Spruill 1938, 330–31). These disparities in punishment and in sanctioned forms of speech suggest that colonial women's verbal assertiveness was more threatening to the social order than men's. Against this backdrop, the ideals of meekness and modesty that women were expected to emulate acquired heightened political meaning. In addition to serving a religious purpose, these ideals served an ideological purpose, enforcing and defending women's subordination not simply to God, but also to men.

Middle-Class Reserve

In the early part of the eighteenth century, religious and social changes weakened the value placed on submission among men. These changes included the religious movement known as the Great Awakening, which promoted the idea of personal independence and questioned the worth of a static social hierarchy (Rotundo 1993, 15). Male meekness was no longer a virtue in a society which increasingly valued individual male initiative. This contrast between meekness and initiative formed the centerpiece of the new, revolutionary, national male character. As constructed by authors of fiction and political essays, this mythic new American man was bold, resolute, independent, and frugal, the exact opposite of the timid, dependent, feeble, effeminate, and self-indulgent British man (Kimmel 1996, 19–21; Wilkinson 1986, 95–96). Once the United States established independence from Britain, upper-class American men served as the negative reference point for American manhood. Consequently, Thomas Jefferson was branded by his opponents as an aristocratic Southern gentleman, "timid" and "whimsical," a man who "took counsel in his feelings and imagination" (Kimmel 1996, 27). Similarly, moralists advocated travel to the West as an antidote to the "shrinking and effeminate spirits" engendered by the fashionable life in eastern cities (Kimmel 1996, 61).

Yet even in this climate of masculine toughness, the ideal of modesty, for men as well as women, lived on, in slightly altered form, in the notion of "reserve." The key to reconciling "reserve" with notions of American manhood was to distinguish it from timidity and shyness, the former tainted by its association with effeminacy, the latter by its association with awkwardness. Thus, reserve consisted of a *strategic* reticence and wariness, a "hanging back" from others until a degree of trust could be established (Hemphill 1996, 324). Where timidity implied fearfulness, reserve suggested judicious caution. Reserve also carried with it notions of grace, something that was decidedly lacking in the shy. Authors of Revolutionary-era conduct books written for the middle classes defined shyness, or bashfulness, as an absence of grace, particularly in terms of bodily comportment (Hemphill 1996, 325–26). To be bashful was to be awkward, stiff, and ill-at-ease in company; to be reserved was to be prudent in choosing one's company (Hemphill 1996, 324, 326–27). Both became important markers of class status, with bashfulness—defined as gracelessness—associated with the lower classes and reserve with the middle and upper classes (Hemphill 1996, 328).

Drawing distinctions between behaviors that, on the face of it, had much in common was an important way to preserve this class hierarchy. Silence, for example, could be interpreted as a symptom of timidity or reserve; likewise, wariness, though linked to reserve, could also be a sign that one was uncertain about how to behave in the company of others, that is, that one was bashful. To acknowledge these similarities, however, would undercut the rationale for regarding reserve as superior. By distancing reserve from timidity and bashfulness, authors of conduct texts helped to create a hierarchy of "shylike" behaviors that corresponded to the class hierarchy.

For men who hoped to ascend the economic ladder, avoiding ungainly bashfulness and displaying a "modest assurance" before others were important means of cultivating a "creditworthy reputation" (Hemphill 1998, 40, 43). The key was to appear to be open and at ease with everyone, while actually revealing little, thus concealing information from competitors (Hemphill 1998, 36–37). The ultimate goal was to master one's emotions, presenting to society a visibly cool, calm, and collected demeanor (Hemphill 1998, 39). Thus, an emotionless silent reserve linked to power, rather than an awkward shyness or timidity linked to fear, was the behavioral goal for middle-class men.

Middle- and upper-class women were encouraged to behave in a similar controlled manner, but with important modifications—the "market" they were dealing with was the marriage market, and the shyness they were expected to manipulate was regarded as "natural" to women. In order to attract eligible men, middle- and upper-class women were encouraged to be friendly and relaxed, and to refrain from awkward displays of shyness. Yet they were also expected to be somewhat reserved and delicate in order to check men's passions (Hemphill 1998, 41; Norton 1980, 112). A woman's modesty was considered her best defense against any attempted impropriety, an outward sign of her purity and chastity (Hemphill 1998, 42). Yet, while acting to keep men at arm's length physically, a woman's blushing reserve was a powerful emotional attraction, one that "forced men to love them" (Gregory 1774, 36, cited in Taylor 1958, 98). When a woman ceased to blush, she had "lost the most powerful charm of beauty" (Gregory 1774, 36, cited in Taylor 1958, 98).

Despite the fact that a modest reserve was thought to come naturally to women, authors of conduct literature found it necessary to spell out how it was to be achieved: through blushes, downcast eyes, a moderate tone of voice, timidity, and occasional silences—particularly on topics that might reveal a woman's intelligence (Hemphill 1998, 41–43; Norton 1980, 112; Ryan 1975, 110). Although these behaviors smacked of the very shyness that was condemned for women, the key seemed to be in the degree of awkwardness displayed: as long as a woman's shyness was graceful, delicate, and dignified, it was acceptable. Women's reserve, like men's, could be used to manipulate others, but it offered women a more limited form of power: whereas men's silent reserve was a means of establishing independence, self-control, an air of command over others, and a hint of hidden reserves of strength, women's silent reserve was a means of establishing dependence and vulnerability, since it invited men's protection by acting as proof of sexual innocence.

The idea of "reserve" provided important justifications for class and gender hierarchies at a time when revolutionaries were espousing notions of equality and freedom. Middle- and upper-class "reserve," in contrast to shyness, was a sign of superior breeding, a justification for class power and privilege. At the same time, the idea that women's reserve was "natural" to them legitimated women's lack of power, by suggesting that they were too delicate to withstand the rough and tumble of public life. A writer who called for the repeal of New Jersey women's newly established right to vote drew on this image,[12] arguing that "female reserve and delicacy are incompatible with the duties of a free elector" (Philbrook 1939, 96, cited in Coontz 1988, 152).

Anglo-Saxon Masculinity

In the mid-nineteenth century, timidity became a mark of race as well as class.[13] According to the increasingly popular ethnologic theories of race and racial hierarchies, timidity was one of the characteristics that distinguished white men[14]—now labeled "Caucasians" or, ironically, given Revolutionary antipathy toward British men, "Anglo-Saxons"—from "Negro" men. This new racial logic characterized white men as naturally independent, aggressive, and domineering. Negro men, by contrast, were characterized as timid, meek, docile, and submissive—all qualities that marked them as effeminate and, more importantly, incapable of self-government (Fredrickson 1972, 98, 106, 108). In 1864, a white government official declared of Negro men that "with their African blood, they may have inherited more of womanly than of manful dispositions; for Africans have more of womanly virtues than fiercer peoples have. Indeed, it may be said that, among the races, Africa is like a gentle sister in a family of fierce brothers" (cited in Fredrickson 1972, 163). While white abolitionists regarded this gentle timidity as a virtue that justified protection rather than enslavement, they did not question the idea that timidity marked one as unmanly. Indeed, white abolitionists themselves were loathe to embrace this apparent virtue: William Lloyd Garrison claimed that (white) abolitionists were "bold" and "hardy" and might justifiably be regarded as "violent [and] perturbed" (Wyatt-Brown 1975, 223–24).

Thus, white abolitionists and slave owners alike drew on the notion of a racial hierarchy, in which the races were distinguishable by the presence or absence of certain characteristics such as boldness or timidity. For supporters of slavery, this racial hierarchy justified slavery within a democracy, by suggesting that only whites were capable of fulfilling the demands and reaping the benefits of democratic government (Fredrickson 1972, 100). For white abolitionists, the racial hierarchy was reversed: the idealized "Negro" was considered to be spiritually superior to the aggressive Anglo-Saxon, since he "carrie[d] within him . . . the germs of a meek, long-suffering virtue" (Fredrickson 1972, 106). Yet the fact that white abolitionists resisted adopting this black ideal as their own suggested that male meekness remained more of a stigma than a virtue—boldness and aggressiveness, for all their flaws, constituted the proud centerpiece of Anglo-Saxon manliness.

Yet this manliness did not consist entirely of unchecked boldness and aggression. Among the middle classes in particular, white men's ability to control, direct, and restrain powerful passions was considered an important source of their strength and authority (Bederman 1995, 408). A dignified reserve remained central to the middle-class white man's ability both to achieve success and to maintain control. Thus, he was counseled to control his emotions in public, to discipline his face, to wear sober colors, to walk "like a gentleman," neither hurrying, shuffling, or mincing, and to avoid, when possible, speaking to others on the street (Kasson 1990, 119, 123, 149). This verbal, physical, and emotional self-possession was a source of power in the world of business, and a sign that the man was "well bred" (Hilkey 1997, 147–48; Kasson 1990, 149). By definition, those who were loud, unrestrained, and emotional—men from the working classes, for example, who "swagger[ed] along the street, shouting and laughing"—were neither successful nor well bred (Kasson 1990, 123). White men may have shared an "Anglo-Saxon" identity, but class differences remained, with "loudness" rather than awkward bashfulness as the primary mark of lower-class status. A controlled reserve remained a mark of superiority, a justification for middle-class white men's position of privilege relative to working-class white men.

But the ideal Victorian middle-class white male was not expected to be a completely self-controlled being. When he was courting, he was allowed, even expected, to drop his mask of reserve in favor of open disclosure of his thoughts and feelings to his beloved. Middle-class Victorians regarded courtship as a time of intense feeling and self-revelation for both men and women (Rothman 1984, 91); indeed, open and honest communication with one's intended was the ultimate proof of romantic love in nineteenth-century America (Lystra 1989, 33). Despite the fact that Victorians regarded women as more emotional and sensitive than men, in the private arena of romantic love men were expected to abandon rationality, to lay bare their souls to their beloved in order to establish a foundation on which to build a marriage (Rothman 1984, 200–201). Middle-class Victorian men approached friendship with other men in much the same way. "Romantic friendships" between men were in some sense "practice" marriages, since middle-class men had so few opportunities to interact with middle-class women (Rotundo 1989, 14).[15] As in courtship, self-disclosure occupied a central role in these friendships, with friends "shar[ing] youth obsessions, . . . ponder[ing] career plans, and . . . sift[ing] through hopes and fears about their prospects for success" (Rotundo 1989, 2). Rather than threatening to undo the image of the middle-class white male as self-restrained, the intense emotional life he experienced in private lent greater significance to his restrained and unemotional public persona, since it confirmed that he was the master of his emotions in public and not simply a man devoid of emotion.

The Nineteenth-Century "Lady"

There were a number of competing ideas about women's ideal relationship to shyness in the nineteenth century. The ideology of "True Womanhood" celebrated privileged white women's "natural" shyness and timidity, along with their piety, purity, submissiveness, and weakness (Scott 1970, 4; Welter 1966, 152, 159). Pundits encouraged middle-class white women to cultivate their shyness in order to advertise and protect their purity and thereby guarantee an advantageous marriage. According to the author of an 1844 conduct book for young women, "the coldest reserve" was "more admirable in a woman a man wishes to make his wife than the least approach to undue familiarity" (Graves 1844, 140, cited in Welter 1966, 155). Once they were married, True Women were to submit meekly to their husbands, avoiding at all times a "controversial spirit" (Welter 1966, 161). But women also faced the rather contradictory expectation of nineteenth-century romantic love that they be open and self-revealing with their prospective mates. It was difficult for a woman to both declare her feelings and maintain the necessary air of feminine reserve and submission (Rothman 1984, 113). Women tried to accommodate both sets of expectations by peppering their letters to their beaus with apologies for "boldness" and "unmaidenly confidences," thus demonstrating the "unnatural" aspect of candor (Rothman 1984, 228–29).

The impact of the ideology of privileged white women's "natural" shyness extended beyond domestic and class boundaries. Men used this ideology to stymie working- and middle-class women's efforts to enter the workplace on an equal footing. In the mid-1830s, for example, the National Trades Union resisted admitting women to their ranks, arguing that their "natural . . . modesty and bashfulness" made them incapable of pressing the demands of organized labor (cited in Kimmel 1996, 57). The fact that the union also supported the "family wage"—a wage large enough for a male worker to support a dependent family— and women's subsequent withdrawal from the labor force suggests that the ideology of middle-class women's natural shyness was also used to support working-class women's confinement to the domestic sphere (May 1982, 112–13). Similarly, a woman who sought to practice law in Illinois in 1872 was informed by Supreme Court Justice Bradley that "the natural and proper timidity and delicacy which belongs to the female sex unfits it for many of the occupations of civil life" (Bradwell v. Illinois 1872, cited in Reskin and Phipps 1988, 192). The ideology of middle-class white women's shyness was also used to belittle their work in the abolitionist and suffrage movements. Women who spoke in public on behalf of these causes were condemned for "behaving in a manner unbecoming to their sex," indeed, were regarded by some as completely "unsexed" since a true woman's "natural" delicacy and timidity would prevent her from speaking in public (Degler 1980, 304; Douglas 1988, 59).

In the South, the cult of True Womanhood not only provided justification for white women's subordination to men, but also legitimated slavery (Leslie 1988, 19; Scott 1970, 16). By serving as the standard of femininity against which black womanhood was measured and found wanting, the ideology of the True Woman justified the exclusion of black women from the traditional privileges and protections—limited though they might be—that "gentlemen" offered "ladies." The two primary images of black women circulating in antebellum America were the "Jezebel" and the "Mammy" (Jewell 1992; Morton 1988; Mullings 1996, 112–13; White 1985, 27–61). The Jezebel was promiscuous and aggressively sexual, the very opposite of the pure, timid standard set by the True (white) Woman; therefore, she was denied protection from rape—indeed, she could never be raped, given her lustful nature (White 1985, 38). The Mammy was a desexualized, maternal figure devoted to raising and sustaining her white "family" (Morton 1988, 41). But where her white mistress was timid and frail, she was strong and assertive, and thus insufficiently feminine to be considered a "lady" (Morton 1988, 41). Whether labeled as "Jezebel" or "Mammy," black women were regarded as the very opposite of shy, with their sexual and verbal assertiveness placing them beyond the bounds of True Womanhood.

In slave narratives, black women attempted to counter these negative images by creating an alternative image of black womanhood (Carby 1987, 36). They consistently emphasized their honesty, intelligence, defiance, and strength in the service of their *own* families (Carby 1987, 36–38). However, these qualities did not translate into a widely shared positive image for black women because they violated the cult of True

Womanhood's notion of female submission and silence; the image of the strong, assertive, and independent black woman thus became "a figure of oppressive proportions with unnatural attributes of masculine power" (Carby 1987, 39). The black woman's assumption of traditionally male characteristics also contributed to the image of the emasculated, "unmanly" black male (Morton 1988, 41).

White women living in the North had recourse to an alternative vision of womanhood: "Real Womanhood," championed by its mid-nineteenth-century promoters as uniquely American. Unlike the "undue reserve" promulgated by conduct texts imported from Britain—a reserve which included blushing, giggling, keeping one's eyes downcast when addressed by a man, "fraudulent maidenly shyness," and stiffness—this ideal of femininity emphasized the American virtues of self-reliance, common sense, and dignity in interactions with men (Cogan 1989, 139, 159). "Real Women" achieved this dignity by regular socializing with men in which they demonstrated their modesty not through silence, but by refraining from flirting, monopolizing the conversation, or speaking loudly (Cogan 1989, 159). Thus, the goal for Real Women was to negotiate a path between the two extremes of shyness and boldness. To a limited degree, therefore, the Real Woman rejected the link between shyness and white femininity. Yet this challenge to traditional conceptions of woman's "nature" was muted still further by the fact that women's shyness offered them more protection than did its absence. In public, particularly in urban settings, a "loud" woman or a woman who made eye contact with men risked being mistaken for a prostitute, as did a woman who laughed "immoderately" (Kasson 1990, 130, 163). This link between "boldness" and sexuality limited Victorian women's freedom of movement and expression in public; in addition, it had the potential to elicit a silence and timidity from middle-class women that fed the popular view of them as "naturally" shy.

Not every class of woman followed these prescriptions. In fact, "Bowery Gals," who set the standard for New York's working-class women, claimed some of the elements of the prostitute's style as their own: they wore bright and startling combinations of color, called attention to their faces with ornate hats, and gazed openly about (Stansell 1982, 94). Their "very walk . . . [had] a wink of mischief and defiance in it, and the tones of [their] voices . . . [were] loud, hearty, and free" (Foster 1850, 107–8, cited in Kasson 1990, 130). Yet they were not "streetwalkers"; instead, they presented themselves as "members of a high-spirited peer group, reveling in their associations with each other" (Stansell 1982, 93). Their dress and manner were both a celebration of working-class life and an explicit rejection of the middle-class ideology that promoted women's shyness and timidity (Stansell 1982, 93).

Crisis in Masculinity

At the end of the nineteenth century, economic and cultural changes stimulated anxieties about middle-class white men's loss of manliness and growing effeminacy. The traditional foundation of middle-class manliness—self-restraint—had less relevance in an increasingly bureaucratic, interdependent consumer society; in addition, gender divisions in American society were beginning to weaken, calling into question the characteristics that distinguished men from women (Bederman 1995, 409; Greenburg 1988, 387; White 1993, 9). Greenburg (1988, 387–88) argues that "[t]he preservation of male dominance in the face of women's aspirations to equality depended on men possessing qualities that clearly differentiated them from women. It consequently became necessary to police men who lacked these qualities just as much as women who exhibited them. Continued male rule required that male effeminacy be repudiated." This was achieved by embracing a bodily ideal of manhood, one that emphasized physical strength and robust health and vigor. Middle-class men eagerly participated in bodybuilding and athletics, while young boys joined all-male organizations like the Boy Scouts (Gorn 1986, 187; Macleod 1983, 46; Pleck and Pleck 1980, 28; Rotundo 1983, 26–27). These newly invigorated boys and men even had "manly" churches in which to worship: "Muscular Christianity," which emphasized health, endurance, and other "manly" virtues, flourished among American Protestants between 1880 and 1920 (Putney 2001, 1, 11). Proponents rejected the idea that meekness was a virtue, arguing that a Christian man could not be a "spineless" "dishrag . . . [who] lets everybody make a doormat out of him" (McLoughlin 1955, 179). Jesus, after all, was no "dough-faced, lick-spittle proposition," but, according to the Reverend Billy Sunday, "the greatest scrapper that ever lived" (McLoughlin 1955, 179).

A new term was created to identify insufficiently manly boys and men: "sissy." Shyness and timidity were two prominent characteristics attributed to the sissy (Kimmel 1996, 122). For a sissy to reclaim his masculinity, he would have to emulate Teddy Roosevelt, who, though shy, timid, and frail as a boy, "re-made his body and his image by going West," where he became "the embodiment of 'strength, self-reliance, and determination'" (Kimmel 1996, 182). If travel to the frontier proved impractical, the shy, retiring boy could still set out on the road to "independence and true manhood" by learning to fight with other boys (Puffer 1912, 91, cited in Kimmel 1996, 161).

Middle-class white men also sought to shore up their threatened masculinity by distinguishing themselves from black men (Bederman 1995, 410). In the 1890s, the idea that black men were naturally timid and meek competed with the idea that black men were savages by nature, prone to raping white women, docile only when under the control of more "civilized" white men (Fredrickson 1972, 275). Inspired by Darwin, "civilization" was now a racial concept, denoting the highest stage of human development, after savagery and barbarism. Whites believed that only they had advanced to the civilized stage in which women were "womanly"—spiritual and motherly—and men were "manly," or firm of character, self-restrained, and reserved but not timid or shy (Bederman 1995, 411). In essence, whites denied black men the status of men, relegating them instead to the ranks of children, their status starkly illustrated in the South by whites' tendency to address black men of all ages as "boy" (McMillen 1989, 23). This racial ideology provided justification not only for white political and economic supremacy, but also for a great deal of violence against "savage" blacks (including lynching); at the same time, it reinforced the central role that self-control and emotional restraint played in middle-class white men's self-definition.[16]

An Early Twentieth-Century Change

It was not until the early decades of the twentieth century that reserve became a less valued aspect of white middle-class identity, for both women and men. Spurred by a growth in leisure activities and consumerism, a "culture of personality" replaced the previous century's "culture of character" (Susman 1984, 274; White 1993, 17). In the nineteenth century, advice manuals had described the self in terms of "character," the key ingredients of which were self-control, self-sacrifice, discipline, and delayed gratification (Cushman 1995, 64). Around the turn of the century, advice manuals began to describe the self in terms of personality—the ability to appeal to others and to be noticed for one's appearance, poise, charm, and manners (Susman 1984, 274). Developing a "good line"—the capacity to verbally sell oneself to prospective dates, clients, employers, or friends—was central to cultivating an appealing personality (Rothman 1984, 225, 290; White 1993, 100). Maintaining a public reserve was no longer a guarantee of financial or romantic success.

This change had important implications for middle-class white women. No longer bound by demands for displays of shyness and timidity, women may have experienced greater freedom of movement and expression, both in public and in private. Limited evidence from the 1920s suggests that this was the case, although it also reveals some unanticipated negative consequences. Cultural, political, and economic changes, including the century's first "sexual revolution," women's newly won right to vote, women's growing presence in universities and in the labor force added up to a greater sense of freedom and possibility for women (Cott 1987, 148; Kessler-Harris 1983, 224, 229). The sexual revolution was particularly significant for women, as it brought greater (though still limited) access to birth control and more acknowledgment of women's passion (Cott 1987, 157; D'Emilio and Freedman 1988, 229). "Modern" women and men were encouraged to embrace rather than suppress their sexual urges—women to a lesser extent than men, but more so than their nineteenth-century predecessors, who were considered to have been rather shy about sex (Simmons 1989, 162–64, 169–70). No longer, presumably, did a "loud" woman on the street or a woman who made eye contact with male passers-by risk being automatically taken for a prostitute. Yet the loss of the idea of female sexual shyness also entailed a loss of women's power to either control or withdraw from men's sexual demands (Simmons 1989, 164). Women who responded to sexual overtures with fear or timidity instead of enthusiasm were derided as "frigid," a condition that physicians linked to lesbianism (Jeffreys 1985, 169–71; Simmons 1989, 164).

The shift to a culture of personality also had important implications for white middle-class men. To be successful in dating, the more casual form of courtship that had replaced nineteenth-century forms (such as "calling" at a young woman's home), a man had to be verbally skillful (White 1993, 155). The "line" that he developed—a sort of exaggerated flirtatiousness that aimed to "convince the young woman that he has already at this stage fallen seriously in love with her"—was essential to initiating and maintaining any sort of relationship (Waller 1937, 733; see also White 1993, 155). In the arena of romance, shy men were at a decided disadvantage compared to their more extroverted counterparts, since shy men who were tongue-tied around women were unlikely to impress them with their verbal skills; indeed, some complained to newspaper advice columnists that they were too afraid to ask women out (White 1993, 157). This fear would only have added to others' suspicions regarding shy men's sexuality, as any sign of effeminacy was now regarded as a mark not simply of physical and spiritual weakness but of homosexuality (White 1993, 67). As one author of a popular 1926 sex manual pointed out, many people shared the assumption that "homosexuals are invariably timid, shy, retiring, fastidious, dainty even, and what is popularly called effeminate" (Collins 1926, cited in White 1993, 69).

The shift in emphasis from character to personality also put shy men at a disadvantage in the arena of work. Advice givers no longer advocated reticence and self-restraint for the man hoping to achieve business success, but "being people oriented, even a 'glad hander'" (DeVitis and Rich 1996, 61). With the growth of large organizations with numerous employees (and potential competitors), self-confidence and a winning personality were increasingly important means of attracting attention and winning patronage (Cawelti 1965, 183).

Developing this winning personality was increasingly the concern of the psychologists, social workers, and medical personnel who considered themselves child guidance experts. In the second decade of the twentieth century, child guiders had been concerned primarily with the delinquent—girls who were sexually "precocious," and boys who were petty criminals, truants, or ran away from home (Jones 1999, 67). Beginning in the 1920s, they began to focus on the problems of the "everyday child," particularly the child with the "maladjusted personality" (Cohen 1983, 131; Jones 1999, 94). The chief symptom of the maladjusted personality was shyness (Cohen 1983, 129). However, because parents and teachers were more likely to object to assertive children who defied their authority than to quiet, timid and seemingly "good" children, child guidance experts had to campaign vigorously to educate adults about the dangers of the shy, withdrawn personality (Cohen 1983, 131, 133; Jones 1999, 139; Wickman 1928, 78). Experts warned that if left unchecked, shyness could lead to economic dependency, alcoholism, drug addiction, mental illness, and suicide (Jones 1999, 139; Wickman 1928, 139, 147). They argued that the ideal of mental health, an outgoing, peer-group-oriented personality, would not only ward off these afflictions, but would guarantee children social and economic success (Jones 1999, 139).

Parents' role was to provide children with a secure emotional environment in which they could develop non-shy personalities, while the school curriculum was to shift its emphasis from academics to "assisting and guiding the developing personality" (White 1920, 263, cited in Cohen 1983, 130; see also Jones 1999, 208). Educators' recognition of the importance of the latter goal grew throughout the 1930s and 1940s and reached a peak in 1950, at the Mid-Century White House Conference on Children and Youth, which adopted the slogan, "A Healthy Personality for Every Child" (Cohen 1983, 139).

For adult middle-class women, the Great Depression brought with it a return to more traditional views of proper feminine personalities (see Bailey 1988, 28–29). As married women were either urged or forced to give up their jobs so as not to compete with men who had families to support, women's magazines glorified domesticity, attacked feminism, and emphasized "natural" sex differences, including women's inherent timidity (Chafe 1972, 105; Haag 1992, 565). With the advent of World War II, this trend was reversed, as the government relied on the image of the plucky, strong, competent "Rosie the Riveter" to bring housewives into war work (Dabakis 1993, 185). Although media representations of "Rosie" often made sure to note her essential femininity—her reliance on cosmetics, her neat hair, her heterosexuality—none referred to a natural timidity or shyness, emphasizing instead her fearlessness and determination (Dabakis 1993, 193, 194, 199).

The decades preceding the 1950s, then, were marked by both challenges and returns to the ideology of white middle-class women's natural shyness. In the remainder of the book, I explore how later generations incorporated or rejected this ideology into the prevailing conventions and norms that governed shyness in heterosexual relationships, at work, and within friendships. At the same time, I explore how the loss of reserve as a central aspect of white middle-class identity affected men, both at home and at work.

Conclusion

This exploration of Western shyness norms has revealed that at numerous points in history men have regarded women's speech as a threat to men's power and authority. Their efforts to control it have ranged from the physical (the scold's bridle and the cucking stool) to the legal (prohibitions against gatherings of "babbling" women). Idealizing shyness in women as both natural and proper is a more effective means of enforcing women's silence, because it encourages women to regulate and limit their own behavior in an effort to live up to the ideal (see Fox 1977). It also encourages women and men to regard the restrictions on expression and movement created by such an ideal not as socially created limitations but as the unremarkable consequence of women's innate character.

Given the link between shyness and femininity, men's displays of shyness have frequently been interpreted as a sign of weakness. For white middle-class men in particular, shyness has been perceived as a threat to their privileged position in gender, race, and class hierarchies. Thus, shyness norms for men have reflected efforts to remove shyness from the realm of white middle-class masculinity, often by redefining it for men in order to obscure its links to femininity. In the eighteenth and nineteenth centuries, for example, authors of conduct texts were careful to distinguish between shyness and reserve. They associated the former with women, the working classes, and black men, and the latter with middle- and upper-class white men. Whereas shyness was uncontrolled, awkward, and childlike, reserve was dignified and restrained, evidence of white middle-class men's superiority.

The emergence of the culture of personality in the early part of the twentieth century led to changes in shyness norms that, even if temporary, represented a break with earlier eras' emphases on white women's natural shyness and white men's reserve. For white middle-class women and men, shyness was at odds with new demands for personal and sexual appeal. Yet the links between shyness and gender proved difficult to dislodge, as was evident in the return, in the 1930s, of the notion of women as naturally shy. As we will see, the idea that women are or should be naturally shy and that men's reserve is distinct from common shyness are recurring themes in the shyness norms of later decades. Though the norms themselves change, the link between shyness and gender remains a powerful ideological tool in support of gender, as well as race and class, hierarchies.

CHAPTER THREE

"Build Him a Dais"

Shyness and Heterosexuality from the Roles of the Fifties to The Rules of the Nineties

> If woman be formed to please and be subjected to man, it is her place, doubtless, to render herself agreeable to him, instead of challenging his passion. The violence of his desires depends on her charms. . . . Hence arise the various modes of attack and defense between the sexes; the boldness of one sex and the timidity of the other; and, in a word, that bashfulness and modesty with which nature hath armed the weak, in order to subdue the strong.   Jean Jacques Rousseau, *Emile* (1765)

I n their discussions of shyness, self-help authors writing for a white middle-class audience in the last half of the twentieth century focused a great deal of attention on its impact on intimate heterosexual relationships. Indeed, some limited their advice about shyness to this particular arena, further underscoring its importance. Authors regarded shyness as a frequent, even natural aspect of interactions between the two sexes, an emotion that affected both women and men. They suggested that knowing how to properly handle shyness in everyday heterosexual encounters was a key determinant of romantic success. Their advice about how to do so—for example, whether it was appropriate to express, manipulate, or suppress shyness—was linked to prevailing notions about how to achieve emotional intimacy. As talking about emotions began to occupy a more central role in authors' conceptualizations of intimacy, shyness came to be regarded as more of a threat to successful heterosexual relationships.

In this chapter, I explore changes in the relationship between shyness and emotional intimacy in heterosexual relationships. I show that while advice about how to manage shyness in heterosexual relationships varied across time periods, such advice consistently functioned as ideological support and legitimation for women's relative lack of power within those relationships. It did so in two primary ways: (1) by producing and reproducing oppositional gender differences in the meaning and expression of shyness for middle-class whites that justified power differences between women and men; and (2) by creating and sustaining meanings associated with shyness that supported white middle-class women's responsibility for performing unreciprocated emotional labor within heterosexual relationships.

"Be Careful How You Say Things"

Recent scholarship has dispelled the notion that the popular culture of the 1950s was entirely devoted to preaching the white middle-class gospel of domesticity and motherhood known as the "feminine mystique" (Friedan 1963). Instead, historians examining the era's music, films, and popular magazines have found them to contain both radical and conservative messages about women's proper place in society;[1] indeed, the two messages were often reconciled by using evidence of femininity or domesticity to legitimate other behavior that challenged traditional gender norms (Meyerowitz 1994, 234). The advice books I examined reflected this tension: authors of courtship and dating manuals (most of whom were women) frequently acknowledged young women's competence and independence,[2] yet they insisted that in the arena of courtship, male privilege had to be preserved. As one author succinctly put it, "Boys know you for modern, self-sufficient, car-driving, job-holding, money-making, vote-getting women. You can and you do take everything into your own hands *except love and courtship and marriage.*"[3]

Given the traditional association between shyness and white middle-class femininity, one might expect shyness to have been regarded as the ideal emotion for white middle-class girls to experience around boys. But the advice texts told a more complex story, one in which successful heterosexual relationships required that white middle-class girls resist any inner feelings of shyness but at the same time adopt certain characteristics associated with it. According to the advice books, a girl who yielded to internal feelings of shyness experienced self-consciousness, fear, and feelings of inferiority. She communicated these feelings to boys nonverbally, through bodily tension, silence, a "scared expression" in the eyes, and fidgeting.[4] These telltale signs of shyness made her seem unfriendly, unapproachable, and aloof, characteristics which "chase(d) the boys away."[5] Boys were easily frightened since they themselves often felt shy around girls: according to several authors of advice texts, feeling self-conscious and ill at ease around girls was a stage that most, if not all, boys went through.[6] Bashful boys had a difficult time speaking to girls, let alone asking them for dates. If they were faced with an equally shy girl, the "fun and friendship of dating" was stalled before it could begin.[7]

Instead of a "quiet mouse," boys required a friendly, outgoing, and talkative girl who was sensitive to their special, albeit temporary, problem.[8] Yet she could not be *too* friendly or outgoing, because then she might easily cross the line into bold and aggressive behavior, such as calling a boy on the phone for no apparent reason, or asking him to dance. Such behaviors marked her as "cheap," "forward," or a "flirt," and also chased boys away, for although boys preferred "self-confident, poised girls" to those who were "always at a loss to know what to do," they did not like "aggressive girls who too obviously [took] the initiative."[9]

The key to a girl's behavior when faced with a bashful boy who was slow to take the initiative was subtlety: she could take as much initiative as she wanted, as long as it could be classified as "undercover . . . quiet promoting."[10] In fact, she was obligated to do some self-promotion in the name of propriety: "While no girl wants to be cheap . . . neither should she always stand passively by and wait to be selected by the man of her dreams. It is not necessary, and it is not proper."[11] Her strategy was to "make it look as though he, rather than she, is the pursuer. . . . [I]t is all right for a girl to 'chase a fellow until he catches her.'"[12] Once she was "caught," the success of the date that ensued depended upon the girl donning a mask of shyness—consisting of such behaviors as reticence, silence, and meekness—in order to preserve the illusion that the boy was in control of the date. In essence, the boy and girl now switched roles, so that he, formerly shy, was now the talkative one, while she, the active initiator, was now a quiet, appreciative foil. Thus, she allowed him to take the lead in conversation—after initially prodding him along with "leading questions about himself, his hobbies, his school activities, or any work he may be doing."[13] Her flattering attention was guaranteed to make her "a big hit" with her date, who, despite his initial feelings of discomfort, "[would] love to tell [her] all he knows."[14] In donning the mask of shyness, a white middle-class girl was required to hide not just her voice, but also her intelligence, which, like boldness or any hint of aggression, threatened the boy's masculine pride.[15] It seemed that the pride of mid-twentieth-century boys was as delicate as that of their eighteenth-century counterparts, who also preferred to remain ignorant of a young woman's capacity for intelligent thought. Instead of impressing a young man with her knowledge, a young woman in the 1950s devoted her energy to "build[ing] him a dais," a firm foundation for his sense of superiority:

> BUILD HIM A DAIS: . . . give him a chance to lead the conversation. You know—men suffer from an odd sense of inferiority. They're often terrified by smart women. This doesn't mean you have to act the idiot role or the cute little "Oh, aren't you smart!" role. But it does mean that you can let him feel he is superior. This is a good start for a first date. . . . The first evening you are together, don't let him know you read Greek.[16]

Here, the author figuratively "winked" at his female readers, acknowledging that they were indeed smart, and that men were silly to be afraid of women's intelligence. But he suggested that the truly smart woman would do better to surreptitiously manipulate her date into thinking he had the upper hand rather than prove to him how smart she was. Such behavior was justified since the stakes were so high: future dates and, ultimately, marriage. Though unspoken, the specters of spinsterhood and lesbianism lurked behind his and others' advice to girls to tone down their intelligence and any other "mannish" qualities or behaviors that might turn men against them forever.[17] With spinsterhood popularly associated with lifelong unhappiness,[18] and lesbianism associated with deviance and immaturity,[19] many women were only too happy to comply: a study conducted in 1950 found that 46 percent of female students at

Stanford University "played dumb" on dates because they thought the men preferred it (Wallin 1950).[20]

A white middle-class girl built up her date's sense of superiority not only by letting him lead the conversation, but also by contrasting his masculine wisdom with her air of feminine meekness. She achieved this effect by moderating her tone of voice and limiting her talk to humble requests for advice. Thus, girls were cautioned to "be careful how you say things. You are in the habit of knowing. Your voice may have a positive sound. If it has, tone it down with 'I think.'"[21] Clearly, a girl had to be extremely careful about hiding her intelligence—an intelligence this author, too, takes for granted—since it could slip through in the confident way she expressed herself. To completely snuff out a boy's smoldering inferiority complex, a girl had to assure him that any thoughts she did have were only opinions, easily changed by his superior knowledge, and not well-researched facts. Similarly, girls were instructed to speak of themselves only if their dates appeared interested and provided they followed their statements with requests for guidance about their future plans.[22] If their date was not interested, girls were not to insist on sharing the conversational spotlight—to do so might suggest they were overly aggressive and, hence, not feminine.

For these authors, white middle-class masculinity was an extremely fragile achievement that could crumble under prolonged exposure to any girl or woman who displayed ostensibly male characteristics, such as boldness, initiative, and intelligence. To protect this delicate masculinity, white middle-class girls had to hide their resourcefulness, intelligence, and cunning behind a mask of shyness. Ironically, girls' assumption of shy behaviors also ensured that the actual shy feelings of white middle-class boys did not become a problem serious enough to threaten heterosexual relations: by stifling their own voices, girls drew bashful boys out of their shells and created an intimate environment in which boys could feel powerful, in control, and confident of their own appeal and interest. This helps to explain why self-help authors were so blasé about young men's feelings of shyness. In contrast to young women, young men's feelings of shyness did not make them less desirable. One author included the "shy fellow who isn't too sure of himself when the girls are about" on her list of "masculine behavior patterns" and noted that this fellow and other types of masculine boys were "all fine folk."[23] Another author asked young women if they preferred "the strong silent" type of man or "the weak silent," noting that "any man is wonderful if he is the man in your life."[24] Empirical evidence suggests that boys indeed felt less pressure to perform: a national study of high school students conducted in the mid-1950s found that 14–16-year-old boys (59 percent of whom dated) were less likely than girls of the same age (72 percent of whom dated) to express concern about improving their social skills. Boys' major worry was achievement, while girls' was popularity and acceptance (Douvan and Adelson 1966, 371–72, 389).

The behavior prescribed for young girls on a date can be viewed as a form of emotion work—the work of building self-esteem, understanding and managing emotions, and providing emotional support. The fact that only young girls were expected to perform this labor in the 1950s is consistent with recent scholarship, which has found that women are seen as largely responsible for emotion work; it is another form of "women's work" that men take for granted and fail to supply in return (Blumstein and Schwartz 1983; Cline and Spender 1987, 97–98; Ferguson 1989, 97; Hochschild 1983, 165; Mansfield and Collard 1988, 178–79; Peplau and Gordon 1985; Rubin 1976, 114–33). Because men receive this caregiving as "a kind of entitlement," women's provision of emotion work has been described by one feminist scholar as "a collective genuflection by women to men" that affirrims male power and authority in heterosexual relationships (Bartky 1990, 109). It is a "warm" form of deference—instead of offering men a formal bow of submission, women offer them "gestures small and large that show support for [their] well-being and status" (Hochschild 1983, 168). From this perspective, then, the 1950s' emotional culture of shyness helped to enforce the gender hierarchy. By invoking strategic displays of shyness as a resource on which young women could draw to perform unreciprocated emotion work for young men, self-help authors reaffirmed women's lack of power in heterosexual relationships. Thus, shyness remained a powerful symbol of female deference in the 1950s.

The More Things Change . . .

Between the 1950s and 1970s, attitudes toward "proper" gender behavior underwent remarkable changes, spurred in large part by events of the 1960s, particularly the "sexual revolution" and the women's movement. For young women and men, dating was no longer a highly structured ritual that conferred prestige, but was simply "one form of social contact among many"; when they did date, women and men did so at a later age and for "the intrinsic satisfaction the relationship provided" (Modell 1989, 291). The women's movement also contributed to Americans' changing conceptions of proper gender behaviors; through both word and deed, feminists challenged traditional conceptions of (white) femininity and highlighted the exploitative nature of heterosexual relationships.[25] Feminists encouraged women to speak up and out with one another, in consciousness-raising sessions devoted to uncovering the political nature of seemingly individual experiences of oppression (Echols 1989, 83).

Self-help texts published during the 1970s were not deaf to the challenges to traditional conceptions of white femininity posed by the sexual revolution and the women's movement, but they did not embrace them until the second half of the decade. Authors writing in the first half of the decade tended to resist calls for equality in male-female relationships: their advice on courtship and dating echoed the conservative tone of the 1950s in which male privilege in initiating dating had been defended as natural and proper. These authors insisted that the white middle-class woman who had the best chance of appealing to white middle-class men was not a "woman's libber" but a woman who deferred to men, particularly when it came to the initiation of a date. Author Barbara Walters, the well-known television journalist, argued that while feminists were to be commended for some of their views regarding male-female equality, she drew the line at women asking men for a date:

> It seems to me that, Women's Liberation Movement aside, women come on awfully strong these days and men are unhappy about it. A college lecturer told me he was amazed at the applause, cheering and stamping from the young men in his audience when he criticized the aggressiveness of the modern woman. I agree with some of what the new feminists are saying, but I think they're way off in trying to change the biological roles as they apply to the sexes. Why spoil all the fun? It's terribly old-fashioned of me, I know, but I still feel that a woman who wants to win a man should allow him the initiative. Her best bet is to concentrate on making him want it.[26]

Like advice authors of the 1950s, Barbara Walters suggested that the preservation of male privilege in the dating arena would compensate for white middle-class women's gains in other traditionally male arenas, thus reassuring white middle-class men (and women) that these changes posed no real threat to conventional heterosexual relations. Her words also served as a warning to white middle-class women, cautioning them that being "too aggressive" in any arena could earn them the enmity of men; women who wanted to appeal to men should defer to men's "natural right" to initiate.

Of course, if men's and women's mating behavior was, as Walters suggested, preordained by biology, then she had nothing to worry about—feminists' efforts to change them would be unsuccessful. Her insistence on trying to prevent women from tampering with nature highlights one of the essential contradictions of much self-improvement literature written for white middle-class women, which regards femininity as "natural" at the same time that it instructs women in how to be feminine (see Davidoff and Hall 1987, 171; Haag 1992, 574). Thus, self-help books vividly illustrate one of the primary ways that ideology operates to create and sustain relations of domination: by representing a historically specific, socially mediated state of affairs as permanent and natural (Thompson 1990, 65–66).

Author Helen Andelin considered a strategic display of shyness, or, as she put it, "timorousness," to be the primary means by which a woman signaled her submission. She described timorousness as "an air of timid fearlessness, of self-conscious modesty and of pretty confusion," and encouraged women to practice it around men by "first unconsciously performing some task, then when you realize that the man is noticing you, suddenly becom[e] self-conscious and confused. Look first directly up in his face for a moment, and then hastily down or to the side."[27] She assured her readers that this seemingly innocent show of bashfulness would not only make the man at whom it was directed conscious of the woman's femininity but, more importantly, gratifyingly conscious of his own masculinity, which was devoid of such delicate timidity. Confident that he had found a woman in need of his "manly care and protection," the man would most certainly be smitten.[28] Thus, a display of shyness was one method by which white middle-class women could reassure men that they had no intention of challenging the traditional power dynamics of the heterosexual relationship. Andelin's insistence that white middle-class men required these performances as reassuring proof of their own manliness revealed a rather low estimation of men, for it suggested that an encounter with an independent and strong woman could lead a man to doubt his masculinity. How, then, would he fare when faced with an overt display of aggression?

Yet like the advice givers of the 1950s, Andelin cautioned that a woman's air of timidity was to remain at surface level only; middle-class white women were not to succumb to inner feelings of shyness, since the fear and confusion they engendered would interfere with a woman's calculated performance of femininity.[29] A middle-class white woman was to devote her energies toward *appearing* fearful and helpless in order to attract a man. A woman who actually experienced fear and helplessness around men squandered whatever advantage she gained in authenticity by her inability to "play to" the audience—to exaggerate, downplay, or refine her shy performance according to the man's response.

Once a woman had attracted a man through a display of shyness, she was required to maintain the fiction of shyness on the date itself. Andelin expanded the elements of the 1950s' mask of shyness, advising white middle-class women not only to be reticent about expressing their own views, but also to display timidity "in the presence of small dangers" such as mice, insects, or heavy traffic, and to adopt an air of bashful incompetence when confronted with a "masculine" task, like lifting a heavy object.[30] As in the 1950s, such behavior was a form of emotion work: by pretending to be shy and timid, white middle-class women inspired a sense of "strength and manliness" in their date, building his ego by making him feel useful and important.[31] Men were not obligated to reciprocate; women's emotional needs were satisfied simply by knowing that they had succeeded in serving men's needs. From this perspective, an unequal division of emotional labor was not particularly troubling; indeed, it guaranteed happiness for both women and men. It was not until the end of the decade that self-help authors began to question this assumption.

The Turning Point

By the end of the decade, the women's movement was no longer a point of contrast for advice givers, but a seeming source of inspiration. Many authors now rejected the old valorizaton of middle-class white women's shyness and enthusiastically embraced women's assertiveness, which was considered the very opposite of shyness.[32] Middle-class white women were no longer told that their desirability hinged upon their ability to sustain an illusion of meekness and silent awe in the presence of a man; in a dramatic switch, women were assured that men now preferred women who took a more assertive approach to dating.[33] Women were given permission to ask men out, to buy them a drink, to ask them to dance—in short, to boldly approach men without fear of being labeled cheap, flirtatious, or forward. Such behavior, once beyond the pale of white, middle-class respectability, was now the trademark of modern, liberated white womanhood. Of course, not every man welcomed this new approach, but advice givers who advocated it calmed women's fears by arguing that only "stupid" and "weak" men with "hangups" were threatened by a woman's outspoken attentions.[34]

White middle-class women who remained shy in the misguided belief that it was an appropriate strategy for snaring a man, or who experienced genuine shyness on a regular basis, were doomed to a life of celibate loneliness: not only did a woman's shyness interfere with her ability to make social contact with men, but it also inhibited her from making sexual contact.[35] Unlike the dating manuals of the 1950s, those of the 1970s (which were also written for a slightly older audience) assumed that sexual activity was an important, indeed, necessary part of dating. In this, they were in line with widespread public opinion, which embraced (hetero)sexuality for women and men as a "valued, worthy, even necessary component of the good life, a prime means of attaining self-discovery" (Modell 1989, 308). The shy woman, then, was missing out on an important source of self-knowledge. Albert Ellis, author of *The Intelligent Woman's Guide to Dating* (1979), put it somewhat more crudely, arguing that the shy woman's "tied tongue and locked legs are no longer attractive in a world where women commonly open up their heads and hearts to new acquaintances as well as would-be lovers."[36] Now that sex was sanctioned as an important means of establishing rapport while dating, a white middle-class woman's displays of shyness no longer signaled deference to men's emotional needs and desires, but showed prudery, a quality that was guaranteed to turn men off and to destroy a woman's chances of establishing a heterosexual relationship. According to Ellis (1979, 30), the woman who persisted in being shy and unassertive was committing social and sexual "suicide":

> Timidity and unassertiveness are just as healthy for the average young female as is a thrice-daily dose of cyanide. Being alive and kicking means, in the first and final analysis, being and expressing oneself. Self-imposed inhibitions on self-expression are equivalent to suicide; only, in terms of extended suffering, much worse. The woman who

sells her soul for a mess of pusillanimous pottage is, whether she mates or not, a zero. And what man in his sound mind wants to marry and live with a cipher?

Ellis's caustic remarks highlight an interesting shift in authors' attitudes toward their female readers. In the 1950s, both female and male authors of self-help books openly acknowledged that their female readers were smart, competent, and capable. Their aim was to help them play down those qualities in order to win a hopelessly insecure man. But in the mid- to late 1970s, female and male authors viewed their women readers less generously: they assumed that they were damaged, insecure, and in need of help. The authors' goal was to make their female readers smarter and more competent by the time they finished reading the book. Thus, in an ironic twist, the late 1970s middle-class white woman—a woman who had presumably benefited somewhat from the activities of the women's movement—was perceived as weaker than her 1950s counterpart. In teaching her to become stronger and more assertive, self-help authors assumed that their advice was essential in order for her to overcome the social training that had made her timid and unsure of herself.[37] Where 1950s self-help authors regarded white middle-class femininity as a performance a step removed from the performer, late 1970s authors regarded it as an identity that middle-class white women had all too eagerly embraced.

How did the shy, heterosexual middle-class white male fare in this environment? Was he, too, committing sexual "suicide," or did he simply reap the benefits of the demand that women take some responsibility for initiating a date? Despite the change in expectations regarding women's behavior, this shy man did not suddenly find his dating problems solved. Self-help authors portrayed him, like the shy woman, as suffering from a chronic lack of dates; however, his datelessness stemmed not from an appearance of sexual prudishness, but from his inability to take the initiative with women.[38] Self-help authors argued that shy men—unlike some shy women—desired sexual contact, but were simply too timid to make the first move.[39] Yet authors refused to absolve shy men from responsibility for initiating a date by suggesting that newly assertive women would come to their rescue. Fearful, perhaps, that women would fail to find shy men worthy of their attention, authors sternly cautioned shy men that unless they overcame their fears, they faced a lifetime of loneliness and sexual frustration. Thus, in the 1970s, both women and men, shy and not shy, were expected to take responsibility for their dating destinies by directly approaching those who interested them.

Self-help authors' adoption of an "equal opportunity" approach to dating held the promise of a commitment to greater equality in heterosexual relationships. Authors' insistence that white middle-class women and men adopt similar behaviors at the beginning of a relationship could have heralded an insistence that they do so at all stages of the relationship. In what follows, it becomes clear that this promise was not realized; white middle-class women may have been free to boldly pursue men, but they were not free from the expectation that they were responsible for performing the emotional labor that sustained the relationship.

The Joy of Self-Disclosure

The 1970s self-help authors' instructions to middle-class white women to be more assertive did not stop at the initiation of a date. In order to nurture long-term heterosexual relationships, middle-class white women were also required to master new assertive communication skills, skills that were often at odds with shyness. In intimate relationships, assertiveness took the form of self-disclosure, the verbal expression of feelings and emotions. Most self-help authors regarded self-disclosure as essential for heterosexual intimacy, arguing that the verbalization and discussion of emotion fostered not only mutual trust and understanding but also individual emotional growth.[40] A relationship without such disclosures was considered superficial at best, emotionally dishonest at worst.[41] White middle-class men, too, were expected to self-disclose to their female partners since "men have as much need to express their emotions as women."[42]

This emphasis on self-disclosure represented a remarkable development in attitudes toward heterosexual intimacy among middle-class whites. The marriage manuals of the 1950s that I examined did not even use the term "self-disclosure," let alone suggest that long-term heterosexual relationships required this type of emotional expression to thrive. In fact, 1950s advice givers seemed quite wary of emotional expression for both men and women. Rather than sharing negative emotions such as anger with their husbands, wives were told to find an alternate outlet for their aggression—like scrubbing the kitchen floor, pulling weeds, or kneading bread.[43] Emotionally demonstrative wives were cautioned that "many things can be solved without words."[44] Men, too, were advised to divert their negative feelings—perhaps into a letter to be burned upon completion—rather than succumb to the temptation of telling others their troubles.[45] When it came to expressing more positive emotions, such as happiness or joy, authors had little to say on the subject.

The fact that verbal self-disclosure had moved to center stage in white middle-class heterosexual relationships in the 1970s may help to explain why shyness—whose many symptoms included the failure to self-disclose—became an issue of such concern in the 1970s among mental health professionals and lay people. Self-disclosure allowed a couple to drop their masks, to become "transparent," "authentic beings" with one another;[46] shyness was one of the masks to be discarded in the pursuit of unfettered emotional closeness. But at the same time that self-disclosure was being touted as *the* route to intimacy, authors of self-help books that dealt with interpersonal relationships frequently noted that male silence was becoming a serious problem between marriage partners.[47] It appeared that many men would not or simply could not satisfy the new demands to talk about their feelings, and lapsed into stubborn silence at home.[48]

Women, on the other hand, seemed quite equal to the challenge to self-disclose, since there were no corresponding complaints from men about female silence. Men's silence was not labeled shyness despite many similarities to it, both in terms of symptoms (silence) and causes (fear of negative evaluation); rather, it went by the fairly neutral term of "reserve" or "reticence." Ironically, given the fact that shyness was under increased scrutiny during the 1970s, male silence was placed in a separate category altogether. One author went to great lengths to deny any connection between the two. She insisted that while most men were reserved, they were decidedly *not* shy. For her, male reserve was "a barrier that a man builds around himself, making it difficult to 'get next to him.' By reserve we do not mean bashfulness or timidity. The latter peculiarities apply to comparatively few men. Reserve, on the other hand, is an attribute of all."[49] She went on to explain the source of his reserve:

> His reserve is caused by fears, the fears of ridicule, contempt and indifference—those things that we learned about in connection with a man's pride. Because of fears, he forms a wall of reserve which makes it difficult to get him to talk. Although he may long to confide, so that he can be appreciated for his masculinity, he hesitates because of his re-

serve, or his fear of ridicule. Nothing is so frightening to a man as making a fool of himself.[50]

Psychologists writing popular manuals on how to identify and overcome shyness attributed its cause to a similar fear of ridicule. For example, Dr. Philip Zimbardo claimed that "at the core of shyness is an excessive preoccupation with the self, an overconcern with being negatively evaluated," while Dr. Arthur Wassmer made much the same point, stating that "the roots of shyness are negative thoughts that people hold about themselves."[51] Since both male reserve and shyness stemmed from a man's fear that he was making a negative impression on others, the only real difference between the two was in the term used to describe the man's condition.

The choice of the term "reserve" rather than "shyness" to describe male silence was significant for two reasons. First, it allowed self-help authors—most of whom did not acknowledge the fear at the heart of reserve—to suggest that men's silence was a rational response to a poor communication environment rather than an emotional response to the new demands for feeling talk. Where the term "shyness" invoked images of a powerful, involuntary emotion that "overwhelmed" its sufferers and paralyzed them with fear, the term "reserved" suggested a calm, objective decision to remain silent. Second, the use of the term "reserve" allowed self-help authors to blame women for male silence, and thus make them responsible for ending it. In the 1970s, adult shyness was regarded as a psychological problem whose resolution was the responsibility of the individual sufferer; reserve, on the other hand, could be overcome by the efforts of *either* conversational partner—one or both could take responsibility for changing the conversational environment in order to facilitate speech. Since self-help authors identified women as the primary source of the poor communication environment, they carried the burden of improving it. Women were instructed to stop the behaviors that resulted in male silence—interrupting, overempathizing, sniping, nagging, unfavorably comparing their husbands to more successful men, and trying to change their husbands;[52] they were to replace these behaviors with acceptance, admiration, compliments, praise, discretion, brevity, and conversational skill.[53] Self-help authors could feel fairly confident that women would perform this emotional labor since they simultaneously drove home the point that both women's and men's happiness depended on meaningful talk. Unlike men, white middle-class women could blame no one but themselves for failure.

Thus, middle-class white women in the late 1970s were still responsible for performing the conversational and emotional labor necessary to maintain heterosexual relationships despite changing attitudes toward female shyness. No longer bound by demands that they adopt shy behaviors to shore up a fragile masculinity, middle-class white women might have expected to become equal partners in heterosexual intimacy. Instead, despite the recognition that self-disclosure by both women and men was necessary to achieve intimacy, women continued to shoulder most of the burden of performing this emotional labor, thus preserving the power inequities in heterosexual relationships. Their talkative dating partners of the 1950s were now afflicted not with a temporary bout of shyness, but with a lingering "reserve," a label that signaled the transformation of male shyness into a quality that demonstrated not emotion, but its absence or suppression. The removal of male shyness from the realm of the emotional distanced middle-class white men from the chaotic and illogical arena of the emotions, an arena associated with women, one that provides justification for a gender hierarchy in which (rational) men wield power over (emotional) women (James 1989, 23; Lutz 1990, 87). As Jack Sattel has pointed out, "What better way is there to exercise power than *to make it appear* that *all* one's behavior seems to be the result of unemotional rationality?" (emphasis in original) (Sattel 1983, 120). The link between white middle-class womanhood and shyness may have been loosened in the late 1970s due in part to the pressure of the women's movement, but the shift in men's relationship to shyness ensured that the balance of power in white middle-class heterosexual relationships remained undisturbed.

Backlash, but No Turning Back

With the rise of the New Right, the cultural climate framing gender relations in the 1980s and 1990s was more conservative than that of the 1970s. Organized around a "pro-family" ideology that defended traditional family and gender roles, members of the New Right opposed sex education in schools, teenage sexuality, abortion, and gay rights (Herman 1997, 137–69; Oden 1993, p. 1978). Feminism was a favorite target, blamed for the rising divorce rate and for women's continued entry into the paid labor force (Bondi 1996, 399; Mintz and Kellogg 1988, 234).

The sexual revolution likewise came under attack by conservatives, who blamed the spread of AIDS, teenage pregnancy, and sexually transmitted diseases on its excesses (Bondi 1996, 380). Conservative legislators attempted to ban abortion, prohibit the use of certain forms of contraceptives, and cut off funding for schools whose curriculum "denigrate[d], diminish[ed], or den[ied] the role differences between the sexes as they have been historically understood in the United States" (D'Emilio and Freedman 1988, 349).

Despite the conservative cultural landscape, most advice givers continued to tell middle-class white women to be more assertive in initiating relationships with men. Their justifications included the fact that some men now expected it, and that it was an empowering move for women to actively search for Mr. Right rather than simply wait for him to arrive on their doorstep.[54] One author neatly summed up the ideal approach as the following: "[T]he key is not in developing artificial tricks or ploys that will allow a man to feel that he is taking the lead; rather, it lies in developing enough self-confidence to go after what you want without giving off the message that you are needy, dependent, and desperate."[55] At the same time, however, advice givers did place some limits on women's "bold" behavior; unlike their counterparts writing in the late 1970s, they were concerned that women not be too aggressive in their pursuit of men. Perhaps white middle-class women had taken their relatively new freedom to pursue men to dangerously "unfeminine" lengths so that some restrictions were now in order. But these limits did not consist of strategic displays of shyness; instead, they revolved around the ability to recognize when to stop pursuing a man who was uninterested—for example, when a man has turned down three invitations in a row.[56] Instead of invoking displays of shyness to curb middle-class white women's "aggression" as in the 1950s, self-help authors now appealed to women's sense of dignity and self-respect.

But while shyness lost its connection to white middle-class femininity, surprisingly, it was being reevaluated by some self-help authors as a potentially superior form of white, middle-class masculinity.[57] A small minority of authors (18 percent of those who discussed male shyness) offered "very worthwhile but . . . shy men" as a reward to middle-class white women who approached men of their own accord.[58] These authors reminded their female readers that not every man found it easy to approach women; in fact "lots of guys" were "as intimidated and tongue-tied" as women.[59] Rather than marking them as undesirable, their bashfulness was indicative of a gentle, sensitive, loving nature, superior to that of the more uninhibited, aggressive male.[60] In the previous decade, male shyness was exclusively symptomatic of a deeper malaise, but now, for some, it hinted at security and safety for women. Indeed, men who were untroubled by shyness were suspected of lacking all feelings, and, in fact, all sense, since they seemed to be oblivious to the dangers awaiting them in making the first romantic move. This appreciative view of shy men posed a challenge to prevailing conceptions of masculinity by suggesting that timidity was more desirable than aggression.

It is important to note that these men are described as "shy," not "reserved." In contrast to the majority of descriptions of reserved men, descriptions of shy men acknowledge the fear that they experience. This fear does not necessarily manifest itself as an unwillingness to talk about feelings as reserve does, but rather as an unwillingness to make the first move. Once that barrier is overcome, shy men may, in fact, be better able to self-disclose than not-shy (and "reserved") men, given their more "complex" and "sensitive" natures. Thus, these authors contribute to the sense—established by self-help authors in the 1970s—that male "reserve" has little in common with male shyness: where reserve is rational, shyness is emotional.[61]

Ruled by Biology

The political conservatism of the period was noticeable in the tendency of some self-help authors (30 percent) to justify their advice through recourse to biology. A prominent example of this trend appeared in 1995 with the publication of *The Rules*, a dating advice book for white middle-class heterosexual women that quickly made its way to the bestseller list and into the popular imagination. Its premise was that women who took the initiative with men took away the thrill of the chase. Authors Sherrie Fein and Ellen Schneider used vague references to biological difference to justify their advice, claiming that "[i]n a relationship, the man must take charge. He must propose. We are not making this up—biologically, he's the aggressor."[62] Their "time-tested" rules for finding and keeping Mr. Right included letting the man take the lead in conversation, and refraining from phoning a man or speaking to him first—all familiar female dating tactics from the 1950s. But unlike the 1950s, they did not tell white middle-class women to do any "quiet promoting" from the sidelines; since "nature" ensured that men would aggressively pursue women in whom they were interested, such tactics were unnecessary.

Fein and Schneider's advice hinged on the assumption that the only obstacles to white middle-class men's pursuit of women were those posed by rule-breaking women. They rejected outright the notion that men might suffer from shyness: "Perhaps a therapist would say so, but we believe that most men are not shy, just not *really, really* interested if they don't approach you. It's hard to accept that, we know."[63] In other words, "naturally aggressive" men were biologically incapable of being shy; therefore, white middle-class women had no excuse for taking the initiative with men.

Yet being relieved of this burden did not relieve white middle-class women of the responsibility for overcoming any tendencies toward shyness. Fein and Schneider argued that a woman needed to be cool, calm, and collected in the presence of a man, not shy and timid. At a singles' bar or party, she circulated with brisk purposefulness, hiding her nervousness, and acting "as if everything's great" even if she was quaking with fear on the inside. When approached by a man, she was to smile and be "nice," but say very little; such a strategy made her seem "demure, [and] a bit mysterious" and left him "hungry for more, as opposed to bored."[64] Her silence was intended to be alluring and seductive, a signal not of feminine meekness, as it was in the 1950s, but of feminine self-confidence. It was central to *The Rules* strategy of playing hard to get, since it left men off-balance and unsure of the woman's interest. According to Fein and Schneider, this uncertainty was the very spark that awakened men's innate "ambition and animal drive." Ironically, however, silence did not come naturally to women, who "love[d] to talk."[65] It appeared that in the world according to *The Rules*, only men were ruled by biology; women who wanted to find and keep Mr. Right had to train themselves to accommodate men's "instinctual" behavior.[66]

Biological arguments were also popular explanations for differences in white middle-class women's and men's propensity to self-disclose. To an even greater extent than in the previous decade, advice givers of the 1980s and 1990s were committed to the idea that men were reserved when it came to talking about feelings, while women were loquacious. But where inadequate practice communicating about feelings was seen as the cause of men's reserve in the 1970s, now the cause was believed to be a biological difference in the way men and women communicated.[67] Not only were men naturally quieter than women, but when they did speak, they spoke different languages.[68] Author John Gray suggested that their communication differences were so great that, figuratively speaking, men were from Mars, women were from Venus. He summed up the fundamental difference between them by claiming that "[s]ilence is a man's birthright, while talking is a woman's."[69] When men chose to break silence, they spoke in the ancient "male" tongue, "a language of few words" created by contemporary man's warrior ancestors to meet the minimal verbal requirements of the hunt.[70] Unlike women's language, which was indirect and emotional, men's language was rational and logical: "Men are more focused on results and completion, or closure, than women. Women are more concerned about relationships and the process of communication than men."[71] In contrast to the 1970s, when neither middle-class white women nor men were presumed to have a *natural* advantage in "feeling talk," it was now a well-established fact that middle-class white women were, and always had been, better at it than men.

Of course, given that every author agreed that self-disclosure was essential to intimacy, men were not relieved of the burden of speech despite their supposed "natural" deficiencies. It fell to middle-class white women—naturally, given their inborn proclivity for speech—to teach men "female" and, at the same time, to learn "male." This advice had serious implications for heterosexual relationships. If women spoke "male," they would lose their distinctive difference from men; they too would lapse into silence, and neither partner would perform the emotional work that was now required to sustain the relationship. The other possibility was that women would be unable to speak male—given the apparently intractable biological imperative that compelled them to speech in the first place, this was not an impossibility. Instead, they would turn away from uncommunicative men and look to women to satisfy their intimacy needs (see Rich 1980). Gray dealt with these issues by arguing that women need only learn "male"—they were not required to actually speak it with their male partners. At the same time, they had to teach men how to properly interpret women's speech, and how to listen.[72] Through this apparent compromise, Gray rescued men and women from a communication impasse that seemed to require the abandonment of heterosexual relationships and thus ensured men's continued access to women's bodies, as well as their emotional labor.

The development of an ideology of natural communication difference between middle-class white women and men marked the rupturing of the traditional relationship between "proper" white, middle-class femininity and shyness. No longer required of middle-class white women to help secure heterosexual relationships as it had been in the 1950s and early 1970s, shyness ceased to be invoked as a means of women deferring to men. Instead, it was replaced by the very different conviction that middle-class white women were naturally talkative, possessing verbal skills that dictated their dominance in an arena increasingly defined as feminine—the arena of talk about one's emotions. Although the recognition of this feminine skill suggests that middle-class white women may hold some power over men within heterosexual relationships, several scholars suggest that such verbal and emotional power is illusory, since men undervalue such skill and deny their need for it (Bartky 1990, 106; Cancian 1987, 78; Duncombe and Marsden 1995, 164). In fact, given that women report a great deal of dissatisfaction in heterosexual relationships in which men silently withhold from them the emotional care giving they desire, it appears that many women do not experience their apparently superior skill at feeling-talk as a form of power (Duncombe and Marsden 1995, 158; Rubin 1976, 114–33). Instead, "women appear to win only limited and precarious victories through emotional or 'relational' power. And while these may soften the face of male power, the overall balance is tilted not only by men's greater 'extrinsic' economic or 'structural' power, but also usually by a gender asymmetry which leaves women more emotionally vulnerable" Duncombe and Marsden (1995, 161).

Conclusion

As ideas about how to achieve emotional intimacy in heterosexual relationships have changed over time, so, too, have ideas about white middle-class women's and men's ideal relationship to shyness. What has not changed is the idea that women are primarily responsible for performing the emotional labor deemed necessary to achieve intimacy. In the 1950s, when the arena of courtship was regarded as the last bastion of male privilege, ideas about how to achieve intimacy on a date were explicitly one-sided. Young middle-class white women were expected to suppress their own interests and adopt certain shy behaviors to create an intimate environment in which even bashful, awkward young men could feel powerful, confident, and in control. In the mid-1970s, when feminists were challenging male privilege in many arenas, mutual self-disclosure was established as the new standard of intimacy. Yet given that white middle-class men were increasingly afflicted with a shyness labeled "reserve," women were still considered responsible for performing most of the emotional labor in heterosexual relationships, disclosing their own emotions while at the same time attempting to elicit emotions from their silent male partners.

In the conservative 1980s and 1990s, mutual self-disclosure continued to be held up as an ideal, but it was undermined by the development of a biological explanation for middle-class white men's and women's communication differences. With men's tendency toward silence rooted firmly in biology, white middle-class women's unreciprocated emotional labor was not only necessary for a satisfactory relationship, but impervious to challenges by women demanding change. In doing this labor, white middle-class women faced the prospect of disempowerment not only by performing labor without compensation, but, more importantly, by consistently placing men's interests and needs before their own, thus colluding in their own oppression (Bartky 1990, 112).

In the move from shyness facilitating white middle-class women's performance of emotional labor to shyness interfering with it, middle-class white women were transformed from relatively silent actors performing a role scripted by society into more vocal creatures possessing a "natural," emotional language. This transformation had contradictory implications: on the one hand, white middle-class women's assumption of speech had liberatory possibilities, including the ability to speak for and about themselves; on the other hand, their association with the "chaotic" and "irrational" language of emotions offered further justification for their subordination to "rational" men (Lutz 1990, 87). White middle-class women may have gained a voice, but it wasn't necessarily a powerful one. As white middle-class men so ably demonstrated in the 1970s and 1990s, silence may sometimes be more powerful than speech.

Indeed, Michel Foucault ([1976] 1990, 61–62) makes just this point, arguing that the silent listener who witnesses the self-disclosures or "confessions" of another holds the power to "judge, punish, forgive, console, and reconcile." Perhaps, therefore, feminists need to reconsider women's relationship to silence and speech, to claim the power of *both* in undermining patriarchy. Heterosexual women might, at strategic moments, choose silence as a form of resistance, a way of refusing to provide verbal emotional sustenance to men—a new form of "shock" therapy for men and self-improvement for women.

CHAPTER FOUR

Assertive Women and Timid Men?

Race, Heterosexuality, and Shyness

> [W]e were told in the same breath to be quiet both for the sake of being "ladylike" and to make us less objectionable in the eyes of white people.
>
> Combahee River Collective,
> *Combahee River Collective Statement* (1979)

Black women and men have had to contend with a very different set of assumptions about their "natural" proclivities for shyness than have whites. In contrast to "naturally shy" white middle-class women, black women of all classes have long been assumed to be naturally assertive. In the nineteenth century, this ideology took shape in the image of the "mammy," the loyal, nurturing slave with a sharp tongue whose "verbal assertiveness [was] tolerated when she [was] giving advice to her mistress" (Jewell 1992, 42). In the mid-twentieth century, this ideology was represented by the image of "Sapphire," a "sassy," "verbose," and assertive black woman, devoid of compassion, who used her words to belittle and "emasculate" black men (Jewell 1992, 45; Mullings 1996,

116; White 1985, 166). First introduced on the *Amos n' Andy* television show, Sapphire became "the most pervasive image [of black women] white people shared at that time. . . . [S]he became a popular epithet to be used in place of less jovial ones" (Gilkes 1983, 294–95). The "mammy" and "Sapphire" images were created by whites, and were used to rationalize racialized gender hierarchies—black women were "unfeminine" compared to white women, and were thus excluded from the privileges and protections offered to "true" women (Mullings 1996, 112). These images also reinforced racial solidarity among whites, masking class and gender divisions, as black women occupied the role of "bad" or "unfeminine" women and white women the role of "good" women (Mullings 1996, 114).

Yet African Americans have sometimes subverted damaging images like Sapphire, turning the negatively regarded trait of women's assertiveness into a positive one in order to challenge assumptions of black women's inferiority (see Jones 1985, 269; Mullings 1996, 121). In the late nineteenth century, for example, although black women and men embraced some aspects of the white ideal of "true womanhood," the "true" black woman was more assertive than her demure white counterpart, an outspoken activist whose words benefited the black community (Carlson 1992, 62). The fact that whites themselves have, since the late 1970s, revalued women's assertiveness has also offered African American women the opportunity to occupy the position of standard setter rather than negative reference point for white women (see, for example, Robnett 1997, 123).

In contrast to black women, black men have frequently been assumed to be naturally timid. This quality, coupled with childlike docility, simplicity, and dependency, was central to the "Sambo" image that first developed in the last decades of slavery (Williamson 1986, 15).[1] Whites imagined Sambo as their adopted child. Properly cared for, he was appealing and manageable; without such care, he reverted to his dangerous and wild "bestial" nature, a personfication of the other prevailing image of the black man—the uncivilized brute (Williamson 1986, 15).

These two images of black men—docile and nonthreatening versus savage and threatening—remained at the heart of popular representations of black men well into the twentieth century. In the 1950s, television's Kingfish, husband of Sapphire, was simple, inept, and unmanly, lost without the direction of his domineering wife (Gilkes 1983, 294). In the Blaxploitation films of the 1970s, black men, though portrayed as heroes, were highly sexualized criminals (Miller 1998, 26). These images allowed whites to feel superior, justifying the subordination of black men, who were not seen as men, but as children or savages, and thus in need of control or surveillance. The gender reversal implicit in the image of timid Sambos and assertive Sapphires also divided black women and men by suggesting that black women had too much power over black men. This division became particularly salient during the struggle for civil rights, as black men sought to be taken seriously by whites as powerful men deserving of respect.

In what follows, I examine how African American advice givers have regarded the issue of black women and men's shyness and assertiveness in the 1950s, 1970s, 1980s, and 1990s.[2] I explore how they have challenged or appropriated the images of "Sapphire" and "Sambo," and to what end, and also how their advice subverts or legitimates race and gender hierarchies. I show that African American attitudes toward the relative value of shyness and assertiveness have been highly charged: not only have these attitudes frequently been tied to the struggle for civil rights, but they have also been linked to issues of loyalty between black women and men. I rely for evidence on a small sample of self-help books and magazine articles written specifically for a black audience. Since these texts were concerned primarily with intimate relationships between black women and men, rather than with relationships at work or between friends, I explore representations of shyness and assertiveness only in the context of heterosexual relationships. Given these limitations in size and scope, my analysis is tentative and provisional; nonetheless, the data provide a starting place for a more nuanced exploration of the race and gender implications of the emotional culture of shyness.

"Acquire Manners: The Rest Will Come"

I was able to identify only one advice text written specifically for a black audience that was circulating during the 1950s—Charlotte Hawkins Brown's *The Correct Thing To Do—To Say—To Wear.*[3] The author, a prominent African American educator and public speaker, argued that white prejudices could best be overcome by young black women and men learning proper social graces. As she explained in a 1940 radio broadcast, if black youths were to "practice the little courtesies, the gentle voice, a knowledge of when to sit, when to stand, how to open and

close a door," then the "wheels of progress" would move "with great ve-
locity . . . toward equal opportunity and justice for all" (Brown, March
10, 1940, cited in Smith and West 1982, 204). To that end, she encouraged black women and men to adopt the prevailing (i.e., white middle
class) codes of respectable behavior. Thus, her advice on how young
black women were to behave around young black men echoed that of her
counterparts writing for a white middle-class audience in the 1950s.

On the one hand, Brown regarded shyness as a conversational handicap and encouraged those suffering from it—men and women alike—to
overcome it by practicing their conversational skills to the point that
they could "speak with assurance on subjects in which they [were] interested."[4] Once they had mastered that skill, they were to strive to become
conversational leaders, choosing topics of interest to all and asking
thoughtful questions of others. But at the same time, Brown expected
black women, in the presence of black men, to adopt certain characteristics associated with shyness, such as silence and reticence, in order to
show the proper degree of deference to men. She instructed young black
women to take no initiative in meeting young men or in planning dates;
it was the man's prerogative to ask to be introduced to particular women,
and to decide how best to entertain them.[5] On a date, women were to
avoid "do[ing] all the talking. It is the nature of man to dominate."[6]
When women did speak to their dates, they were to discuss topics that
would "swell his ego," including his friends, his sports prowess, and his
academic achievements.[7] They could inflate his ego even further by behaving like a "clinging vine"—hanging on to his every word and displaying their helpless dependency on his gallant courtesies.[8] Instead of embracing the assertiveness traditionally associated with black womanhood,
Brown encouraged black women to adopt a mask of shyness like that advocated for white women, thereby reaffirming male power in heterosexual relationships. In doing so, she was guided by her belief that blacks'
adherence to the rules of etiquette—in this case, the etiquette of gender
relations—was an essential means of achieving racial equality.

Adhering to this etiquette also allowed black women to pay lip service
to the domestic ideology of the 1950s. The material circumstances of
many black women's and men's lives were such that they could not adhere to the basic premise of this ideology: that husbands provide financial support for wives, who confined their labors to the home. Black men
were nearly twice as likely as white men to be unemployed, and those
who were employed received lower wages, on average, than white men;[9]

thus, many married black women simply could not afford to stay home.[10] While black periodicals generally lauded black women's work outside the home in paid jobs and in the civil rights movement, regarding them as a form of racial uplift, black women's work outside the home was not without controversy (Jones 1985, 268–74; Meyerowitz 1994, 233). Black scholars investigating the rise in the number of black households headed by women frequently invoked the image of Sapphire, blaming black women for driving men away by being too domineering and ambitious (Frazier 1948).[11] By following Brown's advice and donning a mask of shyness, black women could refute this criticism, demonstrating their willingness to defer to black men.

Black women and men active in the civil rights movement provided something of a counterpoint to Brown's view of the proper means of achieving racial equality. Not only did they favor direct action over acquiring good manners, but women as well as men occupied leadership roles. Although the 1955 Montgomery bus boycott propelled Martin Luther King, Jr., into the spotlight as the leader of the civil rights movement, black women initiated and sustained it (Barnett 1993, 168). Women like Ella Baker and Septima Clark organized and trained movement volunteers (Barnett 1993, 169). They could not have been effective leaders by following Brown's advice and behaving like a "clinging vine." Yet, in some senses, Brown's view of the importance of "proper" gender relations was mirrored in relations between black women and men civil rights activists. As one veteran civil rights leader explained, "When you're dealing with Black men and women and the fragile position of Black males, you can expect that Black women, even though they might do all the work, will not be recognized as doing the work or leading anything. . . . Black women had to work hard, but *never ever* threaten the fragile position of their Black men" (emphasis in original) (Barnett 1993, 175). Acting as the sole, undisputed leaders of the black community offered black men one source of the power and authority that they were regularly denied by whites. Black women could play their part by displaying some degree of deference to black men—by adopting a mask of shyness or by some other means. Thus, while they might be acting as leaders, they would at least be paying lip service to the idea that their proper role was a supportive one. As the civil rights movement progressed, the question of black women's proper relationship to black men—both in the movement and out of it—continued to be a central one.

"We Are Tired of Our Men Being Emasculated"

In the 1970s, relationship advice for black women and men reflected the era's tensions over the implications of a pattern of "nontraditional" gender relations within black families.[12] This issue was raised most famously by the 1965 publication *The Negro Family: A Case for National Action* by Harvard sociologist Daniel Patrick Moynihan.[13] Putting a scientific gloss on the Sapphire image, Moynihan (1967, 76) identified the "matriarchal structure" of black families as the "principal source of most of the aberrant, inadequate, or anti-social behavior that did not establish, but now seeks to perpetuate the cycle of poverty and deprivation." Evidence for this "black matriarchy" included black women's greater representation in higher-paying occupations, relative to black men,[14] their higher educational attainment,[15] and a study which claimed that black wives were the "dominant" partner in the majority of black families (Moynihan 1967, 76–79).[16] Moynihan (1967, 62, 75) argued that these factors "impose[d] a crushing burden on the Negro male" since "[t]he very essence of the male animal, from the bantam rooster to the four-star general, is to strut." Moynihan's choice of the terms "male animal" was telling, invoking as it did emasculated Sambo's opposite—the black man as animalistic savage. He proposed separating black men from black women in the "utterly masculine world" of the military as one method guaranteed to rebuild their manhood, since, as one recruiting poster succinctly put it, "In the U.S. Army you get to know what it means to feel like a man" (Moynihan 1967, 42, 43).

The report had a powerful impact in black communities. Black women leaders were asked to "step aside and let a man take over, not because they were incapable but because their being female and competent 'looks bad for the race'" (Gilkes 1983, 295). Similarly, *Ebony* magazine, which had traditionally been quite supportive of black women's work outside the home, changed its tune: in 1966, its editors argued that "the immediate goal of the Negro woman today should be the establishment of a strong family unit in which the father is the dominant person." They urged black women to follow the example of the Jewish mother "who pushed her husband to success, educated her male children first and engineered good marriages for her daughters" (cited in Murray 1970, 92).

The idea that successful claims to black manhood depended on the subordination of black women was also evident in the civil rights and Black Power movements. In 1968, during the Memphis sanitation strike, black male strikers equated their struggle for better working conditions and an end to racial discrimination on the job with a defiant assertion of their manhood, most evident in the placards they wore that proclaimed "I *Am* a Man!" (Estes 2000, 158). In making this claim, the strikers served notice that they would no longer abide by the rituals of social deference that denied them any form of verbal self-assertion and consigned them to the role of Sambo—childlike, timid, and servile (McMillen 1989, 23–26). Central to their claim of manhood was the ability, through higher wages, to support a dependent wife and family in the "traditional" patriarchal manner (Estes 2000, 160–61). Instead of black women being forced to work outside the home to help support their families, black men's higher wages would allow black women to occupy their "rightful" positions as wives and mothers, with black men as the undisputed heads of household.

Members of the Black Panthers claimed a more militantly aggressive version of black masculinity than that claimed by civil rights leaders. Their goal was not egalitarianism, but black power; thus, while Martin Luther King, Jr., tried to "challenge dominant racist stereotypes by claiming black men as citizen-subjects," the Panthers, through their dress, art, and political culture, "reconfigur[ed] and romanticiz[ed] black men as the very embodiment of revolutionary rage [and] defiance" (Doss 1998, 491). In so doing, they did more than challenge the image of black men as naturally childlike, incapable, timid, and passive—they "declared war" on it (Doss 1998, 490). This newly invigorated black masculinity was too fragile, however, to support the presence of black women as equals. Black nationalists urged black women to play a limited, supportive role in the revolution, strengthening black manhood by leaving the political and economic arenas to black men and devoting themselves to domestic and family concerns (Giddings 1984, 318; Jones 1985, 312). For the Panthers, black power was black *male* power, and patriarchal authority was a central component of this objective (Doss 1998, 484). The militant image the Panthers cultivated may have put the image of Sambo to rest, but the ideology that replaced it was not entirely liberating, as it drew on the equally constraining idea, created by whites a century before, of black men as uncivilized, threatening savages.

The assumption that patriarchy was an essential ingredient of black nationalism did not go unchallenged by black women. Although the early period of the second-wave women's movement has been characterized as predominantly white and middle class, women of color participated with white women both in large, mainstream feminist organizations like the National Organization for Women, founded in 1966, and in smaller ones (Giddings 1984, 303–4). Women of color also founded their own feminist organizations. In 1973 a group of black women established the National Black Feminist Organization to address both racial and gender oppression; by 1974, it had a membership of two thousand spread among ten chapters (Chafe 1977, 125). Between 1973 and 1975, the San Francisco Bay Area's Black Women Organized for Action grew from fifteen to three hundred members (Schneir 1994, 172). A smaller, more radical group organized by black women in Boston was the Combahee River Collective. They explicitly rejected the idea put forth by black nationalists that "[the man] is the leader of the house/nation," arguing that racial equality went hand-in-hand with gender equality (Combahee River Collective 1979, 365).

Dee Williams made the implications of feminists' call for gender equality the starting point of her 1974 book, *How to Get and Keep Your Black Man in Spite of Women's Lib.* Although she embraced many of the goals of the women's movement, including equal pay for equal work, day care, and women's political representation, she argued that black women could ill afford the "experiment with social and sexual lifestyles" that women's liberation represented.[17] According to Williams, black women had not yet established strong and secure ties to black men—"neither side is sure of love and acceptance by the other."[18] When black women insisted on equality and were too strong and independent, they alienated black men, "commit[ting] love suicide."[19] Black men, she argued, were easily alienated by black women's strength due to their pronounced need to be the dominant partner in the relationship, a reaction to the reversal of traditional gender roles under slavery.[20] Relationships survived only when the black man felt that he was "the boss."[21]

With that in mind, Williams scolded her black women readers for being too assertive, strong, and determined. These qualities were at odds with the ideal of feminine behavior she proposed: a calculated mix of helplessness, innocence, and bashfulness that would call forth a man's protective instincts and thus ensure a healthy, happy relationship.[22] White women were the implicit and, at times, explicit models for this feminine ideal; at one point, Williams even recommended that black women emulate the white slave-owning heroine of *Gone with the Wind,* Scarlet O'Hara, who made an art of using tears to get what she wanted from (white) men.[23] The author addressed the potentially contentious nature of such a role model when she asked her readers, "Sounds like I'm trying to make you act like a white woman?" Her answer was to suggest that, in this instance, race was irrelevant: "Well, I'm only trying to make you act like a *woman*, period."[24] Her scolding also implied a rather low opinion of black women who, without Williams's guidance, did not behave like women at all.

Williams need have looked no farther than the 1950s for her feminine ideal, since her advice to black women was largely in keeping with that of the earlier decade. Just as the 1950s generation of young white women had been advised not to "stand passively by and wait to be selected by the man of her dreams,"[25] Williams urged her black women readers to be quite proactive and assertive about finding a man. Thus, she counseled them to move to a state with an oversupply of men, switch to a male-dominated occupation, find an apartment complex that catered to singles, or organize their work schedules around their man hunt.[26] Once they had found their man, assertiveness was no longer required; indeed, it was a marked handicap. Instead, as in the 1950s, the appearance of shyness and a willingness to perform deferential emotional labor were the qualities that would nurture and sustain the relationship.

Williams referred to this emotional labor as the "art of making men feel good about themselves."[27] Developing this art required women to listen, to let the man take the lead in conversation, to allow a man to educate them on some topic, and to be prepared to act as silent, approving witnesses to his every endeavor.[28] Williams claimed that white women were much better at this labor than black women, at least in the eyes of most black men. Citing a survey of black men's attitudes toward women, she asserted that 90 percent of black men felt white women were "more feminine and understanding" than black women.[29] Black women, by contrast, were seen by many of the black men she interviewed as "bossy," "aggressive," and "demanding." One interviewee who dated white women explained that he did so

> only when he tired of battling strong-willed black women who didn't always know how to make him feel big. He's really attracted to ambitious professional black women, but finds a little of them goes a long way, like good medicine. When he wants to relax and just feel like a man, he goes to a white woman who waits on him like a servant. He feels that black women are so afraid of any semblance of servitude that they refuse to do anything for their men that reminds them of the master/slave roles. What they're failing to realize is that this is the only way they will get, keep, and please him.[30]

The contrast between black and white women presented here re-created the nineteenth-century dichotomy between the shy, submissive white "lady" and the assertive black "mammy," but with a twist—the white "lady" was now the servant of the black man, rather than the reverse. Although this man felt that, "like good medicine," he should prefer black women, they could not provide him with the proper sense of manliness, which seemed to require some degree of deference from a woman, including the offering of her emotional labor. Thus, the message to black women who wanted to keep a black man was to adopt the shy, submissive, emotionally nurturant characteristics of the white "lady" as their own. To do so was to demonstrate not only their femininity, but also their loyalty to black men and to their needs. If they insisted instead on being "strong and independent," they risked permanently alienating black men.[31]

Unlike authors writing for a white audience in the 1950s, Williams was not concerned that some of her readers might actually suffer from feelings of shyness; from her perspective, black women's assertiveness, not shyness, was the major obstacle to romance. Thus, she offered no advice on how to overcome shyness in the pursuit of a man, and she failed to caution readers against displaying certain shy characteristics that might make them appear aloof or unapproachable. Instead, she emphasized the dangers of boldness, a quality that she assumed all black women naturally possessed.

Black men, for their part, were portrayed by Williams as confident, verbally skillful, and dynamic—there was no trace of the shyness and timidity of the Sambo stereotype. Yet despite their apparent repudiation of this emasculating stereotype, their masculinity was not entirely secure. According to Williams, a history of a reversal of "sexual leadership pattern[s] among blacks" meant that "the Black Man, more than any other man, has to feel that he masters his woman."[32] Only by following "traditional" (i.e., white) patterns of gender relations could black men prove their manhood; it was up to black women to loyally support their efforts by downplaying their strength and assertiveness and willingly taking the subordinate role. Women who resisted and tried in some manner to control black men were destined to lose them.[33]

The value and implications of the tradition of black women's strength and assertiveness were also debated in the pages of *Essence* magazine throughout the 1970s. A number of articles raised the issue of a long-standing tension between black women and men, one that was rooted in slavery, when whites had disrupted gender relations in black families by giving black women more power than black men.[34] As a result, black men felt very insecure about their manhood, especially in relation to strong and independent black women.[35] The *Essence* articles, written primarily by men, debated the view that the subjugation of black women was central to black men's efforts to prove that they were no longer the "shuffling Uncle Toms of yesteryear."[36] According to these authors, many black men subscribed to the view that, in order for the "revolution" to succeed, black women must "sit down, shut up, and let us lead."[37] By stifling the once-assertive voices of black women, black men could banish the infantilizing image of the passive, timid Sambo and reclaim their masculinity. Ultimately, the authors argued against this position, explaining that "[a]ll this talk about 'the woman has to walk two paces behind the man and she can't talk back' is bullshit. If your woman has something to say, she says it."[38] *True* revolutions did not insist on women's silence, but "affirm[ed] the equality of women in the building of the new nation."[39] Black women did not need to be subservient to men to demonstrate their loyalty to black men and to build up black men's trampled egos.

Indeed, a series of articles suggested that it was only by learning to communicate with black women that black men would be able to truly heal their wounded psyches. The authors, two psychologists, portrayed black men, like their white counterparts, as having difficulty expressing their emotions due to a fear of ridicule. As was the case with authors writing for a white audience in the 1970s, they expected women to play a role in helping men to disclose their emotions. But this role was more limited than that envisioned for white women; it consisted primarily of encouragement and understanding in the struggle to express emotions. Ultimately, it was up to black men to take primary responsibility for engaging in "feeling talk."[40] The authors explained that the benefits far outweighed any risks: "Talking things out with your woman is essential if you hope to improve your relationship. You need to check out what's going on with her and let her know what's going on with you. Holding feelings in won't improve your relationship, it may just give you an ulcer."[41] Thus, while these authors, too, saw self-disclosure as the key to a healthy relationship, they did not blame black women for black men's hesitancy to self-disclose. Moreover, in assuming that black men and black women were equally responsible for the emotion work required to sustain a relationship, they offered readers a more egalitarian view of heterosexual relationships than that offered to middle-class white audiences.

Taken together, the *Essence* magazine articles and Dee Williams's book of advice presented black women and men with both sides of the debate about black female and male relationships. On one side, Williams, like some black nationalists, argued that black women needed to embrace the shy, submissive qualities of the "lady" and quietly perform deferential emotional labor for black men in order to restore men's masculine pride. On the other side, authors of *Essence* magazine articles argued that black women's submission was out of character with a true revolutionary spirit and emphasized the need for reciprocal emotion work. In many ways, this debate was in no way unique to black Americans; whites were likewise rethinking the value of shyness for women during the 1970s. What was different about the debate within black publications was that the stakes were considered to be so much higher. With the quest for civil rights tied to definitions of black masculinity and femininity, the strength and survival of an entire community were implicated in the standards of behavior that black women and men chose to endorse.

The Controversy Continues

Advice texts concerning heterosexual relationships written for a specifically black audience in the mid-1980s to mid-1990s were more numerous and more diverse than they were in the 1970s. They ranged from those that were practically indistinguishable in tone and content from those written for a middle-class white audience,[42] to those that were focused on black women's particular relationship problems,[43] to those written for black men that were full of invective aimed at black women.[44] Articles on male-female relationships occupied more space in *Essence* magazine than they had in the 1970s and covered five main themes: relationship conflicts between black women and men, interracial relationships, ways to boost self-esteem, the importance of communication, and positive perspectives on being single.

In many of the advice texts and the magazine articles, black women continued to be represented as the opposite of shy—that is, as verbally assertive, even aggressive, in keeping with the Sapphire image. Black women's perceived assertiveness was a source of controversy primarily to the extent that it was thought to interfere with their "duty" to perform emotion work for black men. For some conservative authors, black women's speech was a powerful symbol of their disloyalty and failure to support black men emotionally, a failing that led to serious problems for black men.[45] Yoshua Barak (1992, 23, 29, 42) characterized (American) black women as "loud," "sassy," "hostile," "disgraceful bitches" who

sapped black men's energy by constantly arguing with them and question-
ing their authority; ultimately, this lack of energy made it far easier for
"the white man" to control black men. Similarly, Shaharazad Ali (1989,
66) argued that vocal black women with "electrical shock tongue[s]" led
many black men to abuse alcohol or drugs. Both authors agreed that
black women needed to put black men's needs before their own, to quietly
submit to their greater power and authority, since nature had decreed
that "the Blackman must always be the main focus of the relationship."[46]

Although these authors represented the extreme view, men quoted in
the relatively mainstream magazine *Essence* frequently made similar
points about black women's verbal aggressiveness and unwillingness to
provide emotional support for black men, characterizing black women as
"bitchy," "angry," "Amazon[s]."[47] One member of an all-male discussion
group argued, "Sisters, they're kinda rough. I think they should learn to
be softer, less hostile and argumentative. Carrying so much responsibility for so long has made them very bitter."[48] Another made the implied
threat behind these characterizations explicit, asserting that he preferred
to date less demanding white women,[49] a move that would be perceived
by some as a denial of the bond, forged by a shared history of racism, between black men and women. Although none of these men suggested
that the advancement of civil rights was dependent upon black women
giving up "unfeminine" assertive behaviors, racial solidarity was clearly
still at issue. Black women's failure to heed this advice to become more
quietly feminine carried the risk of abandonment by black men.

Black women authors writing in *Essence* as well as the women they interviewed tended to have a different perspective on their apparent lack of
shyness and its implications for male-female relationships. First, some
authors argued that black women were not assertive enough: afraid of
the stereotype of the emasculating black "matriarch," some black women
failed to communicate their own needs and desires or remained silent
when they should have spoken.[50] One author spoke for many black
women when she asked, "How many of us have remained silent about a
man's money making scheme, however disastrous we knew it to be, in
order to be supportive? Who among us can say that she hasn't stifled a
criticism and kept her mouth shut about something that really bothered
her, under the guise of standing by her man?"[51] Second, those authors
who did accept the idea that black women were generally assertive saw it
as a source of strength in heterosexual relationships.[52] If black men were
threatened by it, black women could always date white men[53] or remain
happily single.[54] Thus, these authors challenged the assumption that

gender inequality was a small price to pay to guarantee successful relationships with black men.

Some authors put part of the blame for problems in black female-male relationships not on black women's assertiveness, but on black men's emotional distance. Like white men, black men in the 1980s and 1990s were frequently perceived as unable to express their feelings to their partners, a difficulty that was regarded as an integral aspect of the "cool" masculine pose, in which men hide their feelings beneath a tough exterior. Some saw this as a particular problem plaguing black men, who experienced more societal pressure than other men to be "strong" and "macho."[55] By contrast, black women, like white women, were regarded as generally quite skilled at "feeling talk."[56] But where these gender differences were often explained through recourse to biology in advice books written for a primarily white audience, those written for a black audience regarded these behavior patterns as a consequence of socialization: black women, by virtue of the fact that they were women, simply had more license to talk about their feelings than black men.[57] This was a handicap that black women had to acknowledge, and that black men had to overcome. There was no mention of black men being "naturally" reserved about discussing their feelings, or of an ancient male tongue offering them few words for expressing their emotions, as was the case among self-help authors writing for a white audience. An ideology of natural difference may have been less appealing to black authors as an explanation for gender differences given the history of its use in the service of racism (see, for example, Gould 1981; Haller 1971).

References to the hazards of the cool masculine pose suggested that the efforts of an earlier generation of black activists to redefine black male identity had been successful, at least from blacks' perspective. Black men, it seemed, had indeed repudiated the Sambo stereotype, with its accompanying notion of a timid, childlike dependency. The problem was no longer how to achieve masculinity, but how to mitigate its negative effects.

The fact that the Sambo image had lost much of its relevance by the 1980s and 1990s may have helped to explain why the issue of black women's apparent assertiveness had fewer political implications in this period compared to the 1970s. With black men's masculinity more secure in the larger culture, black women's assertiveness had less power to disrupt black men's attempts to be taken seriously as leaders. Thus, black women's assertiveness was no longer considered either an impediment to or method of achieving racial equality; instead, self-help authors focused exclusively on its implications for successful relationships with black men.

Yet, even with this narrower focus, black women's assertiveness continued to be a divisive issue, with some self-help authors offering highly negative views of such assertiveness. At a time when black men were increasingly likely to be absent from black families—due to high rates of divorce,[58] incarceration,[59] and death[60]—this perspective could be regarded as a cautionary tale to black women that sought to enforce their silence. Black women, in effect, were being told that by being quiet and submissive, they could restore both black men's affections and their presence in black households. The more positive view of black women's assertiveness offered by other self-help authors was a form of resistance to this effort to enforce power relations between black women and men.

Conclusion

For African Americans, advice regarding shyness and its perceived opposite, assertiveness, has had a level of urgency missing from the advice offered to whites. With definitions of masculinity and femininity tied to the quest for civil rights, African Americans' very survival has been implicated in how they incorporated shyness and assertiveness into those definitions. In the 1950s, black women's displays of shyness in the presence of black men were thought by some to demonstrate the proper feminine manners that would overcome prejudice and discrimination. For black women to be too assertive was a threat both to black men's fragile egos—a consequence of being treated as less than men by whites—and to the advancement of civil rights, which depended upon dispelling notions of blacks' essential difference from whites.

In the 1960s, as the civil rights movement intensified, debate grew over the implications of assertiveness on the part of black women. Some civil rights leaders and black nationalists argued that black men's ability to repudiate the timid Sambo image and to claim both their manhood and equal treatment with whites depended for its success on black women abandoning their assertive behaviors. This view was reflected in 1970s' author Dee Williams's book of advice to black women. She embraced the 1950s' version of black (and white) femininity, urging black women to be less assertive, and to instead quietly perform deferential emotional labor for black men. This view was also debated in the pages of *Essence* magazine, where it was ultimately rejected in favor of a more egalitarian approach that emphasized reciprocal emotional labor and assertive behavior for both women and men. The authors of the *Essence* articles attempted to redefine black femininity in a manner that challenged negative stereotypes about black women's assertiveness. They also challenged the idea that black masculinity needed to repudiate all seemingly feminine elements, such as talk about emotion, in order to be a force to be reckoned with.

In the 1980s and 1990s, black men appeared to have successfully laid the image of Sambo to rest, replacing it with a "cool" image. With their masculinity more culturally secure, black women's assertiveness might have been perceived as less of a threat, both to black men and to the quest for civil rights. But while assertiveness on the part of black women was no longer regarded as an impediment to racial equality, it remained, for some self-help authors, a sign of disrespect and disloyalty to black men. They implied that if black women did not learn to curb their tongues, they risked abandonment by black men, their traditional allies, in favor of other, more accommodating groups of women. They used the negative image of Sapphire to try to silence and control black women.

Other 1980s and 1990s self-help authors saw black women's assertiveness as a strength, one that they should draw upon more often. If it threatened black men's masculine pride, so be it. These authors encouraged black women to find alternatives to relationships with black men rather than be silenced out of fear of rejection. By urging black women to hold on to a tradition of assertiveness, these authors questioned the legitimacy of male dominance within heterosexual relationships. They embraced assertiveness as a model of empowerment for black women.

African Americans' debate over the meanings of shyness and assertiveness shows how women's assertive behavior can be perceived as a threat to men, not simply because women can use their words against men, but also because male power is enhanced by a monopoly on public speech. In the 1960s and 1970s, when the civil rights and black nationalist movements were at their peaks, black women's assertiveness was frequently regarded as an impediment to black men's efforts to create a more powerful masculinity. Now that this masculinity has been established, there is somewhat less public concern about black women's assertiveness; however, the fact that it remains a point of contention suggests that it retains its power to divide black women and men.

CHAPTER FIVE

Shyness from Nine to Five

> Whoever desires constant success must change his conduct with the times.
>
> Machiavelli, *The Discourses* (1531)

In this chapter I explore the relationships among shyness, gender, and popular ideas about how to achieve success in the workplace. The workplace that I focus on is decidedly white collar, since most self-help authors, regardless of time period, directed their advice to executives, administrators, managers, and, occasionally, salespeople. Consequently, the manipulation of people, rather than things, played a large role in self-help authors' ideas of success. The idealized workplace that I focus on is also largely white: although the 1970s saw the increased presence of minority women and men in white-collar jobs from which they had historically been excluded,[1] authors writing advice books on work success continued to target a largely white audience that was aspiring to or already in the middle classes. Therefore, I limit my analysis to what these books reveal about the relationship between shyness and success for white middle-class women and men.

In each time period, self-help authors' attitudes toward shyness at work were shaped, in part, by conceptions about how best to achieve a friendly, sociable intimacy in the workplace. In the 1950s, deferential emotional labor was the key to intimacy, and shyness was an important element of this labor. This changed in the 1970s, 1980s, and 1990s, as more women entered the workplace and the focus moved from an intimacy achieved through deference to one achieved through the assumption of equality. Shyness came to be regarded as antithetical to the communication style that demonstrated this equality. These shifting shyness norms both legitimated and challenged gender hierarchies in the workplace. In the 1950s, the conventions governing shyness at work reflected and supported a gendered occupational structure in which men routinely held positions of authority over women. The shyness norms of the 1970s posed a challenge to these power relations, a challenge that was muted in the 1980s and 1990s as these norms came to conceal rather than contest gender hierarchies at work.

"The Man with the Smile Is the Man Worthwhile"

In the 1950s, most (72 percent) self-help authors directed their advice about how to achieve success at work to the most upwardly mobile members of the white-collar workplace, white middle-class men; however, a few addressed white middle-class women as well, thus acknowledging that women, too, might have career aspirations.[2] But their support for women's ambitions was rather limited, since they, along with those authors writing exclusively for men, routinely depicted women as occupying subordinate positions in a gendered job hierarchy. Men were presidents, vice-presidents, top executives, managers, and small-business owners,[3] while women were secretaries, stenographers, bookkeepers, receptionists, filing clerks, and "salesgirls."[4] Given that these clerical and sales jobs rarely led to promotions for women,[5] the idea of "success" that self-help authors were selling was a more static concept when applied to women than when applied to men: the successful woman worker simply managed to keep her job and do it well, whereas the successful businessman advanced up a career ladder, was recognized as a leader, inspired others to succeed, or became wealthy.[6] With women having such limited opportunities to compete with men, men's success was measured primarily in relationship to other men.

Success for the white middle-class businessman hinged, above all, on his mastery of social skills and his development of a "pleasing" personal-

ity.[7] According to self-help authors, education, experience, or job-re-
lated skills counted for only a small portion of a businessman's success.
"[P]ersonality factors, the ability to deal with people effectively" ac-
counted for a far larger portion of success. Authors who wished to drive
home this point relied on "various scientific studies" to argue that personality was in fact responsible for anywhere from 67 to 90 percent of
the businessman's success.[8] Every author urged readers to immediately
begin developing the ideal business personality, one that was friendly,
sociable, self-confident, and enthusiastic,[9] that attracted friends quickly
and easily,[10] and that appealed to coworkers, clients, and customers.[11]
Parents could set this process in motion early in life by teaching their
children to be sociable and to "fit in" with groups of other children.[12]
The goal was to become a "magnetic," "charming" individual, thus securing the goodwill and friendship of those in a position to aid one's rise
up the ladder of success.[13]

This advice was in keeping with the "personality ethic" of success that
had developed at the turn of the century, a phenomenon that Cawelti
(1965, 183) attributed to the growth of the large, impersonal organization.[14] To attract notice in large, anonymous firms where every coworker
was a potential competitor, early twentieth-century self-help authors had
advised businessmen to develop a dynamic personality, arguing that it
played a larger role in determining success than business acumen (see
Biggart 1983, 300; Cawelti 1965, 183; DeVitis and Rich 1996, 49; Lasch
1978, 57–59; Susman 1984, 274).[15] What was unique in the 1950s was
how white middle-class men were expected to win over others in order to
get ahead: through a degree of deference quite at odds with traditional
norms of American masculinity, which fashioned the ideal "self-made
man" as an aggressive competitor who tested and confirmed his manhood in the capitalist marketplace (Kimmel 1994, 124; 1996, 23). Shyness both inhibited and supported this new, deferential success strategy,
playing much the same role that it did in establishing a young woman's
heterosexual appeal. On the one hand, a businessman's feelings of shyness were thought to drive clients and coworkers away, but on the other,
self-help authors embraced certain qualities associated with shyness—
such as silence, reticence, and humility—as key ingredients of the emotional labor required to please others and thus achieve success.

A businessman's feelings of shyness threatened his career prospects
for the same reasons that it threatened a young girl's ability to appeal to
boys: it made him seem aloof, unfriendly, and "hard to get to know."[16]

Self-help authors argued that coworkers and customers would respond poorly to the shy man's apparent cold and indifferent manner, taking their ideas and their business to "some 'easy to know' fellow" instead.[17] If not fired outright, the shy businessman might remain stuck in a low-level job, or take home an inadequate salary.[18] These were risks not to be taken lightly in a decade which considered the "breadwinner" role to be "the only normal state for the adult [white] male" (Ehrenreich 1983, 15). These potential blows to male pride and identity help to explain why 1950s self-help authors were more concerned about white-collar men's shyness than they were about young boys' feelings of shyness around girls. Much more was at stake, and the shy white-collar man hoping to succeed could not rely on others to draw him out of his shell.

Self-help authors advised shy men that instead of interacting with a "timid, lukewarm Caspar Milquetoast,"[19] customers, coworkers, and superiors preferred to do business with a man with a "smile in his manner and a warm eagerness in his handshake."[20] This man could not be *too* eager or aggressive, however. Echoing the advice given to young girls to be discreet in advertising their interest in a particular boy, self-help authors argued that the key to appealing to others in the business world was to show just the right amount of self-restrained interest in them.[21] Too much eagerness was a sign of desperation, raising suspicions in the other person's mind as to "why you [were] trying so hard" to win his approval;[22] on the other hand, playing it cool by standing on the sidelines waiting to be noticed carried the risk of being overlooked completely.[23] By taking the middle road and adopting an air of calm self-assurance and "enthusiasm used with wisdom and discretion," readers were assured that they would inspire confidence in others, thus guaranteeing success.[24]

Feelings of shyness interfered with the businessman's ability to properly manage his own emotions and perform emotional labor for coworkers, superiors, and customers, labor that further enhanced his success. Like young women on a date, white-collar men were told to suppress negative feelings (like fear or timidity) in favor of positive ones, letting those around them "see only the optimistic side of [their] personalit[ies]."[25] Suppressing feelings of fear or timidity also facilitated the businessman's ability to provide his fellow employees, superiors, and clients with unstinting emotional support—encouraging them, sympathizing with them, refraining from criticizing or disagreeing with them, sending them notes of support, felicity, or reassurance, or simply smiling at them.[26] Like an anxious lover hoping to elicit some sign of reciprocal interest from the beloved, the success-seeking businessman was to shower everyone in the workplace with attention and concern.

But while *feelings* of shyness were a hindrance to performing this emotional labor, characteristics associated with shyness were central to businessmen's use of emotional labor to advance their own interests. Several authors stressed that silent attention was a useful strategy for allowing the businessman to "find out what the other fellow wants, what he will settle for, before showing your own hand."[27] Others argued that reticence and humility were important means of ingratiating oneself with the speaker, ultimately helping to secure a business deal. In a passage with striking similarities to dating advice for young women, Earl Prevette (1953, 150) explained the proper approach for the success-seeking businessman to take with a client:

> By listening to what he says, you compliment him. You please him. Praise his point of view and be hearty in your approbation. On the other hand, if he says something you do not like, don't tell him. Agree with him. His opinion may only be temporary, but respect it. Try to be considerate of his feelings. A kind word gently spoken is a quick means of relieving strain and tension. . . . [A]pproach him with a spirit of humbleness and kindness. . . . Make him feel that any idea you are giving him is his own.[28]

In the economic marketplace, no less than in the marriage market, adopting a mask of shyness—by deliberately displaying silence, reticence, or humility—was a strategy of deference, intended to create feelings of self-satisfied superiority in the men to whom the performance was directed. By donning this mask, businessmen were advised that they would reap tangible rewards, such as a sale or a promotion, just as young women were advised that their assumption of deferential shy behaviors on a first date secured a second one.

Viewing the prescribed behavior of the businessman at work as a form of deference akin to that expected of a young woman on a date underscores the power dynamics at play not only in relationships *between* white middle-class women and men, but also *among* white middle-class men. As Connell (1987, 186; 1995, 76–79) has pointed out, there is more than one type of masculinity. "Hegemonic masculinity" is the form of masculinity that is culturally exalted, that which preserves and institutionalizes men's power over women and some men's power over other men;

"subordinated masculinities" are those masculinities that are stigmatized or prohibited. The white middle-class men reading success manuals for advice on how to achieve prosperity occupied a subordinate position in this hierarchy of masculinities—albeit a (hopefully) temporary one—while those men who had "made it," whose behavior presumably influenced the advice proffered, occupied the dominant position.

In order to move to the top of the hierarchy, success-seeking businessmen had to "pay their dues" by showing the proper degree of deference and subordination to their superiors through their performance of emotional labor. Like apprentices in the manual trades, if they performed well, they were granted the rewards that enabled them to move up the ladder of success, securing the "master" status that confirmed their manhood and made them part of an elite, all-male club (see Cockburn 1983, 45–46). Since large firms generally relied upon internal promotion ladders to fill positions in the 1950s, the secure environment necessary for such a system to work was in place (Goldin 1990, 116).

Self-help authors' embrace of a success strategy that featured the decidedly nonmasculine quality of deference created alarm among pundits in the 1950s. A diverse group of writers and scholars argued that the "feminine" behaviors demanded of the "company" man irrevocably compromised the masculine ideal of the self-made man (see Mills 1953, xii; Packard 1959, 9; Riesman 1950, 23; Whyte 1957, 150; Wylie 1955, 243). These critics longed for the days when success was epitomized by boldness, independence, and daring, when men struck out on their own and refused to abase themselves to anyone. They disparaged the new company man as innocuous and benign, a man who was conditioned against taking initiative or risks. C. Wright Mills (1953, xii) succinctly summed up the critics' case with the argument that the new success strategies had led to the ascendancy of "the little man," a "pitiful" creature who "never talk[ed] loud, never talk[ed] back, never [took] a stand." At the heart of these reproaches lay critics' rejection of the notion of a temporary subordinated masculinity. From their perspective, the man who rose to the top of the ladder by deferring to other men knew no other way of behaving; thus, there was no distinction to be made between subordinated and hegemonic masculinity. Successful men remained "little men."

Yet, regardless of how small he was when compared to men of previous generations, the white middle-class businessman remained a large, commanding figure in relation to women at work. As envisioned by self-help authors—and reflected in the workplace itself—white-collar men routinely occupied positions of authority over women in clerical or sales positions. This authority entitled them to a show of friendliness, under-standing, and flattery, the anticipation of their every want and need, and the suppression of any grievance by the women working for them.[29] In essence, white middle-class women were expected to behave as "office wives," performing the same type of emotional labor expected of them at home. They were to suppress any feelings of anxiety-producing shyness that might mar the requisite pleasant working relationship between themselves and their male bosses, yet also limit their role to that of a quiet supporter of their bosses' ideas and demands.

But unlike white-collar men, whose deferential emotional labor took place within a context of competitive advancement, white-collar women's emotional labor took place within a context of survival; if they wanted to keep their jobs, they had to accept a degree of humiliation as part of their duties. As Elizabeth MacGibbon (1954, 46–47) explained:

> I know a girl whose superior indulged his mean disposition by yelling and swearing at her, even though he liked her and her work. One day he shouted at her from another room, "Come here!" in much the same tone he would have used in calling a dog. It seemed the crowning hu-miliation, and she was tempted to put on her hat and walk out. Instead she went quietly to his door and smilingly asked, "Did you call me, Mr. Smith?" Now, that was tact, and common sense too, for she happened to need the job. . . . A clever secretary I know says that she is, among other things, a butler, a doormat and, at times, a nurse to her boss.

The clever secretary's status as "doormat" was unlikely to change since she was not an "apprentice" using deferential emotional labor to gain en-trance to an elite club, but an invisible "helper" who ensured that the club ran smoothly. The ideal of feminine behavior that she was expected to emulate centered on submission; there was no more powerful version of femininity akin to hegemonic masculinity to which she could aspire (Connell 1987, 187). Thus, where white-collar men's deferential emo-tional labor was a "ritual of induction into . . . [hegemonic] masculinity" (Connell 1987, 186), hers was a symbol of her powerlessness, a ritual that supported and reinscribed a gender hierarchy in which white middle-class men dominated white middle-class women.

The 1950s' success strategy of businessmen performing deferential emotional labor for others on the way up the ladder relied upon women's (and non-white men's) absence from the ranks of both the success seekers and the successful, since it ensured that white middle-class men took orders only from other white middle-class men. When women and non-white men began to enter these ranks in the 1970s, self-help authors abandoned this strategy for one based on the presumption of equality among employees.

"One May Smile and Smile, and Be a Villain"

In the 1970s, women's presence in the labor force rose steadily.[30] Aided by federal commitment to work-based gender equality,[31] women managed to make significant inroads into traditionally male occupations, so much so that the rate of decline of sex-segregated occupations was three times greater in the 1970s than in the 1960s (Beller 1984). Self-help authors responded to these trends by making it standard practice to include white middle-class women as members of the intended audience of success manuals.[32] Indeed, instead of writing exclusively for men, as most of their 1950s' counterparts had done, self-help authors now either wrote success books for a mixed audience, or for women alone. They also expanded the notion of success for white middle-class women to incorporate both a wider variety of white-collar occupations, including supervisor and manager, and movement up a career ladder.

Whether they wrote for both women and men or women alone, 1970s' self-help authors sent a consistent message to their readers: "communication" was the new gospel of success.[33] Claiming that communication was "what much of business is all about," authors urged male and female success seekers to learn to manipulate a complex array of verbal and nonverbal communication skills, including being direct, building rapport, using proper body language to support one's verbal message, controlling one's voice, and listening.[34] Likewise, parents were urged to teach their children good social skills at an early age, skills that included assertive communication, positive affect, and eye contact.[35] Readers were instructed to "state facts clearly and concisely in a moderate but firm tone. Emphasize appropriate words, concentrate on a smooth delivery, and pause for attention. Avoid a whiny, high-pitched sound; a harsh, hard, tight voice; a monotone; or those 'gosh,' 'gee,' 'uhs' that go with many hesitations."[36] Self-help authors claimed that mastering these skills would bring greater productivity, better work relationships, "personal power," promotions, and higher salaries—as much as $40,000 higher, according to one author.[37] When such social skills were mastered early in life, they ensured that children would get along well with other children and adults.[38]

This emphasis on communication was not so much a departure from the "personality ethic" of success evident in the 1950s as a variation of it—both people pleasing and communication required good interpersonal skills. But as envisioned by self-help authors, communication lacked one important aspect of people pleasing: deference. The goal of communication was to maximize understanding, not to make the other person feel superior. Rather than remain silent or simply agree with a client or coworker in order to avoid conflict and enhance the other's self-esteem, good communicators were expected to be assertive with superiors and inferiors alike, stating their opinions, needs, and instructions clearly and forcefully.[39] Accordingly, Michael Korda (1977, 193) urged, "When someone makes a mistake, point it out! When you're not satisfied, say so! When you've got a point to make, make it!"

Self-help authors were now of the opinion that clarity and honesty offered more direct routes to success than deferential silence and reticence.[40] The fact that the American economy was at its weakest since the Great Depression may have played a part in this shift: with unemployment on the rise and major American industries in decline, long-term employment prospects were in doubt, even for white-collar workers (Bondi 1995, 125; Winkler 1993, 221). Many companies were abandoning internal promotion ladders and bringing in upper-level executives from outside (Jennings 1971, 12). With less job security and assurance of promotion, there was no longer any guarantee that an "apprentice/master" relationship would have time to develop and bear fruit. Thus, blowing one's own horn and asking for rewards outright may have indeed been a wiser strategy to follow.

With the loss of deference as a means of achieving success, self-help authors considered all aspects of shyness—both feelings and behaviors—to be off limits for success seekers. Self-help authors cautioned that feelings of shyness interfered with one's ability to communicate well, by inhibiting speech, fostering nervous body language, and producing excessive self-consciousness and anxiety.[41] As Arthur Wassmer (1978, 6–7) explained, when overcome with feelings of shyness,

> your attention focuses on the turmoil going on within, rather than on the person you are with. . . . Part of this self-concern is an attempt to control your anxiety. You struggle to stop your voice from shaking,

calm your trembling hands, and keep yourself under control. But with the focus of attention so powerfully drawn inward, you often fail to hear accurately what others are saying, let alone really make contact with them.

Failure to "make contact" with others was signaled by a lapse into silence, now regarded not as a sign of pleasing deference, but of communication failure. Failure to communicate, in turn, seriously limited the shy person's chances of obtaining a position, remaining in it, or advancing to greater heights. Thus, self-help authors cautioned readers that shyness on the job was more than a "handicap"—it was a "total disaster."[42]

Shyness at work was particularly troublesome for white middle-class women. In an era devoted to women's liberation, shyness had heightened political significance for women given its association with subservience, deference, and passivity. These were qualities considered incompatible with career ambition, leadership, and competitiveness.[43] Liberal feminist authors writing exclusively for white middle-class women encouraged them to reject shyness as an aspect of traditional femininity, and embrace assertiveness instead. Being assertive was primarily a matter of verbal communication, the direct statement of a woman's rights, needs, and wants. Assertive women were "authentic," "confident," and "open," capable of "acting in their own behalf" and taking "the initiative in meeting their needs."[44] They did not engage in deferential emotional labor for others.

Assertiveness also involved a particular nonverbal communication style, the hallmarks of which were a steady, "uncompromising" gaze, a firm tone of voice, and calm, purposeful gestures.[45] Several authors equated assertion with power, suggesting that power was, in large part, a matter of style of presentation:

> The powerful person walks into a room standing straight with her head up. She seeks eye contact, chooses a chair close to the speaker, and introduces herself immediately. She sits relaxed, with her hands in her lap. She is free of nervous, fidgety gestures. The powerless person knocks timidly at the door, and waits hesitantly until she's invited in. A powerless person always needs instructions. She walks slowly and chooses a chair that's removed from the group and looks to the others to speak and to invite her to introduce herself. She looks down and avoids eye contact. Her nervous gestures include fidgeting and clutch-

ing her arms across her chest. While the powerful person brings life and energy into a meeting simply by her presence, the powerless person will drain a conversation. In fact, one wants to get rid of her quickly.[46]

If power was indeed a performance rather than a "perk" associated with a particular job title, white middle-class women had only to act powerfully in order to be powerful. Thus, the shy, powerless woman simply needed to replace her silence, timidity, lack of eye contact, and nervous gestures with assertive gestures and behaviors in order to gain authority at work.

While this approach to ending women's subordination to men might seem simplistic, its basic premise is in keeping with current sociological perspectives on how gender is maintained as a relationship of inequality. According to West and Zimmerman (1987, 146), gender is a product of microlevel behaviors and interactions in which men "do" dominance and women "do" deference. These individual behaviors, in turn, help institutionalize gender as a larger structure which shapes the form that individual gender performances take (Connell 1987, 94). White middle-class women's abandonment of shyness and embrace of assertiveness would be tantamount to a refusal to "do" deference, thus challenging the foundation of gender. If this challenge were sustained and supported by other challenges, gender as a structure of inequality could be undone. Thus, whether they realized it or not, self-help authors' advice to women to be more assertive had the potential to contribute to a radical alteration of gender relations.

"There's Daggers in Men's Smiles"

What were the implications for white middle-class masculinities of the new emphasis on communication as the key to success?[47] Mastering communication skills required the 1970s businessman to perform some emotional labor: he had to listen to others and build rapport with his audience by, for example, remembering a subordinate's name, or engaging in small talk about his pet or home with other employees.[48] But the emotional labor expected of him lacked the critical ingredient of deference that had signaled his subordination to a more powerful group of men in the 1950s. The 1970s communication model of success urged both white middle-class women and men to be assertive, to refuse to be a powerless, deferential victim.[49] As Wayne Dyer (1978, 39) explained, "You just don't have to be passive or weak as you walk through your life steps. . . . Be a worthy, important you, rather than a sniveling permission-seeking victim who believes that everyone is more important than you are." Self-help authors of the 1970s clearly rejected the idea of success-seeking white middle-class male executives as temporarily subordinated to the more powerful; instead, these executives were instructed to act *as if* they were in a position of dominance, regardless of their actual place in the work hierarchy. Feelings of shyness and behaviors associated with it were considered to be at odds with this portrayal of dominance.

Thus, the shift in success strategies from people-pleasing to communication skills held out the possibility of changing the nature of relations between and among white middle-class women and men at work. No longer bound by demands for deference, women and men were instructed to behave in an assertive manner normally reserved for the privileged, treating subordinates and superiors alike, and expecting others to treat them as equals. While most would no doubt consider this to be a positive development, it is important to note that the elimination of deference as a success strategy for white middle-class men—at a time when women's presence in male-dominated occupations was growing—relieved them of the potential burden of having to defer to a woman. This is not to suggest that women's entry into male occupations *caused* success strategies to shift away from deference. As Reskin and Ross (1995, 136) found with women managers in the early 1980s, women may enter white-collar male occupations but still be limited to exercising authority solely over other women, thus posing no real threat to male strategies for advancement or to the gender hierarchy. Nonetheless, self-help authors' rejection of the strategy of deference for white middle-class men in favor of assertiveness ensured that, if there was an advantage to be gained through assertive communication, women were not the only ones who had access to it.

"Feeling Alone against Smiling Enemies"

Women's overall progress in making inroads into male-dominated occupations slowed somewhat in the 1980s compared to the precedent-setting 1970s,[50] stymied, in part, by a conservative political climate that offered less institutional support for women's employment in nontraditional occupations.[51] At the top levels of management, little had changed: in 1978 two women were heading Fortune 1000 companies, and in 1994 there were still only two (Brooks and Groves 1996). In 1990, women made up less than one-half of one percent of the most highly paid officers and directors of 799 of the largest American industrial and service companies (Fierman 1990). But women's desire to compete in the upper echelons of the white-collar world remained difficult to stifle. Women entered business schools in rising numbers throughout the 1980s, fueled partly by the cultural celebration of "yuppies," the young (mostly white) urban professionals who were unabashedly materialistic and highly focused on their careers (Bondi 1996, 391–92). By 1989, women constituted one-third of all recipients of the MBA, compared to a meager 3 percent in 1971 (Bondi 1996, 392). Women also swelled the ranks of lawyers: in 1995, women were 23 percent of all lawyers, a fifteen-point increase since 1980 and a twenty point increase since 1970 (American Bar Association Commission on Women in the Profession 1995).

Liberal feminist self-help authors writing in the 1970s had assumed that once they were given the opportunity to compete with men, white middle-class women's advancement would be secured by women rejecting shyness and passivity in favor of assertiveness. Their counterparts writing in the 1980s and 1990s were of the same mind, although a few preferred the term "bitchiness" or "gutsiness" to describe the type of behavior they were advocating, in which a woman "stands her ground and speaks her piece," and "doesn't try to please everyone but herself."[52] They argued that assertiveness training was still necessary for adult women, given the persistence of traditional female socialization practices, which favored deference, submission, and shyness over self-assertion or aggression.[53] (These socialization practices were not reflected in the child-rearing manuals of the period, which regarded both girls' and boys' shyness as a problem to be overcome.) It seemed, then, that either an earlier generation of women had failed to pass along the assertiveness ethic to their daughters, or that power relations were more difficult to dislodge than 1970s feminist self-help authors had anticipated.

Research suggested that the problem lay in the unanticipated strength of gendered power relations. In a study of the communication styles of a sample of 442 matched pairs of managers, Donnell and Hall (1980, 74) found no differences between women and men: both were equally likely to communicate feelings and factual information to superiors and subordinates, as well as solicit information from them. Likewise, subordinates' reports of their bosses' behaviors revealed no gender differences in managerial communication styles. Thus, it seemed that white middle-class women had indeed followed the advice of 1970s self-help authors to become assertive communicators. The source of women's difficulty became clear when the researchers examined subordinates' behavior toward their bosses. Subordinates with a female boss interacted with her differently than subordinates with a male boss, treating the woman boss *as if* she were a poor communicator. Similarly, Seifert (1984) found that male and female participants in an experiment who believed that they were receiving written communication from a female leader rated the notes as less clear than those who believed the communication originated from a male leader.[54] Thus, women were disadvantaged not by their own behaviors, but by others' perceptions—wrong though they might be—that they lacked communication competence.

This situation is an example of what Ridgeway (1997, 221) refers to as the pervasiveness of "gender status beliefs," "widely held beliefs that evaluate one sex [men] as generally superior and diffusely more competent than the other." Ridgeway (1997, 222) argues that these beliefs are so ingrained in our society that men (and sometimes women) are less likely to notice or give credence to behavior—such as women's assertiveness—that challenges them. Thus, encouraging white middle-class women to abandon shyness and to be assertive would not guarantee their future success, because women who followed this advice would not necessarily be perceived by others as assertive, competent communicators. In other words, women's behavior might change, but gender as a structure of inequality remained unchanged.

I make this point not to expose self-help authors as "wrong," but to highlight the difficulties faced by contestatory symbolic forms—those ideas that challenge the status quo (see Thompson 1990, 68). Ideologies incorporate and co-opt contestatory symbolic forms in order to diminish their disruptive potential (Williams 1982, 40–42). At the same time, the fact that gender ideologies are so pervasive and so flexible means that threats on one front are easily muted by shoring up another front (see Reskin and Roos 1990, 51). Thus, 1970s' feminist self-help authors' challenge to workplace gender hierarchies may have succeeded in helping to encourage more women to enter nontraditional occupations, but gender ideologies pervading the workplace prevented women's assumption of powerful behaviors from having its intended effect. To constitute an effective challenge to gender hierarchies, self-help authors would have to address the ways in which the liberatory possibilities available to individual readers are foreclosed by an environment structured by discriminatory practices and the gender ideologies that support them.

"Damn the Men with Careful Smiles"

Like feminist self-help authors, authors who wrote for a mixed audience in the 1980s and 1990s were attuned to the workings of power in the workplace;[55] however, they were more likely to offer success strategies that aimed to reduce its effects than to suggest ways to harness it. Mastering good verbal and nonverbal communication skills remained a central tenet of their advice,[56] but instead of arguing that assertive communication brought success, they linked success to the ability to create a comfortable, nonthreatening, respectful communication environment at work, one devoid of anger, power differences, or ambiguity.[57] The key to doing so was "empathic listening," a type of emotional labor that involved placing oneself almost literally in another person's shoes:

> Empathic (from empathy) listening gets inside another person's frame of reference. You look out through it, you see the world the way they see the world, you understand their paradigm, you understand how they feel. . . . The essence of empathic listening is not that you agree with someone; it's that you fully, deeply, understand that person, emotionally as well as intellectually.[58]

Empathic listening required a great deal of emotion work and was expected of bosses as well as subordinates. To attain such a deep level of understanding one had to "restate the ideas and feelings of the previous speaker accurately and to that speaker's satisfaction," synchronize one's "mood, body language, speech rate, and even breathing with the other person," display the proper degree of "non-judgmental acceptance," and offer interpretations of the "core" thoughts or emotions underlying the speakers' words.[59]

According to self-help authors, shyness, both as a feeling and as a set of behaviors, hampered one's ability to perform this labor. Feelings of shyness led to self-consciousness, a "self-absorption trap," which caused shy people to "be so concerned with what [they were] going to say next, or with what others [were] thinking of [them]" that they failed to listen properly.[60] In addition, silence, though clearly an important aspect of listening, became a hindrance to understanding when it was sustained for very long, since so much verbal encouragement was needed to be able to truly understand the speaker's point of view. As self-conscious, overly quiet communication partners, the shy were considered to be failures at empathic listening, unwilling or unable to do their share of emotional labor in the workplace. Thus, they failed to reap the rewards it could bring: business deals that satisfied both parties, greater trust, mutual respect, better working relationships, and greater productivity.[61]

Thus, despite the fact that a success strategy of listening opened up the possibility for greater tolerance for shyness at work, self-help authors remained committed to a highly negative view of shyness. Listening, after all, was often the one area in which shy people were considered by their peers to excel (Daly and Stafford 1984). The shy were also well known for their failure to self-disclose, which was considered an asset in the context of empathic listening, since it ensured that the spotlight would remain fixed on the empathy-seeking speaker. While these two skills on their own did not constitute the whole of empathic listening, they were not entirely at odds with it, either. But rather than suggest that the shy simply develop these skills more fully, self-help authors argued instead that being shy was "disastrous to winning" at work, and urged shy readers to read on in order to effect a cure.[62]

It seemed that self-help authors were intent not on rehabilitating shyness where possible but on eradicating it. This was, after all, the approach of pharmaceutical companies. If self-help authors wanted to compete with the quick fixes promised by anti-shyness drugs such as Paxil, they, too, had to suggest ways to eliminate shyness, not simply ameliorate some of its symptoms. Indeed, even authors who argued that children's shyness was largely a matter of genes—and thus, presumably, impervious to change—were unwilling to advise parents simply to let their shy children be. Shy children could become sociable, successful adults through appropriate parental intervention.[63]

It is important to note that white middle-class men as well as women were expected to become empathic listeners in order to succeed at work; authors made no allowances for men's supposed deficiencies in language and communication skills as their counterparts did in regards to intimate heterosexual relationships. Indeed, white middle-class men showed no signs of suffering from a lingering "reserve" at work as they did at home, despite the fact that empathic listening, like self-disclosure, was a form of emotional labor. This apparent inconsistency may be resolved by considering that empathic listening drew on different communication skills: as a listener, one's goal was to understand the thoughts and feelings of another person, not—as was expected in intimate relationships—to explore or necessarily verbalize one's own. Thus, a man could be a good empathic listener and a poor self-discloser, willing to listen to his intimate partner's or his colleagues' opinions and feelings, but still resistant to the idea of making his own feelings the subject of discussion. Indeed, one author likened the role of empathic listener to that of therapist or "sounding board," suggesting that the ideal listener was someone who elicited speech but remained somewhat of an enigma.[64]

Self-help authors' embrace of empathic listening for men was in keeping with a more sensitive form of white middle-class masculinity that emerged in the 1980s—the "New Masculinity" (Hondagneu-Sotelo and Messner 1994, 204). "New Men" were characterized by a higher level of involvement in child care and greater emotionality, including public weeping and open displays of affection toward other men. While this new masculinity seemed to signal the dawn of a more egalitarian era in gender relations, Hondagneu-Sotelo and Messner (1994, 214) argued that the New Man's overt displays of nonaggression and sensitivity often deflected attention from white middle-class men's institutional power over women and other men. Empathic listening could function in the same manner, serving to obscure rather than eliminate gendered power relations at work. Indeed, the goal of empathic listening was centered on creating a comfortable communication environment by reducing the *appearance* of power differences between a boss and his subordinates, not on reducing structural power inequities such as pay.

While the same mechanisms would apply when women superiors were interacting with their subordinates, as we saw with women's assertiveness, subordinates might choose to interpret women's behavior in light of traditional gender ideologies. In this instance, a woman boss who engaged in empathic listening could be labeled as "overly emotional" rather than "refreshingly sensitive." It is precisely these kinds of differences in the evaluation of women's and men's performance that can, as they accumulate, easily result in large disparities in promotion, salary, and status (Valian 1998, 3). Thus, far from signaling a more egalitarian era, empathic listening might have little effect on gender hierarchies in the workplace.

Conclusion

This analysis of changes in cultural norms surrounding shyness at work has shown how, even in the workplace, prevailing ideas about intimacy help to explain prevailing ideas about shyness. In the case of work relationships, the level of intimacy required to achieve success is somewhat less intense, in terms of emotional revelations, than that required to achieve success in heterosexual relationships; nonetheless, it is a type of intimacy, one based on friendliness, sociability, and smooth interpersonal relationships. In the 1950s, self-help authors argued that this intimacy was best achieved by performing deferential emotional labor for others; acting shy was a central component of this performance. The fact that white middle-class men as well as women were expected to engage in this labor in the 1950s was unusual, given women's sole responsibility for emotional labor in the context of heterosexual relationships. But for men, such deferential behavior was intended to be temporary, a necessary step on the ladder of success. Women, who had no such opportunities for advancement—at least as envisioned by self-help authors—were expected to hide behind a mask of shyness indefinitely. This changed in the 1970s, as more women entered the ranks of professionals. For women and men, smooth workplace relations were no longer to be achieved through deference, but through assertiveness. Shyness, conceptualized as the opposite of assertiveness, was now completely off-limits to success seekers. In the 1980s and 1990s, success strategies for women and men emphasized greater workplace intimacy and featured the labor-intensive strategy of empathic listening. Since self-help authors regarded shyness—despite some affinities with listening—as incompatible with this approach to workplace intimacy, shyness continued to be perceived as antithetical to success.

The norms governing shyness frequently functioned as ideology, legitimating and defending gendered power relations as worthy of respect, or concealing their existence. In the 1950s, these norms legitimated power relations between women and men as well as among men. White middle-class men, like women, were expected to act shy in the service of performing deferential emotional labor for other men. But for men, deference was not a survival strategy; instead, it was a strategy intended to give them access to positions of power over other men. Even if they failed to reach those positions, men could count on occupying positions of authority over women at work. Thus, they might "do" deference, but it posed no threat to fundamental gender hierarchies in the workplace. Women, on the other hand, were lodged firmly on the bottom rung of the ladder of success, with little hope of moving up; thus, in performing deferential emotional labor for their male superiors, they both acknowledged and reproduced this power difference by continually enhancing men's status in the workplace.

In the 1970s, self-help authors sought to reorganize these power relations along more equitable lines. They did not question the need for hierarchies, but feminist self-help authors in particular challenged the institutionalization of hierarchies based on gender. Thus, they replaced relationships based on one-sided deference with an emotional and behavioral style that assumed one of the prerogatives of power: the direct communication of one's needs and wants and the expectation that others will take them seriously. The goal was no longer to engender good feelings in those in a position to aid one's rise up the ladder, but to act as if one was already at the top, and to expect to be treated by others accordingly. In urging women as well as men to behave in this powerful manner, 1970s' self-help authors challenged the assumption that only men were entitled to positions of authority in the workplace.

In the 1980s and 1990s, as self-help authors paid renewed attention to accommodating others' needs in the workplace, the norms governing shyness posed less of a challenge to power relations. Although non-shy, assertive communication remained an important element of these norms, the addition of empathic listening to the required communication skills shifted the focus away from repudiating gender hierarchies. Instead of limiting their attention to acting powerfully, women and men were to be engaged in creating the appearance of a power-free workplace by actively seeking out, listening, and responding to the needs of subordinates and superiors. While self-help authors argued that women and men could benefit equally from such behavior, the fact that empathy is regarded as a highly feminine quality suggested that women would receive fewer rewards for doing it well, and greater sanctions for doing it poorly than men would. As Valian (1998, 2) discovered in attempting to explain the scarcity of women at the top levels of organizations, "Whatever emphasizes a man's gender gives him a small advantage, a plus mark. Whatever accentuates a woman's gender results in a small loss for her, a minus mark." By promoting empathic listening as a "gender-neutral" success strategy, self-help authors simply concealed the gendered power relations that were at work.

CHAPTER SIX

"Intimacy Is a Difficult Art"

The Changing Role of Shyness in Friendship

> Speak not but what may benefit others or yourself;
> avoid trifling conversation.
> > Benjamin Franklin, *Thirteen Virtues* (1741)

In addition to its role in dating and work success, self-help authors considered shyness to play an important role in one's ability to make friends.[1] Although authors devoted less textual space to friendship than to business or heterosexual romance, they nonetheless regarded friendship as an important source of companionship, intimacy, and ego support. Thus, success in making friends was essential for the shy and nonshy alike. Authors' advice about how to succeed at friendship followed a familiar pattern: deferential, selfless behavior played a central role in the 1950s, only to be replaced by more self-focused behavior, self-disclosure, in the 1970s, 1980s, and 1990s. Changes in ideas about how best to achieve intimacy with friends brought changes in ideas about shyness. Though never officially sanctioned as a friend-making strategy, shyness was much more compatible with 1950s' ideals of deference and modesty than with the ideals that replaced them, helping to explain why shyness was regarded as less of a social problem in the 1950s.

In writing about friendship, self-help authors in each time period often made no gender distinctions: they did not direct readers to choose same-sex friends, and, until the 1980s and 1990s, they did not assume that women and men had different friendship styles. Self-help authors' assumption that men and women were equally capable of and responsible for performing the emotional labor that established intimacy challenged gendered divisions of emotional labor. Friendship was one arena in which men were given no opportunities to avoid, cut short, or downplay the labor required to achieve intimacy. Perhaps in reaction to this threat, in the 1980s and 1990s a small but vocal group of authors argued that men, unlike women, were incapable of establishing and maintaining intimate relationships with friends. Men, it seemed, were naturally reserved on the subject of emotions, even with other men; women, on the other hand, had no such difficulty in disclosing emotions in order to attract friends. By invoking these "essential" differences, these authors reaffirmed the ideology of male rationality, an ideology used to justify (rational) men's power over (emotional) women.

"A Hedge between Keeps Friendships Green"

Attitudes toward friendship and shyness in the 1950s were conditioned by Americans' desire to secure the approval and liking of others, a national character trait that Riesman (1950, 431) labeled "other direction." The other directed person "wants to be loved rather than esteemed; he wants not to . . . impress . . . others, but . . . to relate to them; he seeks less a snobbish status in the eyes of others, more an assurance of being emotionally in tune with them." Child-rearing goals reflected this group orientation, with child guidance experts warning parents to "watch carefully the child who prefers solitary amusements to being with other children."[2] As we have already seen in the context of work and heterosexual relationships, for 1950s' self-help authors the primary means of securing the love of others and of achieving emotional rapport with them was by making them feel good about themselves. Thus, self-help authors advised friend-seeking readers to devote themselves tirelessly to others, following guidelines such as those offered by Mary Beery (1957, 70): "Ask questions. Listen to what [others] have to say. Try to understand people, to accept them and their differences. Do things for others rather than for yourself. Be willing to help; to lead and to follow; to take your turn; to share unselfishly."[3]

As suggested by the author's admonition to "share unselfishly," readers were also advised to avoid any behavior that interfered with the goal of suppressing their own impulses in deference to the needs of others. Such "antisocial" conduct included bragging about "the money you spend, the grades you make, the dates you have," trying to "gain advantages for yourself at the expense of other people," "babbling" on and on about oneself, criticizing, sulking, making sarcastic remarks, gossiping, expressing anger, being impatient or intolerant, and imposing one's will upon others.[4] It also included being selective about the objects of one's selfless attention: authors firmly believed that everyone—man or woman, pleasant or unpleasant—deserved to be considered a potential friend, and that one could, in turn, "learn to like all kinds of people."[5] Willingly taking second place to everyone, all the time, was the key to this process, allowing one to quell or discount any negative thoughts that might hinder one's liking for others, and demonstrating to others one's worthiness for the role of friend.

The attention that readers were advised to lavish on others—listening, understanding, offering praise, and "being more conscious of the other person than of yourself"[6]—were all forms of emotion work, that "effort to understand others, to have empathy with their situation, to feel their feelings as part of one's own" (England and Farkas 1986, 11). While such labor was in keeping with the decade's emphasis on other-direction, friendship was the one arena in which men, like women, were expected to perform this labor indefinitely for others. Men's deferential emotional labor at work took place in the context of a status hierarchy: once they reached the top of the ladder, they became the objects, rather than the providers, of deference. Moreover, given gender divisions of labor, they could count on *not* having to perform deferential emotional labor for women at work. In intimate heterosexual relationships, women were expected to perform emotional labor for men. But self-help authors offered men no similar escape routes when it came to friendship.

Encouraging men to perform "women's work" indefinitely for other men and women posed somewhat of a challenge to male authority. It suggested that men were equally capable of and responsible for creating and maintaining intimacy, at least among friends. Men could not rely on the excuse that this labor was temporary, or that it was damaging to their masculine pride. One possible, and somewhat pessimistic explanation for this turn of events is that self-help authors could afford to give men some flexibility when it came to performing emotional labor for friends because their masculinity was secured elsewhere. According to Ehrenreich (1983, 20), in the 1950s, white middle-class masculinity was proved by being a successful breadwinner—being married and holding down a job that supported a family. Only when a man failed to fulfill this role was his manhood called into question. Thus, provided that he was a successful breadwinner, a man could perform "women's work" for his friends without detracting from his status and authority. A less pessimistic view is that *any* symbolic threat to male power should be taken seriously, especially one that highlighted contradictions in what was expected of men in different arenas. If men could perform emotional labor for male and female friends, then why not for female partners?

A number of authors considered shyness to interfere with one's ability to perform emotional labor properly for potential friends. For some, shyness was a form of selfishness: the shy were too busy comparing themselves unfavorably to others to perform the selfless emotional labor that guaranteed popularity.[7] A *degree* of self-consciousness was acceptable, since it indicated a "fine, sensitive nature," but when self-consciousness prevented one from performing one's social duties, it became a "fault" in need of correction.[8] Other authors regarded shyness as a barrier to friendship because feelings of shyness resulted in *too* much deference to others, particularly in conversation. While shining the conversational spotlight on others was an important means of winning them over, at some point one was required to participate with more than leading questions or humble agreement with what was being said.[9] Those, like the shy, who failed to contribute their own opinions or ideas to a conversation never quite "meshed into the group," making others uneasy.[10] Alternatively, their silence made them appear "indifferent" or "uninteresting," preventing the shy from exciting the reciprocal interest that would lead to lasting friendship.[11] The behavioral ideal was to appear modest rather than shy.[12]

Distinguishing between modesty and shyness could prove difficult, however, given that both were characterized by a degree of reticence, self-consciousness, and self-effacement. Self-help authors did not spell out the precise differences between the two, forcing readers to navigate on their own the fine line between amiable modesty and disagreeable shyness. Shy people's task was made more difficult by the fact that if they tried to overcompensate for their shyness, they might be accused of boldness, behavior for which authors had even less patience. Self-help authors characterized boldness as the opposite of modesty, sternly warning readers not to be "too eager, too pushing, or too hasty," to be "approachable without being forward," and to be "unobtrusive" and "reasonably reserved" rather than "brassy," "brazen," "bold," or "nervy" in their efforts to make friends.[13] "Forward," unrestrained behavior was taboo because it was a form of selfishness—in being forward, one implied that one's own desires were more important than those of the other; one pushed oneself forward rather than deferring to others, thus reversing the order of priorities considered necessary for friendship.

Authors' championing of modesty above boldness was also, implicitly, a championing of white, middle-class standards of behavior. As Sacks (1994, 90) has observed, the postwar period was a time when generous housing and education benefits offered to returning male soldiers allowed many Jews and other white "Euroethnics" to enter the ranks of the largely white middle class. Self-help books provided these new members of the middle class with knowledge of the established rules for social interaction. Modesty was a particularly important white middle-class standard, since it was the behavioral opposite of the "uncouth, unrefined, loud and pushy" behavior that elites attributed to the white working classes and to African American women (Sacks 1994, 82; Gilkes 1983, 294). "Bold and nervy" behavior was therefore unacceptable not simply because it implied that one was selfish and insensitive; it also suggested that one was "low class." Thus, as in the eighteenth century, a type of reserve was an essential element of white middle-class character, a quality that provided ideological support for a race and class hierarchy. A gracious modesty, particularly when contrasted with the "unrefined" brazenness of the working classes, offered proof of the social superiority of the white middle classes, legitimating their claims to privilege and power.

Middle-class modesty also required a degree of reticence about oneself, particularly one's worries, emotions, or concerns. Several authors considered revelations about one's personal troubles, secrets, or general affairs to be inappropriate between friends; one went so far as to argue that such matters were best left to lawyers and doctors, who were "paid to deal with trouble."[14] Most, however, simply had nothing to say about self-disclosure, suggesting that self-help authors did not consider it to play an important role in forming and maintaining friendships. Thus, while one was required to perform emotional labor in order to make and keep friends, this labor did not encompass "feeling talk," the hallmark of emotional labor in later time periods. In the 1950s, self-help authors envisioned intimacy as simply being with others, trying to make them happy by making them feel good and by doing what they wanted to do (see Kidd 1975, 34–35).

For younger readers, sharing group activities was an especially important means of establishing friendly intimacy. Self-help authors urged both young women and men to become proficient at sports and games in order to feel that they belonged.[15] As Allen and Brigs (1950, 158) explained, "The best way to be one of the gang is learning to do the things they do. Learn to dance, swim, play badminton and tennis, drive a car, and play the popular games." These pastimes did not demand self-disclosure, but they allowed one to participate in group activities, thus promoting group enjoyment. By mastering a range of physical skills, the shy could learn to hide, if not overcome, their discomfort around others, since sports "divert[ed] the mind from feelings of insufficiency and inferiority."[16] Of course, this assumed that the shy person could easily master a range of sports; if not, a poor performance in physical games could be another source of feelings of inadequacy.

Empirical evidence suggests that self-help authors' attitudes toward self-disclosure were shared by many Americans. Veroff, Douvan, and Kulka's (1981a, 481–82) national study found that in 1957, few American adults turned to friends for help when they were feeling unhappy or worried.[17] Based on their national study of high-school students, Douvan and Adelson (1966, 188) argued that "intimate and confiding" friendships were common only among one group in the 1950s: young girls. Once young girls formed attachments to boys—an event the authors viewed as inevitable—their friendships with other girls became "calmer [and] more modulated" (191), that is, less marked by the sharing of confidences.

In advocating a "reasonable reserve" above brazen and immodest behavior, authors left some breathing room for the shy. I do not mean to suggest that authors approved of shyness—we have clearly seen that they did not—but shyness was not as far removed from the ideal of modesty as was boldness. Indeed, it might, at times, be difficult to distinguish between shyness and modesty, creating a degree of uncertainty that might permit some shy people to reap the benefits of the modest personality—in this case, friendship—without undertaking any "cure" whatsoever.

The similarities between shyness and modesty help explain why 1950s' self-help authors did not demonstrate the same level of concern about shyness as did their counterparts in later decades. When modesty fell out of fashion, concern about shyness grew.

"I Get By with a Little Help from My Friends"

Self-help authors of the 1970s had a remarkably different approach to building friendships than their 1950s' counterparts.[18] The deference and suppression of self that had characterized the friend-making advice of the 1950s was replaced by a celebration of self: instead of doing things for others, authors urged readers to tell others about themselves, disclosing their emotions, goals, attitudes, secrets, and troubles.[19] Authors argued that in the short run, "getting personal" made you "more personable" and allowed others to get to know you;[20] in the long run, a willingness to self-disclose created stronger bonds between friends.[21] The basis of intimacy within friendship was no longer simple companionship and ego support; now it was the ability to communicate one's deepest feelings to another. Those who failed to do so were not regarded as admirably modest and unassuming, but tragically detached both from their true selves and from others.[22] As Arnold Lazarus and Allen Fay (1975, 39) explained, "If you hide behind a façade . . . you will never know what it is like to be loved for what you really are."

Self-help authors devoted little space to friendship strategies other than self-disclosure. Unlike their 1950s' counterparts, they did not advise readers to advertise their suitability for the role of friend by helping, sharing, or being patient and kind. While they did acknowledge that the pursuit of friendship would require readers to listen to the conversation and self-disclosures of others, they emphasized the friend-making power of speech over listening.[23] This was a rather dramatic change from the 1950s, when selfless behavior had been the order of the day. Instead of performing emotional labor for others in order to attract friends, now the essence of friendship was a demand that others perform emotional labor for you, by listening and responding to your thoughts, feelings, and fears. Why did a willingness to talk about oneself—considered a highly selfish act in the 1950s—mark one as worthy of friendship?

A consideration of the era's well-known preoccupation with the self and self-expression helps to answer that question. A number of factors contributed to the level of introspection that marked the "me decade": the rise of self psychology, with its emphasis on the "cohesion, autonomy, esteem, and emotional validity of the self" (Cushman 1995, 263); the embrace by the women's movement of consciousness-raising as a tool of empowerment (Echols 1989, 87); the economic uncertainty of the decade, which featured three recessions, double-digit inflation and unemployment, the collapse of the manufacturing sector, and two oil embargoes (Bondi 1995, 324); the disillusionment with politics in the wake of Vietnam and Watergate; and a general sense of a loss of intimacy in modern urban society (Schur 1976, 98). Self-disclosure was an effort to create a sense of community with others; it established that you were "real" and "psychologically open" and thus worthy of friendship. Without it, relationships were considered phony, dry, and inauthentic (see Sennett 1974, 222, 259).

The shift in ideas about how to make friends in the 1970s resulted in a corresponding shift in self-help authors' conceptions of why shyness was a barrier to friendship. Authors no longer framed shyness as an impediment to one's ability to perform emotional labor properly for others; now shyness inhibited self-disclosure, preventing others from performing emotional labor for you.[24] The shy person's silence was portrayed as an impenetrable barrier to meaningful contact with others, who were unable to build rapport with someone they viewed as enigmatic, impersonal, and cold. Parents of shy children were warned that shyness inhibited the development of full and satisfying friendships.[25] Self-help authors warned their readers that failure to self-disclose led inexorably to loneliness, isolation, and depression.[26] As Ken Keyes (1975, 32) explained, "Hiding [your deepest feelings] in any degree keeps [you] stuck in [your] illusion of separateness from other people." The remedy they offered was straightforward: they encouraged the shy to begin immediately to reveal their feelings to others, promising that "[w]ith a little time and patience, disclosing yourself more openly . . . will lead you into an experience of deeper contact, and that means new joy and pleasure for both of you."[27] Yet they offered few specific details on how to find appropriate others to whom to disclose. One author recommended joining a political party or enrolling in a course in order to meet people,[28] while another urged readers to turn casual acquaintances into friends,[29] but the rest suggested by their silence on the subject that there were no rules governing the choice of a friend to whom one could self-disclose.

The abandonment of the 1950s modest personality as the ideal to which all those seeking friends should aspire had important implications for the shy. Shyness was no longer an extreme version of the ideal personality, but its opposite: it signaled coldness, rather than exceptional sensitivity. The shy could no longer occasionally "pass" as the ideal friend; therefore, they had to undertake some sort of remedy if they wanted to make friends. Indeed, the proliferation of remedies made available to the shy for the first time in the 1970s (see chapter 1) suggested that potential friends would be less tolerant of their condition than they might have been in the 1950s. Shyness was now considered to be completely incompatible with friendship. Advice to parents of shy children also reflected this shift, as self-help authors conceptualized shyness as problematic primarily because it prevented children from making friends.[30] With the transformation of standards of intimacy, shyness was transformed from a minor to a major flaw.

Shy women and men were both urged to self-disclose in order to attract friends; 1970s' self-help authors did not suggest—as they had in the context of intimate heterosexual relationships—that men were less equipped than women to self-disclose. In fact, authors made no references to gender differences at all, suggesting that they expected men and women to be equally capable of following their advice. Yet according to cultural feminists and male liberationists, the style of friendship promoted by self-help authors was particularly suited to women's capacities for emotional expression; men had a much more difficult time baring their souls to other men due to homophobia, competitiveness, and a fear of intimacy (Balswick and Collier 1976, 58; Daly 1978; Farrell 1974; Fasteau 1974, 6–19; Pleck and Sawyer 1974, 74; Rich 1977). Male liberationists encouraged men to overcome these barriers and establish emotionally richer relationships with other men. Self-help authors' advice about how to make friends was in keeping with these efforts, posing a challenge to prevailing notions of hegemonic masculinity as entirely aggressive, rational, unemotional, and tough, and undermining the centuries-old link between an absence of emotion and male power. Men, self-help authors suggested, had emotions just like women, and they could learn to be just as emotionally revealing with their friends as women were with theirs. Self-help authors did not, however, acknowledge that men might have more obstacles to overcome on the road to friendship than women. To do so might have detracted from the simplicity and power of their message to readers: that immediate change was possible, regardless of the circumstances, as long as the right amount of effort was applied.

In contrast to the 1950s, the 1970s' friendship ideal did not reproduce class or racial divisions. Self-disclosure had more in common with the "loud," "brazen" behavior associated in the 1950s with the white working classes and with African American women than with middle-class modesty and reserve. Moreover, an absence of self-disclosure did not have the same kind of implications for class and race hierarchies that an absence of modesty did: as the reaction to "cold" shy people showed, failure to self-disclose was more likely to be interpreted as a sign of aloofness and elitism than a sign that one was "low class." The goal of self-disclosure was to break down barriers between people, not to emphasize distinctions between them.

Research suggested that men's and women's actual behavior was in keeping with the general spirit of self-help authors' advice, at least to a degree. While no studies assessed how women and men went about making friends, several measured the importance that self-disclosure played within established friendships. For example, Veroff, Douvan, and Kulka's (1981a, 482) study comparing the subjective experiences of Americans in 1957 and 1976 found that both men and women were more likely in 1976 to deal with any worries by talking to friends and family about them. But they also found that women were more likely than men to do so on a fairly regular basis (Veroff, Douvan, and Kulka 1981b, 47). This finding was consistent with Jourard's (1971, 6–7) study of a (nonrepresentative) sample of Alabama college students, which found that women reported more self-disclosure to both opposite and same-sex friends than men. Thus, it appeared that while Americans had adopted new patterns of self-disclosure with their friends in the 1970s, men were more likely than women to resist this new standard of friendship. Some may have hoped that the end of the "me decade" would bring an end to demands for self-disclosure, but the passage of time brought only modifications of such demands rather than outright rejection of them.

"The Only Way to Have a Friend Is to Be One"

Self-help authors writing in the mid-1980s to mid-1990s remained convinced that self-disclosure—"opening up," sharing "values, opinions, and goals" and positive and negative feelings—was an important element of friendship.[31] Like their 1970s' counterparts, they argued that true friendship was possible only when others knew "the real you," the person revealed in the course of confessing your innermost thoughts and feelings. Those, like the shy, who failed to self-disclose faced the specter not only of shallow, inauthentic relationships, but also, according to several authors, damage to their physical and mental health.[32] As Diana Booher (1994, 114) breezily put it, "Emotional distance creates mental illness. To disclose improves your mental health." These occasional references to the harmful physical- and mental-health effects of shyness foreshadowed the acceleration, in the mid-1990s, of the medicalization of shyness (see chapter 1).

Yet authors of the 1980s and 1990s also sounded a note of caution about self-disclosure, warning readers that while it was acceptable to express negative feelings about oneself, it was important to "resist the temptation to criticize, condemn, or complain" about others.[33] Instead, authors urged readers to include expressions of "appreciation, approval and admiration" in their talk with others.[34] They also informed readers that friendship was about more than self-disclosure. Unlike their 1970s' counterparts, self-help authors writing in the 1980s and 1990s emphasized that friendship was about *reciprocal* emotional labor: performing emotional labor for others was just as important in building friendships as offering others the chance to perform emotional labor for you.

Listening ranked high on the list of emotional services one should render a friend. Listening conveyed interest in others, which inspired liking, since "nothing is so flattering as to have someone show personal interest in our job, our background, our experience, or our views."[35] Admiration and kindness were other important forms of emotional support one offered to friends.[36] Echoing the advice of the 1950s, Brian Tracy (1993, 284) urged the reader who wished to become popular and likable to "get out of yourself and get into the lives and concerns of others. Become genuinely interested in them. . . . Think of ways that you can help them. . . . Do unto others as you would want them to do unto you." The admonition to "get out of yourself" made plain 1980s' and 1990s' authors' turn away from the more "selfish," "me-focused" friendship strategies of the previous decade. The more conservative political climate of the 1980s may have been responsible for this seeming "return of the 1950s" (Thomson 1992, 498). The New Right placed on the national political agenda the idea that the traditional "family values" of selflessness and commitment to others had been dealt devastating blows by political and cultural events of the 1960s and 1970s, including the rise in the divorce rate, women's continued entry into the paid labor force, and the legalization of abortion (Diamond 1995, 232; Klatch 1987, 127–29). Although their advocacy of a return to "traditional" values sometimes sparked controversy, it also inspired a sense—seemingly shared by self-help authors—that a missing feeling of community could be regained.

A new concern about shyness that arose in the 1980s and 1990s provides further evidence of self-help authors' advocacy of more selfless friendship behavior. Shyness, a number of self-help authors now contended, was a threat to friendship because the shy were overly dependent on others. Eager to expend as little friend-making effort as possible due to their discomfort with strangers, the shy had an alarming tendency to cling to one or two friends.[37] These friends then became overburdened with the shy person's demands for companionship and emotional support. As Jonathan Cheek (1989, 134) explained, "When you count on one person to be everything—constant companion, confidant, helper, advice giver—he or she often burns out. You're asking too much from one person. You need to build up a network of friends and acquaintances." From this perspective, shyness was a sign of selfishness; as in the 1950s, it indicated a refusal to take others' needs into account.

Yet while the shy were counseled to show moderation in their attentions to established friends, they were encouraged to take an aggressive approach to finding friends. The basic rule to follow was straightforward: the shy were to treat every encounter with a stranger as an opportunity to make a friend. To speed things along, they had to make the first conversational move. As Susan Roane (1988, 193) exhorted, "Don't wait; initiate."[38] Lest the shy worry that such behavior was too forward, authors reassured them that there were new rules governing social interactions: where one was once barred from talking to strangers, eavesdropping, or interrupting, now one was required to "talk to everyone, everywhere . . . [and] break in on other people's conversations."[39] Thus, if the shy wanted to make friends, not only did they have to force themselves to speak to others, they also had to be prepared to do so anytime, anywhere. Authors made no allowances for environment or mood: when in public, the shy were expected to always be "on," to present a friendly, conversational face to the world. They had to maintain this pose with established friends, resisting any tendency to "show their true colors" by expecting a few friends to satisfy all their needs. Despite some similarities with advice of the 1950s, contemporary authors were unwilling to leave any breathing space for the shy by allowing them time off from playing the role of confident extrovert. The stakes were higher now that shyness had been identified as a serious social disease with numerous negative consequences ranging from loneliness to pedophilia (see chapter 1); thus, it had to be eradicated, not, as in the 1950s, offered safe haven.

Women, Men, and Friendship

While most authors (69 percent) made no gender distinctions in their advice about how to make friends, a vocal minority (31 percent) did, claiming that, either due to biology or socialization, women and men had dramatically different capacities for emotionally supportive friendships.[40] Echoing 1970s' male liberationists, these authors asserted that because men's "training to be competitive and mistrustful of one another [made] real emotional bonding difficult," they had fewer and less intimate friendships than women did.[41] Authors explained that male friendships, where they existed at all, were marked by shared activities ("poker games, racquetball, or a fishing trip") or general talk ("the exchange of factual information," "telling stories and jokes"), rather than shared feelings. As in their intimate relationships with women, men suffered from a profound "reserve" when it came to the subject of emotions.[42] By contrast, this group of authors regarded women's relationships with one another as remarkably cooperative and talkative; women, they claimed, cemented their friendships by engaging in the very activity that men spurned—sharing "intimacies, "secrets," "problems," and emotions.[43] Indeed, author John Gray (1992, 19) characterized women, but not men, as expert psychologists and counselors who regarded "open and intimate" talk with one another as the foundation of their friendships. In doing so, he implied that reserve was never a problem for women the way that it was for men.

Yet these authors did not share 1970s' feminists and male liberationists perspective on the implications of this dramatic difference in women's and men's capacity for intimate friendships. Reflecting the backlash against feminism that was underway in the more conservative 1980s (Faludi 1991), this group of authors did not urge men to change their potentially damaging behavior; instead, they counseled women to accept men's different—and from women's perspective, less satisfactory—definitions of intimate friendship. For some authors, this simply meant that women were barred from criticizing their husbands' friendship styles. As Barbara De Angelis (1990, 267) explained, "Your husband might spend three hours with a buddy talking about his new stereo system, and tell you that that filled his need for closeness. You might think 'Is he kidding?' He's not. Remember: Men can't fathom why women like to go shopping together either!" Other authors argued that "because [men] hold back from other men, a tremendous hunger builds up in them" for friendship with their wives;[44] thus, they urged women to perform double-duty as both best friend *and* spouse. In essence, women were being told to help men maintain their reserve with other men. Women's reward would be even more intimacy with their male partners. Such a scheme maintained women's role as emotional laborers for men, and sidestepped the revolutionary potential of 1970s' egalitarianism.

The most common response, however, was to suggest that women's relationships with their male partners would never match the emotional depth of their relationships with their female friends.[45] Deborah Tannen (1986, 143), for example, criticized women who wanted their partners to be "a new and improved version of a best friend," while John Gray (1992, 77) urged women seeking nurturance from a reserved, withdrawn husband to "call a girlfriend for a good chat" instead. Thus, women were to rely on their women friends to fill the emotional gaps in their marriages. This approach had contradictory implications. On the one hand, authors' acknowledgment of women's greater satisfaction in same-sex relationships represented a challenge both to compulsory heterosexuality and to male authority within intimate relationships. By affirming women's superior intimacy skills and validating women's commitment to relationships outside of the family, self-help authors undermined male authority, credibility, and status (see O'Connor 1998, 132; Rich 1980, 657). On the other hand, authors' insistence that men were as reserved on the subject of emotions in their relationships with other men as they were with women shored up heterosexuality by suggesting that men's reserve was natural and inevitable. There was no point in challenging men to live up to women's intimacy expectations because it was impossible for them do so. Women's intimate friendships with other women could compensate for their male partners' shortcomings. Indeed, research showed that married women's friendships did tend to buttress, rather than threaten, their marriages by providing women with an alternative source of emotional intimacy, thereby easing marital tensions (Oliker 1989, 55). This view of men as incapable of self-disclosure also offered implicit support for power inequities—men were rational, at all times, while women were emotional, therefore, power clearly belonged in men's more capable hands.

Thus, self-help readers in the 1980s and 1990s encountered two contradictory friendship ideals: one that established self-disclosure, listening, and admiration as the basis of both women's and men's friendships, the other that regarded this style of friendship as the province of women only. Research suggested that while the former was more reflective of women's and men's actual behavior with their friends, the latter retained a powerful ideological pull. Studies comparing the levels of self-disclosure in men's and women's friendship found that while women often engaged in more self-disclosure with their friends than men did, men's friendships were not completely devoid of self-disclosure (Camarena, Sarigiani, and Peterson 1990; Dindia and Allen 1992; Hays 1985; Wright 1982, 17). Yet, as is often the case, similarities between women's and men's behavior were often overlooked, and their differences amplified to support a conception of gender as a relationship of opposites. Walker (1994), for example, found that among the fifty-two working- and middle-class women and men she interviewed, the men shared feelings with their friends *more* than they were initially willing to admit, while the women shared feelings *less* than they initially claimed. Despite their own behavior to the contrary, both groups espoused the belief, promulgated by self-help authors such as John Gray, that men friends shared activities, women friends, emotions. Their acceptance of gender ideologies in the face of behavior that challenged them points to the powerful role that ideas regarding male reserve and female expressiveness continue to play in Americans' conceptions of masculinity and femininity. These "commonsense" ideas help individuals to make sense of the persistence of gendered power relations in society, by linking men's power to their lack of emotion.

The widespread appeal of the notion of male reserve also provides men with the opportunity, denied to women, to claim that they are not shy. Men who fear ridicule in intimate situations and are reduced to silence have the option of considering their behavior to be an unremarkable, "natural" condition shared by other men. As reserved rather than shy men, they do not need to seek treatment. Indeed, the fact that their fearful inability to talk about emotions has been normalized means that it falls to those who object to their "reserved" behavior—namely, women—to try to change it as best they can. Women, then, become "reserved" men's unpaid therapists, assuming responsibility for managing and expressing men's emotions.

Conclusion

Examining self-help authors' advice regarding friendship since the 1950s reveals, once again, that attitudes toward shyness are linked to ideas about how to achieve intimacy. In the 1950s, intimacy between friends was achieved by doing things with and for others; talking about feelings played no part in ideals of intimate friendship. Although shyness was considered to hinder one's ability to make friends, shyness differed only in degree from the ideal friendly personality, suggesting that shyness was more acceptable in the 1950s. Such acceptance changed with the introduction in the 1970s of a new means of attracting friends: self-disclosure. According to self-help authors, shyness not only interfered with self-disclosure, but it was now the very opposite of the outspoken, self-revealing personality that was required to make friends. While 1980s and 1990s self-help authors moderated these demands somewhat, they still considered self-disclosure to be the key to friendship. Thus they continued to regard shyness as a serious barrier to friendship, a problem that had to be cured completely, rather than—as in the 1950s—something that could be adjusted to suit the demands of friendship.

In each time period, most self-help authors' advice about friendship constituted a challenge to hegemonic masculinity, since this advice established friendship as an arena in which men were not expected to be tough, competitive, and unemotional. In the 1950s, this challenge was muted somewhat by the fact that masculinity was affirmed primarily in the workplace and in heterosexual relationships. But in the 1970s, a decade marked by widespread job insecurity and changing gender norms, masculinity was less firmly tied to the arenas of work and romance; thus, challenges to hegemonic masculinity in the arena of friendship might have more easily spilled over into other arenas. Indeed, male liberationists saw male friendship as an important site in the struggle to both free men from the restrictions imposed by norms of masculine toughness and, ultimately, to create a more egalitarian society. It was hardly a surprise, then, that the more conservative 1980s and 1990s witnessed the appearance of a group of authors who tried to mute this threat by claiming that men were just not cut out for intimate friendship. They relied on the idea of an essential, natural male reserve on the subject of emotions, a reserve that prevented men from establishing the kinds of intimate friendships that "emotional" women easily established with other women. Thus, they reclaimed the link between masculinity and rationality that acts to sustain male power.

The notion that men were "naturally" reserved, even with other men, also introduced a note of inevitability into women's dissatisfactions with men's styles of intimacy. If men were, indeed, reserved by nature, women's efforts to change men's behavior would be futile. While heterosexual women might conceivably use this argument as an excuse to abandon men altogether, research suggested that it simply let men off the hook: women relied on other women to fill in the emotional gaps in their marriages. Reserved men, unlike shy men, suffered no appreciable threat to their romantic lives due to their failure to self-disclose.

CHAPTER SEVEN

Conclusion

I don't think that people should get over being shy. It is a blessing in disguise. The shy person is the opposite of the aggressive person. Shy people are seldom the great sinners. They allow society to remain in peace.

Isaac Bashevis Singer (1976)

I began this book by pointing out that, beginning in the 1970s, mental health professionals sounded an alarm about shyness.[1] This previously undetected "social disease" had the potential, we were told, to doom the millions of Americans who suffered from it to a life of loneliness and depression, even criminality. Such warnings increased over the years, as more research was carried out and more negative effects were discovered. Experts now warn that technology threatens to swell the already teeming ranks of the shy, since reliance on ATMs, answering machines, self-service gasoline pumps, telecommuting, and the Internet provides Americans fewer opportunities to practice their social skills, "creating a socially awkward generation" (Raghunathan 1999, C1). We have arrived at the point where scientists are attempting to identify the shyness gene, in order, presumably, to one day switch it off (Groopman 1999, 49).

119

I questioned these developments, asking why shyness seemed to suddenly elicit so much interest, most of it negative. Tracing historical changes in popular advice about shyness since the 1950s has provided one explanation, namely, that the cultural norms governing shyness are shaped by prevailing attitudes towards intimacy. As ideas about how to achieve intimacy in platonic, romantic, and workplace relationships changed, so too, did ideas about shyness. High levels of concern about shyness coincided with periods when shyness was perceived as being directly at odds with the emotional labor required to achieve intimacy. In the 1950s, when achieving intimacy depended upon qualities and behaviors associated with shyness, such as modesty, reticence, and humility, self-help authors did not conceptualize shyness as a major social problem. They did not approve of it, to be sure, but being bold or forward was often considered more of a barrier to intimacy than being shy. In the 1970s, 1980s, and 1990s, when intimacy seemed to depend upon skills that the shy were considered to lack, such as verbal self-disclosure, empathic listening, or assertiveness, self-help authors conceptualized shyness as a serious, even fatal, barrier to intimacy.

Why Intimacy Norms Changed

For each time period, intimacy ideals both reflected and shaped other social patterns. In the 1950s, Mills (1953, 68) identified the decline of entrepreneurship and the rise of bureaucracies and the service sector as factors contributing to the growth of the "personality market." By the 1940s, the middle class was no longer composed primarily of independent businessmen, but of salaried white-collar workers, working at jobs which required them to handle people rather than things (Mills 1953, 65). Thus, friendliness, courtesy, and attentiveness to others were marketable qualities, which, Mills argues, diffused throughout society, becoming models for social interactions of all sorts (Mills 1953, 187). The effect, Riesman (1950) claimed, was that by the 1950s, middle-class Americans were "other directed," highly attuned to the feelings and opinions of others, and anxious to secure their approval (see also Whyte 1957, 52). This diffuse, "other-directed" ethos was evident in 1950s self-help authors' approach to intimacy in heterosexual relationships, in the workplace, and with friends. In each of these arenas, intimacy was to be achieved largely by pleasing others, making them feel good about themselves, and managing their emotions. In other words, by performing deferential emotional labor for others, one proved one's value as a friend, worker, or, if you were female, girlfriend.

Although the service sector continued to grow throughout the 1960s and 1970s, the "personality" marketplace that it fueled underwent some changes, shaped, in part, by the women's movement, the growth of psychotherapy, and the sexual revolution. Each of these cultural "events" emphasized the importance of the "self," particularly the importance of asserting the self by communicating one's needs, desires, thoughts, and concerns. The women's movement encouraged women to make their voices heard, and, through consciousness-raising and assertiveness training sessions, gave women the tools do so. Psychotherapy—particularly a form known as "self psychology"—offered women and men another forum in which to explore and assert their feelings and needs (Cushman 1995, 263). Once reserved for the mentally ill, by the 1970s psychotherapy was a routine aspect of many Americans' lives, a way to cope with everyday problems and anxieties (Herman 1995, 262). The turn toward self-expression encompassed sexual expression, which came to be regarded as an important means of self-knowledge; its opposite, sexual modesty, was no longer an admirable sign of good character but a shameful mark of repression (Modell 1989, 308). In keeping with the "me" decade's focus on the self, asserting one's own needs and desires, rather than deferring to others', took center stage in intimacy ideals. One proved one's value to others by proclaiming one's worthiness, not by reassuring others of theirs.

Events of the 1980s and 1990s brought some important changes to these ideals. The most significant political and cultural event of the period was the rise of the New Right, whose members advocated a return to more traditional, "other-directed" family values in which one sacrificed one's own needs for others. As suggested by the term "family values," the primary site where such service took place was the traditional family, comprised of a husband who worked to support his dependent family, and a wife, who, in return, performed unpaid child care and housework. The New Right's call for more traditional values was felt in the renewed emphasis in intimacy ideals on taking others' needs into account, along with one's own—for example, by learning to listen to others while also learning to assert oneself. It was also evident in some self-help authors' claims regarding biologically determined differences in intimacy styles between women and men, differences that justified as "natural" women's position in the traditional family as unpaid domestic laborers for men.

The skills now required to achieve even a friendly intimacy are very complex: we have to exhibit control over our emotions and speak up for ourselves and our desires, yet also consider others' needs and desires and reconcile them with our own. We are, in short, highly dependent on getting along well with others, or at least appearing to do so. It is hardly surprising, therefore, that psychologists have identified a large group of people—the shy—who seem to be incapable of managing these demands. The fact that their problem has been labeled a "phobia" rather than a problem of "relational management" reflects the influence of the psychology profession. De Swaan (1981, 365) argues that a similar process occurred at the turn of the twentieth century, with the "discovery" of agoraphobia, anxiety about leaving one's home or entering a crowded place. The emergence of agoraphobia coincided with the loosening of restrictions on the movement of middle-class women in public in the late nineteenth century. While many women welcomed the new freedom to appear in once-forbidden public places, some experienced fear and discomfort. Their anxiety in public places, once a "token of laudable modesty," was now regarded by others as "inexplicable . . . an idiosyncratic inability to move around as everyone else did" (De Swaan 1981, 365). The emerging psychotherapy profession provided a vocabulary for understanding these women's anxiety, which was labeled "agoraphobia" (De Swaan 1981, 375). This vocabulary and clinical label transformed some women's refusal to adhere to the new rules of social behavior into a psychic problem suitable for treatment by psychologists. Similarly, the shy can be regarded as a group of people whose unwillingness to meet increasingly complex demands for intimacy has been transformed into a "phobia" subject to intervention by the mental health profession.

The Implications of Changes in Shyness Norms

The changes I have outlined in the emotional culture of shyness are consistent with broader twentieth-century changes in emotional style. Stearns (1994) has shown that in the early twentieth century, Americans moved away from the nineteenth century's emphasis on emotional intensity. The Victorians relished a disciplined emotional intensity, regarding emotions as basically good, although in need of control (Stearns 1994,

20). For example, anger for men was regarded as vital within the confines of the public arena, where it acted "as an emotional spur for the competitive zeal and righteous indignation desirable in the worlds of business and politics" (Stearns 1993, 44). But in the home, a man's anger was considered to be dangerous, since it threatened to disrupt the domestic harmony of his only haven from the cut-throat world of commerce (Stearns 1994, 29). Similarly, Victorians regarded romantic love as an intensely passionate experience, but frowned upon passionate displays of jealousy, particularly on women's part, since such displays might alienate men and destroy the family (Stearns 1994, 38).

Beginning in the 1920s, Americans became much less tolerant of emotional intensity, preferring instead an emotional coolness, or restraint, which "shelter[ed] the whole personality from embarrassing excess" (Stearns 1994, 1). Due, in part, to Americans' growing anxiety about the relationship between emotion and physical health, as well as to the expansion of managerial bureaucracies with their emphasis on smoothly functioning "teams," emotions came to be regarded as highly disruptive (Stearns 1994, 214–15, 221–22). Positive emotions such as love came with new warnings about the ways in which they could be abused and manipulated by others (Stearns 1994, 171). The ideal basis of marriage was no longer intense passion but equable companionship (Stearns 1994, 176). Similarly, Americans came to view negative emotions such as fear, grief, and guilt as potentially damaging to one's health or emotional equilibrium; consequently, they were to be talked out rather than experienced (Stearns 1994, 146).

As I have shown, the contemporary attitude toward shyness is similar: shyness is regarded as a threat to one's mental health and well-being, and those who suffer from it are urged to undertake some sort of cure to ensure that they no longer experience it on a regular basis. Even in the more tolerant 1950s, self-help authors' distinction between feeling shy and acting shy was in keeping with this approach toward emotional restraint. Feeling shy was prohibited because it entailed a loss of physical and emotional control, but acting shy was permissible since it was a controlled performance.

Yet, while shyness is currently prohibited for both women and men, I found important gender differences in shyness norms which work to disadvantage women. In particular, the notion, first emerging in the late 1970s and gathering strength in the 1980s and 1990s, that men are "reserved," rather than shy, provides men with an important "crutch" to lean upon. As I argued in chapter 3, the ideology of male reserve relieves men of the responsibility of performing their share of emotional labor in heterosexual relationships, placing the burden on women instead. Women who want a successful relationship are informed that they must elicit and manage their male partners' emotions, as well as their own. Given the importance that self-help authors place upon one's ability to disclose emotions, women's responsibility for performing this labor might work to their advantage, enhancing their status in heterosexual relationships.

But self-help authors' insistence, in the 1980s and 1990s, that women were naturally suited for performing this kind of emotion work for men ultimately denies women any advantage. First, it eases the pressure on men to change. Women report a great deal of dissatisfaction and poorer mental health in relationships whose emotional life is sustained solely through their efforts (Cutrona 1996, 23–24; Duncombe and Marsden 1995, 158); a view of men as permanently reserved suggests that this discontent is simply part of the heterosexual bargain. Second, in making biological claims regarding women's superior skill at feeling-talk, self-help authors disguise and trivialize the labor and skill involved. Women, they imply, are good at talking about emotions because they are emotional creatures, lacking men's reason and rationality (see Hochschild 1983, 169). Men, they imply, have difficulty talking about emotions because they do not have any. By linking women and emotion, men and reason in this way, self-help authors' advice reproduces an ideology dating to the seventeenth century that has acted as a justification for men's claims to power and authority over women.

Whether they regarded women's affinity for emotional self-disclosure as a natural or learned ability, since the 1970s self-help authors have suggested that women have nothing to lose and everything to gain by assuming responsibility for self-disclosure. In doing so, they ignore the implications of unreciprocated self-disclosure. As Foucault ([1976] 1990, 62) points out, the ritual of self-disclosure, or confession, is a power relationship, in which "the agency of domination does not reside in the one who speaks . . . but in the one who listens and says nothing." In this case, the "reserved" male partner occupies the role of silent listener who witnesses the "confession." His silence is a strategy for keeping the upper hand as demands are made upon him; revealing only strategic portions of himself allows him to "intentional[ly] manipulat[e] . . . a situation when threats to the male position occur" (Sattel 1983, 122). Thus, male silence may not simply be a source of dissatisfaction and frustration for women in heterosexual relationships, but a central element of male dominance. Despite self-help authors' claims to the contrary, women's self-disclosures may not hold the key to "healthier" relationships.

The fact that men, but not women, can classify at least some of their shy behaviors with the non-shy label of "reserve" suggests that ultimately, men's shyness is acceptable while women's is not. Men who experience fear in the presence of others and lapse into silence have the option of regarding their behavior as unremarkable—a "natural" condition shared by many men. Women who feel the same way will have little option but to conclude that they are shy. This, coupled with the fact that women tend both to be diagnosed with social phobia and to seek professional help for shyness more often than men do, suggests that women will be more likely to be medicated for shyness symptoms (Langlieb 1995, personal communication; Schneier et al. 1992). Given that the side effects of Prozac, Paxil, and Zoloft include sexual and motor dysfunction, and, occasionally, suicide and murderous impulses, as well as withdrawal reactions when discontinuing the drugs, women's inability to consider their shy behaviors as evidence of reserve poses a serious disadvantage to them (Glenmullen 2000; Goeder et al. 2000; Kennedy et al. 2000; Trenque et al. 2002; Zourkova, Hadasova, and Robes 2000).

The ubiquity of the ideology of male reserve means that when men's behavior challenges this ideology, they or others can always define this behavior otherwise. For example, studies of male friendship showed that even when self-disclosure occupied an important place in men's friendships, they claimed that it did not (Walker 1994). They preferred to believe that men and women had radically different styles of intimacy. The entrenchment of the notion of a "natural" male reserve also allows men who choose to self-disclose to limit their responsibility for any difficulties that might arise from such self-disclosures—as an "unnatural" act, men should not be held to the same high standards as women. If, however, they do succeed, they may well be lavished with praise, a reward denied women who, after all, are only doing what comes "naturally."

But the transformation of intimacy standards did not entirely disadvantage women. As I have shown, beginning in the late 1970s, self-help authors urged women to speak up and name their needs, wants, and desires, at home, at work, and with friends. This was a significant change from the 1950s, when women had been advised to embrace their role as the shy, relatively silent cheerleader to those around them. Moreover, it posed an important challenge to male authority, particularly in the workplace. Instead of timidly deferring to those at the top, both women and men were instructed to act as if they were already holding positions of power, communicating their thoughts, opinions, and instructions clearly and forcefully.

This unalloyed victory for women was short-lived, however. Although assertiveness as a standard of behavior for women remained in place in the 1980s and 1990s, it underwent a potentially troubling revision in the workplace—the addition of empathic listening to the required repertoire of communication skills. Empathic listening had much in common with the emotional labor women were expected to perform in heterosexual relationships in the 1980s and 1990s. The empathic listener was required to draw the speaker out, ask pertinent and probing questions, repeat back the speaker's words, and show concern and acceptance. Similarly, in heterosexual relationships, women were expected to elicit talk from their male partners, praise them, and, ultimately, accept them.

Empathic listening differed in one important respect, however: the element of deference was missing. Self-help authors argued that empathic listening was a useful tool for easing the strain caused by power differences in the workplace, and they urged men as well as women, bosses as well as subordinates, to master it. Yet the fact that it was a skill reminiscent of the emotional labor women continued to perform at home for men did not bode well for women. It suggested that women's skill at empathic listening could be taken for granted, regarded not as labor but as *natural* ability; thus, they might receive fewer rewards for doing it. Alternatively, women who are poor empathic listeners might be sanctioned more harshly than men who perform badly, since emotional labor is a recognizably "female" skill.

Indeed, this appears to be the impetus behind a Silicon program designed to teach "tough" and "intimidating" women executives to be softer and more feminine; forced to attend by their employers, participants learn to treat others more gently, display more vulnerability, temper their criticisms of colleagues—in short, they learn to perform for coworkers the emotional labor expected of them as women (Banerjee 2001). "Tough" male executives, on the other hand, were not required to participate; those men who took advantage of executive coaching offered by the same firm did so to learn how to delegate or cope with stress (Banerjee 2001). If they did choose to learn how to become skilled empathic listeners, however, they might receive more rewards than women executives for their "unnatural" abilities. Linstead (1995, 200) points out that when women adopt "masculine" qualities, like being tough, they are not seen as enhancing their femininity but as abandoning it. On the other hand, when men adopt "feminine" qualities like caring and sensitivity, it is regarded as an addition to male virtues which "re-centre[s] rather than de-centre[s] masculinity and further marginalize[s] the feminine by creating a more complete version of masculinity."

While women have often been expected to perform emotional labor for men—through silence and through speech—men, too, have been expected to do this work, most notably in the workplace. This has potentially important implications for hegemonic masculinity, the culturally exalted form of masculinity that sustains men's power over women, and some men's power over other men (Connell 1987, 185). Work is a central site for constructing hegemonic masculinity; since the nineteenth century, masculinity has been defined primarily by "successful participation in marketplace competition," achieved through aggression, risk taking, and daring (Kimmel 1994, 122; 1996, 26).

In the 1950s, critics worried about the implications for hegemonic masculinity of a model of workplace success that required white middle-class men to be attentive and deferential, rather than bold, independent, and aggressive. I argued that white middle-class men's power and status were in no serious danger given that gender divisions in the workplace assured them of occupying positions of authority over women; men may have been required to show deference to others in the workplace, but those others were always men. Moreover, the deference was intended to be a temporary means to a more powerful end. Thus, the relationship between hegemonic masculinity and male power was secure despite the fact that men were expected to "act like women," performing deferential emotional labor for other men.

In the 1970s, the model of work success was more in keeping with traditional conceptions of masculinity. Assertive behavior did not involve deference to others; its focus was claiming the importance of one's own needs. Yet, in certain respects, hegemonic masculinity, at least as "proven" in the workplace, was more precarious than it was in the 1950s. Women, who were entering the labor force in greater numbers, were also expected to be assertive; they were not expected to defer to men. Moreover, there was no longer any guarantee that men would occupy positions of authority over women. The workplace was losing its status as an exclusive male club, throwing into question its central role as a

proving-ground of masculinity. With women and men expected to behave in the same assertive manner, how could men define masculinity in
a manner that underscored its essential difference from the feminine?

In the 1980s and 1990s, this question acquired greater urgency as the
success ideal again emphasized emotional labor skills that were distinctly
at odds with traditional conceptions of aggressive masculinity: coopera-
tion was valued above competition, dependence above independence,
conciliation above aggression. That these seemingly "feminine" skills
should be valued for men suggested that self-help authors were embracing a radically new vision of masculinity, one that might challenge power
differences that stemmed from treating gender as a relationship of opposites.

Hondagneu-Sotelo and Messner (1994, 204–5) find evidence for this
"New Masculinity" elsewhere in American society in the 1980s and
1990s—for example, in the image of the involved, nurturant father, and
in powerful men's public displays of weeping. But they argue that this
new version of hegemonic masculinity fails to transform gender relations.
Instead, it mostly serves to "file off some of the rough edges of hegemonic masculinity . . . while deflecting or resisting feminist challenges to
men's institutional power and privilege" (Hondagneu-Sotelo and Messner 1994, 207). The New Man is encouraged to "act like a woman" by, for
example, engaging in empathic listening at work, but the point of his behavior is to reduce the appearance of power, not to give it up.

Indeed, he appears to have been relatively successful, as the change to
a more "feminine" style of workplace relations has not resulted in men's
displacement at the top: in 1990 and 1995, approximately 5 percent of
senior managers were women, and in 1996, 9.5 percent of board seats of
Fortune 500 companies were occupied by women in 1996 (Online Newshour 1996). It seems, then, that the egalitarian impulses of the 1970s'
workplace ideals were co-opted in the 1980s and 1990s by this new version of hegemonic masculinity which incorporated "feminine" elements
as a strategy to maintain power.

The counterimage of the "New Man" is not women but less privileged men, such as working-class, immigrant, and Latino men, who are
portrayed as embodying the elements of masculinity that the New Man
has rejected—aggression and overt displays of sexism (Hondagneu-
Sotelo and Messner 1994, 207). This juxtaposition is another version of
the ideological pairing of middle-class "modesty" with working-class
"boldness." In the 1950s, a modest demeanor was a mark of middle-class

standing, a signifier of one's social distance from the "pushy" and "loud" working classes. The modest person advertised his or her superiority by willingly taking second place to others, a strategy of attracting attention by deflecting it. Similarly, in the 1980s and 1990s, a middle-class man who engaged in empathic listening advertised both his gentle sensitivity and his distance from the "old-fashioned," implicitly working-class style of aggressive masculinity.

The shyness norms I have outlined thus far are not just middle-class norms, but also white norms. Adhering to these norms has different implications for black women and men than for white women and men. Since the nineteenth century, African Americans' "natural" proclivities for shyness have been assumed to represent a reversal of the ideal, with black women being naturally assertive and black men being naturally shy. This gender reversal was one of many rationalizations for slavery, a way to defeminize black women and emasculate black men and thus exclude them from the rights and privileges accorded to whites. As part of their efforts to redefine black identity and to gain equal rights, African Americans have debated what role shyness and assertiveness should play in black femininity and masculinity. While there was widespread agreement that black men should repudiate shyness, black women's ideal relationship to shyness was more contentious. Some civil rights leaders and self-help authors saw assertiveness as a characteristic that rightfully belonged to one gender only: men. For black men's assertive behavior to have the most impact, black women could not be assertive; instead, they had to be quietly deferential. Others regarded assertiveness as a quality that could benefit both genders equally.

The debate surrounding black women's assertiveness highlights the ways in which, regardless of race, women's assertiveness often has been and continues to be perceived as a threat to men. Assertiveness, the direct expression of one's needs and desires, is a form of power. As the executive training program for "tough" women showed, it is more acceptable on the part of women when it is tempered with a willingness to perform deferential emotional labor. Women who do not perform such labor are rejected as overly aggressive and unfeminine. The ever-present threat of rejection may, in turn, encourage women to police their behavior, softening their words or remaining silent in an effort to appear more feminine, as did one woman participant of the training program. She reported that she now peppered her sentences with "um's" in order to seem less forceful (Banerjee 2001).

Shyness Norms as Ideology

Throughout the book, I have highlighted how shyness norms frequently function as ideology—meaning constructed and conveyed by symbolic forms that serves to establish and sustain relationships of power (Thompson 1990, 7). The self-help texts I examined constituted a body of "commonsense" knowledge about shyness that offered readers a framework for understanding power relationships in society. For example, the insistence of authors of the 1970s, 1980s, and 1990s that most men are "reserved" rather than shy supported a view of men as rational and unemotional, helping to explain why men wield more power than women, since rationality "lends to one's decisions and position an apparent autonomy and 'rightness'" (Sattel 1983, 120). Self-help authors often employed the ideological tool of legitimation, the defense and justification of power relations as worthy of respect. In the 1950s, for example, self-help authors appealed to women readers to engage in unreciprocated emotional labor for men on a date by defending the arena of courtship as the last bastion of male privilege. In the 1980s and 1990s, a number of self-help authors frequently relied on the ideological device of reification. By arguing that there were permanent, biological differences between women and men in their ability to feel and express emotions, they helped to explain their relative positions in the gender hierarchy. Self-help authors also used fragmentation and unification to maintain divisions among as well as between women and men. In the 1950s, for example, white middle-class women were provided with a collective "modest" identity, one that united them with "modest" white middle-class men, and also divided them from "bold" black and white working-class women. Finally, self-help authors concealed power relations by, for instance, urging women to see their superior skill at self-disclosure as a sign of power over men rather than a constraint.

An Age of Transparency

It seems unlikely that contemporary prohibitions against shyness will be lifted in the near future. Indeed, since 1995, fourteen self-help books designed to combat shyness have been published in the United States, including *Triumph over Shyness: Conquering Shyness and Social Anxiety* (Stein and Walker 2002), *The Hidden Face of Shyness: Understanding and Over-*

coming Social Anxiety (Schneier and Welkowitz 1996), and *How I Over-came Shyness: 100 Celebrities Share Their Secrets* (Simon 1999). Although several cultural commentators have, of late, bemoaned Americans' "shameless glorification of self-exposure," their voices are difficult to hear above the din of talk show guests revealing all to a national audience, reality-based television shows giving viewers access to the most mundane aspects of others' lives, and the media delving into every nook and cranny of the private lives of celebrities and politicians (Gates 1997, 123; Soyinka 1997, 49). Americans seem to be more convinced than ever that self-disclosure and openness hold the keys to intimacy and happiness.

At the same time, the possibilities for resistance are greater than ever. Although technological advances may indeed be creating a "socially awkward generation," they also support new forms of communication that are particularly suited to the shy. Computers and the Internet allow a degree of anonymity and reticence in communication that can be put to use in work and in romantic and platonic relationships. Rather than having to speak face-to-face with others, the shy can communicate via e-mail, at their own pace, disclosing as little or as much information as they desire. Instant computer messaging and cell-phone text messaging demand a level of brevity suitable for the reticent, and reduce or eliminate the need for potentially awkward telephone conversations. These forms of communication may ultimately form the basis of a new style of intimacy, one that values gradual self-disclosure and occasional silences. Shyness might thus come to be regarded as a distinct advantage.

Appendix A

Data and Methods

Data

Cultural standards governing shyness are communicated through a number of sources, including songs, television shows, films, advertisements, and novels.[1] Yet most of these sources make only sporadic explicit references to shyness. As a result, identifying a definitive population of novels, songs, ads, or movies that contain representations of shyness might present a daunting task. There is, however, one source that has provided a sustained, readily comparable popular narrative on shyness: self-help books.[2] While not every self-help book contains references to shyness, many do. Those that address shyness directly—whether through an entire book devoted to the topic or, more frequently, through portions of a more general book—dissect its causes and consequences and suggest ways to overcome it or cope with it in a variety of situations. Those that address shyness indirectly do so through discussions of effective communication and interaction skills and ideal personality traits necessary for personal and financial success. Taken together, these books provide a broad perspective on shyness.

Self-help books have a long history in North America; indeed, early British colonists began producing their own brand of prescriptive literature soon after their arrival (e.g., Cotton Mather's *Ornaments for the Daughters of Zion; or, The Character and Happiness of a Vertuous Woman*

[1692]).[3] Given their cost, domestic and imported self-help texts circulated primarily among wealthier colonists until the early nineteenth century,[4] when economic and technological advances in printing made a wide variety of reading material available at lower prices to middle-class Americans (Kasson 1990, 37, 39). Included in the sudden "outpouring" of books made possible by these advances were a great many etiquette books, which were sold through the mail and given away as free accompaniments to products as diverse as soap, aspirin, and soft-drinks (Kasson 1990, 47; Lynes 1957, 71). The early twentieth century witnessed a second "revolution" in the book industry, when the large-scale introduction of the paperback made low-cost books widely available. Self-help books, while frequently popular in hardcover, became a staple of the mass market paperback trade (Simonds 1992, 99). As the popularity of these books has grown, the self-help genre has expanded, so that in addition to its traditional focus on success, character building, personality improvement, and etiquette, it now encompasses topics as diverse as dieting, sex, relationships, psychology, mental health, addiction, recovery, and New Age spiritualism (Crichton 1989, 32).

This expansion of the genre has enabled self-help books to reach an increasingly large audience over the last fifty years. As of 1945, only 10 percent of active readers (approximately one-half of the total population aged 15 and over, a proportion which remained relatively stable into the 1980s) had read a self-help or psychology book within the last month (Link and Hopf 1946, 74). By 1978, 46 percent of book readers had read at least one in the last six months, and by 1983, 54 percent of book readers had read at least one in the last six months (Yankelovich, Skelly, and White, Inc. 1978, 142; Research and Forecasts 1984, 151).

Women are commonly perceived to be the primary readers of self-help books (Simonds 1992, 34), but the only study to address this question using a random sample found that women were only *slightly* more likely than men to have bought a self-help book (Wood 1988).[5] In any case, women are more likely than men to read books in general (a trend evident since 1945); whites, and those with higher incomes and education levels, have also been, and continue to be, overrepresented among book readers (Link and Hopf 1946, 60; Yankelovich, Skelly, and White, Inc. 1978, 26; Research and Forecasts 1984, 74). These findings suggest that, unless otherwise specified, the audience for self-help books is likely to contain more women than men, more whites than minorities, and more members of the middle and upper classes than members of the working classes. A small number of self-help books have been written specifically for non-whites, with the intended audience hailed in the title (e.g., *Chiquita's Cocoon: The Latina Woman's Guide to Love, Money, Status, and Happiness* [1994], *The Black Man's Guide to Understanding the Black Woman* [1989]).

Scholars investigating the current popularity of self-help books have turned to readers to understand not just the size of the audience, but the appeal and impact of the proffered advice. Since these studies rely on nonrandom samples, their findings cannot be generalized to the entire population of self-help readers, but they offer some clues as to why and how *some* readers read self-help books. Taken together, these studies suggest that although some readers may not follow every piece of advice offered, they do regard self-help books as important sources of knowledge regarding ideal models of emotional health and interpersonal behavior. For the thirty predominantly white, well-educated women Simonds (1992, 34, 36) interviewed, self-help books were a way to understand or improve themselves and their relationships with men. Reading these books offered a way for the women to connect to a community of other women readers with similar problems.

Similarly, Grodin's (1991) sample of thirty-three mostly white, middle-class women regarded self-help books as a means of understanding how other people commonly experienced particular problems; for them and for the fifteen men and women Lichterman (1992) interviewed, the books were a resource when the rules of conduct were unclear and when other avenues of help and guidance were unavailable. But despite the fact that readers regarded these books as an important source of aid, they did not accept the advice they were given uncritically: they either rejected outright books that they considered too "sensational" (Simonds 1992, 28), or were selective about which pieces of advice they chose to follow (Grodin 1991, 411).[6]

Given their selectivity, it is perhaps not surprising that readers often found it difficult to remember the overall messages of the self-help books they read (Lichterman 1992, 428; Simonds 1992, 32); generally, readers in these studies tended to glean a few pertinent pieces of information from these books, "one or two sentences . . . that really apply to you in a way that you say, 'that's it. Aha!'" (Lichterman 1992, 430). Yet they continued to read new self-help books on a regular basis (Simonds 1992, 32); in addition, they returned to previously read books in times of personal trouble (Lichterman 1992, 429). One participant in Simonds' (1992, 31) study neatly explained this seeming paradox between readers' poor recall and their continued reliance on self-help books: "When I don't need it, why do I want to remember it? When I don't need it, I don't care. So I really use it when I need it. I don't know anything about them when I don't need them." Thus, it appears that even if the effect is only temporary, readers do occasionally rely upon self-help books as authoritative guides for their own feelings and behavior. Therefore, it is likely that the messages communicated by self-help books about shyness are not falling on deaf ears. Instead, these books may be an effective means of communicating and reproducing cultural norms governing shyness.

Sampling

The Sampling Frame

Ideally, I would have liked to assemble a sampling frame of popular self-help and advice books by obtaining sales information from publishers; however, publishers are loathe to part with sales information for individual titles, releasing instead highly aggregated data on sales figures for particular genres of books, such as "nonfiction" or "textbooks" (available in the Association of American Publishers' annual report on industry statistics).[7] The closest alternative was the yearly list of nonfiction best sellers available in Hackett and Burke's *80 Years of Best Sellers, 1895–1975*[8] and, for the post-1975 period, in the January editions of *Publishers' Weekly*. But reliance on these lists would have severely limited the scope of my project, since only one or two self-help books appeared on them every year.[9] Another source of bestseller lists, the *New York Times Book Review*, seemed the ideal alternative, since it published a weekly list of the best-selling advice, how-to, and miscellaneous books, in both hardcover and paperback;[10] however, I discovered that this list only began in 1984. Thus, while I decided to use the *Times'* list as a supplement for the 1985–1995 period (see below), I was forced to create from scratch my own sampling frame of popular advice books. To do this, I had to perform two steps: (1) define a population of advice books; and (2) determine which of these books had achieved some degree of popularity.

To locate a population of advice books, I first examined the *Publisher's Trade List Annual*, which lists all of the books published in the United States in a given year by title and author. Although this source was certainly comprehensive, I was concerned about the fact that the companion subject index (compiled in *Books in Print)* did not begin publication until 1957. Thus, in order to locate advice books published between 1950 and 1956, I would have had to use book titles as my sole guide. While titles for advice books frequently begin with "How to . . ." (e.g., *How to Win Friends and Influence People*), many offer few clues about the contents of the book (e.g., *Total Joy*, a book for women that offers advice on how to rejuvenate one's marriage); the potential for erroneously excluding some books from consideration and including others based on misleading or ambiguous titles led me to conclude that the *Publisher's Trade List Annual* was an inadequate source for assembling a population of self-help and advice books. I turned to a source that was somewhat less comprehensive but more precise: the Library of Congress. The library does not own or even catalog every book published in the United States: although federal law requires that a copy of every book published in the United States be deposited with the U.S. Copyright Office (a department of the Library of Congress), the library is not required to keep them all. Decisions about which books to accept or reject are guided by the mission of the Library of Congress: "to preserve a universal collection of knowledge and creativity for future generations" (Library of Congress 1996). How this rather vague directive is operationalized is unclear, but the library certainly appears to err on the side of inclusiveness, since it owns over 17 million books and adds materials to the library (including books, maps, video recordings, and photos) at a rate of seven thousand per working day (Library of Congress 1998).

I searched the library's holdings via computer (books could be searched by subject, language of publication, and year of imprint). Since there were few advice books devoted exclusively to shyness in any of the three time periods,[11] I had to explore a broad range of subject categories that could conceivably bear some relationship to shyness, as it has been represented over time. I began my search by focusing exclusively on adult shyness, initially avoiding advice to parents regarding children's shyness. I did so because I assumed that shyness norms for adults would be more revealing than those for children, who are often expected to go through phases of bashfulness on the road to adulthood. As the project progressed, I decided to test this assumption by investigating advice to parents of shy children as well, exploring similarities and differences between shyness norms for children and adults (see below). I started my library search with the subject categories "etiquette" and "manners," since a perusal of contemporary etiquette books at a local bookstore revealed that this type of self-help book consistently devoted at least a small section of the book to advice on shyness. The chapter headings for these books also yielded the subject categories "business etiquette," "conversation," and "social skills." By examining cross-referenced subject classifications, I identified three additional (and somewhat older) subject categories: "young women," "young men," and "conduct of life." This last category led me to an annotated bibliography of American conduct books (Newton 1994, 5–6), which indicated that conduct books were often to be found under the subject categories "success," "character," "courtship," "marriage," and "courtesy."

I identified several additional subject categories by exploring the catalog for all possible variations on a theme that I had already identified as pertinent; thus, I discovered that the subject category "courtship" had evolved over time into the more modern categories of "dating," "single men," "single women," "interpersonal relationships," and "interpersonal communication." I located the remaining subject categories—"solitude," "personality," "assertiveness," "temperament," and "silence"—by exploring the ways in which shyness has been discussed in the social-psychological literature. Together, all of these categories (along with "shyness" and "bashfulness") yielded a total of 916 titles for the 1950–1960 period, 2,450 for the 1970–1980 period, and 7,230 for the 1985–1995 period.

Once I had printed out the cataloging information for each book (which included the title, author, year of publication, place of publication, and publisher), I removed the following kinds of texts from the lists: fiction, humor, books aimed at children or parents, books published solely outside of the United States, academic texts, books with a religious theme, edited texts, textbooks, and books concerned with letter writing or with wedding or diplomatic etiquette.[12] I was left with 338 titles for the 1950–1960 period, 1,088 for the 1970–1980 period, and 3,896 for the 1985–1995 period.

The second step in the process of creating my sampling frame involved limiting the population to those titles that had achieved a certain degree of popularity with the reading public. I focused on popular self-help books for two reasons. First, the fact that certain books reach a larger audience than others suggests that only some books contain ideas that appeal to a large section of the public; those that do may be more likely to influence and reflect readers' perceptions of cultural standards governing shyness. Second, as cultural studies scholars have pointed out, popular culture is an important site in the struggle to secure and resist cultural and ideological hegemony (e.g., Hall 1981; Roman and Christian-Smith 1988, 3). Truly *popular* popular culture seemed more likely to be relevant to this struggle.

I measured "popularity" in three ways: the publication of multiple editions of a book, favorable reviews in trade journals consulted by librarians and booksellers, and an appearance on the *New York Times Book Review* weekly bestseller list. To satisfy the first criteria, a book had to have at least two editions to be included in the sampling frame.[13] I reasoned that the release of a second, third, or fourth (or more) edition signaled that sales were strong enough to warrant another printing. The drawback to this conceptualization of popularity is that it fails to account for differences in the size of print runs: it is possible that a book with a small print run (e.g., 5,000 copies) in its third edition may have sold fewer copies than a book with a large print run (e.g., 100,000 copies) with only one edition. I spoke to several publishers and booksellers to determine if there were any standard policies regarding sizes of print runs.[14] I was told that publishers have no standard policies; instead, the size of a contemporary print runs varies, ranging from 5,000 to 350,000 copies, depending upon advance orders from bookstores. Determining if and when a book will be brought out in a second or third edition also depends upon the particular book.

To find out about policies on print runs during the 1950s and 1970s, I searched biographies and autobiographies of figures in the world of publishing (e.g., Schwel 1984). I found nothing that explained publishing strategies for advice books during those periods. I also searched industry and scholarly work on book publishing (e.g., Dessauer 1989; Lehmann-Haupt 1951; Publisher's Weekly 1976; Tebbel 1975; Unwin 1947). Although Lehmann-Haupt (1951, 413) revealed that in the period after World War II, a traditional first printing was 5,000 to 7,000 copies, neither he nor any other author offered information that explained in detail the policies on size of print runs for particular types of books or when books were released in another edition. Thus, I was unable to adjust the "multiple edition" criteria to account for the size of print runs; instead, I simply identified all those advice books on my list that had at least two editions. As a consequence, I may be excluding from my sampling frame one or more popular and influential works that were released in only one, extremely large, edition. In the 1950–1960 period, 86 advice books had multiple editions; in the 1970–1980 period, 243 advice books had multiple editions; and in the 1985–1995 period, 263 advice books had multiple editions.[15]

The second measure of popularity was a favorable review in one of four trade journals regularly consulted by librarians. In their study of the book industry, Coser, Kadushin, and Powell (1982, 315) assert that positive prepublication reviews in *Publisher's Weekly, Library Journal, Booklist,* or *Kirkus Reviews* result in "substantial" library orders.[16] Although this is no guarantee that patrons of libraries will borrow the books even if they are available, I wanted some way to tap the non-book-purchasing audience. Surveys undertaken in the 1970s and 1980s have shown that readers of self-help books outnumber buyers, with public libraries acting as one of the primary sources of borrowed books (Yankelovich, Skelly, and White, Inc. 1978, 142, 207; Research and Forecasts 1984, 162, 199). The ideal method of exploring the reading habits of library patrons was described by Heath (1978), who reviewed library records showing the number of patrons who had checked out conversation manuals and etiquette books from the Boston Athenaeum. I inquired at the New York Public Library about the possibility of reviewing their records, but was told that this would be impossible. Thus, I turned to the positive review as an alternative method of gauging the potential reading habits of library goers.

I relied upon the *Book Review Digest* for information on reviews for the 1950–1960 time period. It indexed three of the four journals cited by Coser, Kadushin, and Powell (1982) as important guides to librarians choosing books to order: *Booklist, Library Journal,* and *Kirkus Reviews.* In addition to the title, author, and brief summary, the *Digest* frequently included excerpts from various reviews, and signaled the overall favorability of the reviews through the symbols "+," "–," or "+/–." I included in the sampling frame any book that the *Digest* indicated had received a positive review from at least one of the three journals.[17] Forty-two books on my list of 338 1950s' titles were reviewed by one of the journals; of these, twenty-six had multiple editions (and thus were already included in the sampling frame)[18] and sixteen did not. Of the sixteen books without multiple editions, thirteen received positive reviews; I added these to the sampling frame.

For the 1970–1980 and 1985–1996 time periods, I switched to the *Book Review Index* (first published in 1965) to locate book reviews, since the *Book Review Digest* now only indexed two of the four journals of interest to me (*Booklist* and *Library Journal*), while the *Book Review Index* indexed all of them. The *Book Review Index* did not indicate the favorability of the book reviews it cited, so I looked these up myself. If the review contained a positive statement about the merit of the book (i.e., "full value to target audience," or "easily enjoyable"), particularly advice about the advisability of adding it to a library collection (i.e., "This book will be widely publicized and requested. Most libraries should purchase it" or even "Although the book is shallow, trivial, and immoral, most libraries will have to buy it because patrons will demand it"),[19] I included the book in the sampling frame. In the case of multiple (and conflicting) reviews, I included any book that received at least one positive review from any of the four journals. For the 1970–1980 period, 220 of the 1,088 books on my list were reviewed by one of the four journals. Seventy-three of these were multiple-edition books already on the sampling frame.[20] Of the remaining 147 books, 77 received positive reviews, so I added those to the sampling frame. For the 1985–1995 period, 231 of the 3,896 books on my list were reviewed by one of the four journals. Fifty-two were already on the sampling frame as multiple-edition books.[21] Of the remaining 179 books, 100 received positive reviews—I added those to the sampling frame.

To supplement the portion of the sampling frame that covered the 1985–1995 period, I added advice books that made at least one appearance on the weekly "advice, how-to and miscellaneous" best-seller lists (one for hardcover, another for paperbacks, with four to five books on the hardcover list, and four to thirteen books on the paperback list) published in the *New York Times Book Review*.[22] I had planned to use these best-selling books to check the validity of my other measures of popularity by comparing the content of books that I identified as popular to that of the books that made the best-seller lists. As it turned out, many of the best-sellers were also reviewed favorably and/or had multiple editions: seventeen of the thirty-three best-sellers I included in the sampling frame had multiple editions, twenty-one were reviewed favorably in at least one of the four journals regularly consulted by librarians, and thirteen were both reviewed favorably and had multiple editions.[23]

I examined the titles that appeared on the best-seller lists published in the *Review* on the first Sunday of every month during the 1985–1995 period. I rejected outright exercise books, cookbooks, and books of cartoons, and kept everything else—a total of forty-eight titles for the eleven-year period. I then looked up the Library of Congress subject classification for each book and removed those classified as vocational guidance, mind and body, sex, life cycle, spiritual movement, business management, child rearing, or medicine, leaving me with thirty-three best-sellers to add to the sampling frame.

At this point, the sampling frame included only two books specifically addressed to a non-white audience (*Don't Weep for Me*, by Claudette E. Sims, and *Children of the Dream: The Psychology of Black Success*, by Audrey Edwards, both published in the 1985–1995 period). I returned to the Library of Congress catalog and searched each of my original subject categories with the additional terms "African Americans," "Asian Americans," and "Hispanic Americans." I located seventeen self-help books addressed to African American women and men (in addition to the three already on my sampling frame): two published in the 1970s, and the remainder published in the 1985–1995 period. I found no self-help books aimed at Asian Americans, and only one aimed at Latinas.[24] Of the books that I found for a black audience, only three met one of the popularity criteria (all had multiple editions); rather than limit the titles on my sampling frame to this still-small number, I decided to include them all, regardless of popularity.

I also decided to include Charlotte Hawkins Brown's *The Correct Thing To Do—To Say—To Wear* in the final sample of texts from the 1950s. Although this text was originally published in 1940, it was the only text I found written specifically for a black audience before the 1970s. The fact that it was reprinted five times during the 1940s, won the Mark Twain Society Book Award in 1944, was used in many schools and social clubs throughout the country, and was revised for contemporary use in 1965 suggests that it was, in fact, circulating in the 1950s as well as the 1940s (Denard 1995, xxix).

In an effort to add to the self-help material aimed at a non-white audience, I investigated the possibility of including a sample of articles on shyness or related topics published in popular magazines intended for minorities. First, I looked for any English-language popular periodicals geared toward a Hispanic and an Asian audience, but found none.[25] Next, I looked at *Ebony*, a magazine for a black audience that began publication in 1945. (In 1991, its circulation of 1,844,973 placed it among the forty best-selling magazines in the United States; Circulation Leaders 1993, 159). I examined the table of contents of a series of issues published at intervals throughout each of the three time periods (e.g., 1950, 1953, 1957, and 1960; 1970, 1973, 1977, 1980, etc.). Although the content of the articles changed over time, the general structure remained relatively unchanged: the magazine usually included articles covering science, entertainment, race relations, religion, foreign affairs, crime, history, art, education, employment, medicine, politics, and sports. I found no articles that touched on shyness or the subject categories related to it.

I turned next to *Essence*, a magazine for black women which began publication in 1970 (in 1991, its circulation of 868,504 placed it among the 100 best-selling magazines in the United States; Circulation Leaders 1993, 160). I examined the table of contents of a series of issues published at intervals in the 1970s and in 1985–1995. Generally, each issue included an article on education, careers, travel, health, child rearing, music, literature, fashion and beauty, food, home decorating, celebrities, sex, and, occasionally, male-female relationships. The articles in the last category frequently discussed strategies for interpersonal communication, one of the subject categories in which I was interested; therefore, I systematically searched the table of contents of each issue of *Essence* from January 1970 to December 1980 and from January 1985 to December 1995 in order to locate all of these types of articles (or any others that might be related to shyness). If I found a potential article, I read it to determine if it contained a paragraph or more devoted to the following topics: shyness, communication, silence, flirting, dating, listening, body language, assertiveness, timidity, popularity, making friends, fear, reserve, or introversion. I found eight articles published in the 1970s and twenty-eight published in the 1985–1995 period that fit this criteria. I added these to the final sample.

Drawing the Sample

At this point, the sampling frame contained 100 self-help, etiquette, or advice books published between 1950 and 1960, 321 published between 1970 and 1980, and 414 published between 1985 and 1995. I numbered each of the titles on this list and used a random number table to select the books to be included in the sample. My goal was to select one-half of the books published in the 1950s (given the smaller number of books published in this decade), one-third of the books published in the 1970s, 1980s, and 1990s (given the larger number of books published in these decades), all of the books devoted entirely to adult shyness,[26] and as many books as possible written for an African American audience.

In order to be included in the final sample, a book had to contain more than one paragraph specifically on shyness or any of the following: listening, assertiveness, timidity, fear, reserve, introversion, silence, communication, dating, flirting, body language, popularity, and making friends. I located these topics by searching each book's table of contents or index, if available, and by scanning through the pages to determine how much space was devoted to them. I replaced any "inappropriate" texts—those that failed to include more than one paragraph on shyness or related topics, textbooks, religiously oriented books, books on time management, etc.—with another chosen at random. If I chose a book with editions that straddled two time periods (e.g., the first edition released in 1977, the second in 1985), I requested both editions. I planned to include both in my sample if I determined that there were any changes in relevant content. I randomly selected fourteen titles with editions that straddled two or more time periods; seven had no changes (at least to those portions of the text in which I was interested). The remaining seven had an edition that was missing, in use, or not owned by the Library of Congress, so I included in the sample the version that was available. Thus, my sample does not include any "straddlers" whose content changed over time.

Two of the seven books which straddled two time periods, but which had no changes at all in the second edition, were books exclusively concerned with shyness (Phillip Zimbardo's *Shyness: What It Is, What to Do about It* [(1977) 1995] and Arthur Wassmer's *Making Contact: A Guide to Overcoming Shyness* [(1978) 1990]). Given their extensive, in-depth coverage of shyness, I chose to consider them as belonging to *both* time periods; this would enable me to gauge consistencies as well as differences in advice about shyness over time. These two books appear in the final sample twice, once in the period 1970–1980, and once in the period 1985–1995.

I was forced by time limitations to eventually abandon the goal of random selection. Instead, I deliberately requested books with titles that "sounded" more profitable than others, choosing, for example, *Winning with People*, rather than *Inventing the Future*. (Although this strategy generally paid off, it is clear that one "cannot judge a book by its title" since many of the books that made it into the sample at random had titles that I would have judged as unlikely to be appropriate if I were to choose them myself, such as *This Is Earl Nightingale*.) I chose approximately forty books in this nonrandom manner (21 percent of the final sample).

For each book that I selected, I photocopied the portions that concerned shyness or concepts (detailed above) related to it. Frequently, a book contained a clearly labeled chapter or section of a chapter devoted exclusively to shyness, in which case my decision about what part of the book to photocopy was straightforward. For those books which had no separate section on shyness, but which mentioned shyness sporadically, I photocopied the appropriate pages, along with any surrounding material that was necessary to provide context.

Table A.1 shows the revised sampling frame—adjusted after I had examined some of the books and eliminated those that were inappropriate—as well as the final sample that I drew from each category (see appendix B for a list of all of the titles in the final sample). The majority of these books were intended for a primarily white audience. In some cases, these books made their intended audience clear through racial markers such as photographs that uniformly depicted whites, or advice to readers about how to avoid racial prejudice against blacks. The majority, however, had no explicit racial markers. Since silence about race generally signifies whiteness in much the same way that silence about gender signifies maleness, I judged the intended audience of these texts to be largely white (see Shapiro 1982, 718).[27] Table A.2 shows the sampling frame and the final sample of self-help books aimed at an African American audience. Table A.3 shows the number of magazine articles aimed at an African American audience that I used to supplement this small sample of books. Both the self-help books and articles focused primarily on intimate heterosexual relationships; thus my analysis of the emotional culture of shyness among African-Americans is limited to that arena.

TABLE A.1
*Number of Self-Help Books in Revised Sampling Frame
and in Final Sample (White Audience)*

Revised Sampling Frame			Final Sample		
1950–1960	1970–1980	1985–1995	1950–1960	1970–1980	1985–1995
62	196	259	37	60	94

TABLE A.2
*Number of Self-Help Books in Revised Sampling Frame
and in Final Sample (Black Audience)*

Revised Sampling Frame			Final Sample		
1950–1960	1970–1980	1985–1995	1950–1960	1970–1980	1985–1995
1	2	15	1	1	7

TABLE A.3
Number of Magazine Articles in Final Sample (Black Audience)

1950–1960	1970–1980	1985–1995
0	8	28

TABLE A.4
Number of Child-Rearing Manuals in Initial Sampling Frame and in Final Sample

Initial Sampling Frame			Final Sample		
1950–1960	1970–1980	1985–1995	1950–1960	1970–1980	1985–1995
653	1,499	2,300	19	18	41

Child-Rearing Manuals

Due to time constraints, I took a less rigorous approach to identifying a sample of popular child-rearing manuals to be included in the study. I used the Library of Congress's on-line catalog to locate a population of child-rearing texts published in each time period: 1,806 in 1950–1960, 6,691 in 1970–1980, and 11,543 in 1985–1995. Once I had removed inappropriate titles (i.e., fiction, edited collections, humor, religious texts), I was left with 653 in the 1950s, 1,499 in the 1970s, and 2,300 in the mid-1980s to mid-1990s. At this point, I was unable to restrict titles further by popularity, and instead chose books that were owned by San Francisco Bay Area libraries (see table A.4).[28] Thus, the child-rearing manuals that I examined represented a convenience, rather than a random sample of child-rearing manuals that contained references to shyness. Yet, they may still have represented the more popular of these books. Unlike the Library of Congress, the public and university libraries I relied upon had a limited budget for acquisitions; thus, they may make an effort to purchase books that were either popular (or well reviewed) already, or which had the potential to be popular. Moreover, with limited space, over time, they may have held onto only those older texts which had proven to be popular with readers.

Characteristics of Books in the Sample

Most of the self-help books and magazine articles in the sample were written for a mixed audience of men and women (see table A.5). I determined the gender of the intended audience of a particular book by first examining the title—frequently, books written exclusively for women (or, occasionally, men) include words to that effect in the title (i.e., *Smart Women, Foolish Choices; Ten Stupid Things Women Do to Mess Up Their Lives; Smart Cookies Don't Crumble: A Modern Woman's Guide to Living and Loving Her Own Life*). For those books with generic titles, I identified the gender of the assumed audience by examining the text for clues, including pronoun use (e.g., "Don't you hate it when he clams up?"), authorial assumptions (e.g., "As women, we must learn . . .), and the gender of featured "characters" whose stories formed the basis for advice (e.g., "Mary came to me with a serious problem"). I placed only those books which clearly and consistently addressed a female or male audience through these devices into one or the other category. The "mixed" category contained books that specifically addressed their advice to both women and men, or which used both male and female pronouns and/or "characters."

Given that women are perceived to be the primary consumers of self-help books (Simonds 1992, 34), I was surprised that the clear majority of books were intended for a mixed as opposed to a specifically female audience, across all time periods. To determine if women may be the intended audience only of *certain* self-help books, I examined the intended audience of self-help books focused on dating, interpersonal communication, and interpersonal relationships. Table A.6 shows that the intended audience for these types of books, across all time periods, is about

TABLE A.5
Gender of Intended Audience of Self-Help Books, Magazine Articles, and Child-Rearing Manuals

Audience	1950–1960	1970–1980	1985–1995
Female	16% (9)	24% (21)	34% (58)
Male	5% (3)	2% (2)	3% (5)
Both	74% (42)	74% (64)	63% (107)
Unclear	5% (3)	0% (0)	0% (0)
Total	100% (57)	100% (87)	100% (170)

TABLE A.6
Gender of Intended Audience of Self-Help Books and Magazine Articles on Dating, Communication, and Relationships

Audience	1950–1960	1970–1980	1985–1995
Female	43% (3)	50% (17)	64% (52)
Male	0% (0)	3% (1)	6% (5)
Both	57% (4)	47% (16)	30% (24)
Unclear (generic "he")	0% (0)	0% (0)	0% (0)
Total	100% (7)	100% (34)	100% (81)

evenly divided between women and women and men, except in the 1980s and 1990s, when books for women dominate slightly. Particularly in the contemporary period, then, women occupy a more prominent place as the intended readers of these books than among the books in the sample taken as a whole.

Characteristics of Authors

The self-help books in the sample were written by women as well as men, laypersons as well as psychologists and medical doctors. Tables A.7, A.8, and A.9 show that while lay people outnumbered "professionals" in each time period, authors with advanced degrees were more numerous in the 1970s, 1980s, and 1990s, the period when shyness was coming under increased scrutiny by the mental health community.[29]

Coding and Analysis

To code and analyze the text, I used a combination of quantitative and qualitative methods. Since each type of analysis reveals a different facet of the data, using them together promised to yield a more comprehensive portrait of the data than choosing one analytic technique over the other. Quantitative content analysis measures the frequency of media messages, tracking changes in content over time; somewhat contentiously, it assumes that each occurrence of a particular word or theme is of equal importance and intensity (Holsti 1969, 122–23). Qualitative content analysis corrects for this problem by focusing on meaning, intensity, and relationships, revealing subtle thematic shifts that may be invisible in a simple frequency count of key phrases or categories (Altheide 1996, 22).

Coding

I coded the text using the qualitative data analysis program "Q.S.R. NUD.IST," using the sentence as my unit of analysis.[30] I chose the sentence rather than the paragraph because coding schemes based on smaller units of analysis have been found to be more reliable (Weber 1990, 39). In creating my coding categories, I did not follow the tradi-

TABLE A.7
Degree Status of Authors Writing Self-Help Books for White Audiences

	1950–1960	1970–1980	1985–1995
Ph.D.	5% (2)	8% (5)	12% (11)
M.D.	0% (0)	5% (3)	2% (2)
Other advanced degree/unclear[a]	0% (0)	7% (4)	1% (1)
No advanced degree	95% (35)	80% (48)	85% (80)
Total	100% (37)	100% (60)	100% (94)

TABLE A.8
Degree Status of Authors Writing Self-Help Books and Magazine Articles for Black Audiences

	1950–1960	1970–1980	1985–1995
Ph.D.	0% (0)	44% (4)	14% (5)
M.D.	0% (0)	0% (0)	0% (0)
Other advanced degree/unclear[a]	0% (0)	0% (0)	3% (1)
No advanced degree	100% (1)	56% (5)	83% (29)
Total	100% (1)	100% (9)	100% (35)

TABLE A.9
Degree Status of Authors Writing Child-Rearing Manuals

	1950–1960	1970–1980	1985–1995
Ph.D.	21% (4)	17% (3)	27% (11)
M.D.	5% (1)	33% (6)	27% (11)
Other advanced degree/unclear[a]	5% (1)	0% (0)	7% (3)
No advanced degree	68% (13)	50% (9)	39% (16)
Total	100% (19)	100% (18)	100% (41)

tional formula described by Weber (1990, 23–24) of first defining categories, testing their utility on a sample of text and revising them accordingly, and then coding all of the text at once. As Pfaffenberger (1988, 59) points out, this linear, "one-shot" formula was useful for researchers who had to input data on computer cards, and who paid for mainframe computer time; the introduction of personal computers has paved the way for a more recursive method of creating a coding scheme. Since there is no longer any penalty (other than time) for repeated revisions of the coding categories that make up the "dictionary," "[t]he researcher [can go] from text to dictionary and back again, refining the categories and testing the dictionary's usefulness in constant confrontation with the textual data. . . . [T]he emphasis is not on the final product, but on the process of discovery that these techniques can and should entail" (Pfaffenberger 1988, 59–60). This type of coding is one of the hallmarks of ethnographic content analysis, which adheres to the "grounded theory" model of "reflexive movement between concept development, sampling, data collection, and interpretation" (Altheide 1987, 68).

I followed this recursive model, creating coding categories as they emerged from the data, continually refining and expanding them as new themes arose in the text, and recoding previously coded text to reflect these changes. By the end of the coding process, I had identified twenty-six main thematic categories and 501 subcategories. The main themes both reflected and expanded upon the subject categories that had guided my sampling. Thus, for example, they included "shyness," "dating/relationships," "personality," and "success," as well as "fear," "body language," "speech," and "making friends." For the most part, subcategories reflected explicit concepts present in the text, such as "causes of shyness," "who initiates a date," and "how to encourage your spouse to self-disclose." Implicit concepts emerged in the analysis and interpretation stage.

I assigned more than one code to a sentence which had multiple meanings. For example, I coded the sentence "Disclosing your perceptions—your opinions, beliefs and feelings—even if it means confrontation, is fundamental to intimacy and honesty in an open relationship" as both "why one should self-disclose" (to achieve intimacy and honesty) and as "how to self-disclose" (revealing opinions, beliefs, and feelings). The drawback to multiple coding was that it prevented me from employing multivariate statistical procedures (which require mutually exclusive categories) (Weber 1990, 36); the potential benefits were greater flexibility and the discovery of unexpected patterns (Richards and Richards 1991, 51). Given that this was an exploratory study, I was willing to sacrifice statistical finesse for greater versatility.

Analysis

In analyzing the data, I first used the quantitative technique of identifying important themes by performing category and word frequency counts, making comparisons within and across time periods (Weber

1990, 56). Although I do not necessarily report those numeric findings, they formed the basis for much of my analysis, allowing me to make generalizations like "most authors argued . . . ," "in the 1950s, the most common symptom of shyness was . . ." or "the term 'self-disclo-sure' did not come into vogue until the 1970s." To uncover changes in the intensity or focus of specific categories within or across time peri-ods—information that could modify or specify more precisely the quantitative information—I compared narrative data. Performing both steps was revealing, since the numerical predominance of a particular category often did not indicate the intensity of a particular sentence. For example, the category "consequences of shyness: singlehood" in-cluded the statement from a text written in the 1985–1995 period, "Re-search reveals that shy women and men tend to marry later in life or not at all" (Cheek 1989, 165), as well as the statement from a text writ-ten in the 1970s, "What man in his sound mind wants to marry and live with a cipher?" (Ellis 1979, 30). The authorial disapproval lurking in the latter statement is noticeably absent in the former, suggesting perhaps that in the 1980s and 1990s, remaining single due to shyness was no longer regarded as quite such a pitiable condition. Performing a narrative comparison of the texts was the only way to explore this pos-sibility.

A Note on Self-Help Authors

Authors of self-help texts are members of a highly profitable and quite large and competitive industry. While their aim is to grab a potential reader's attention so much that she or he is inspired to buy these books, authors do not necessarily offer unique or highly original ideas. Simonds (1992, 113) reports that self-help books go through fashions, and indeed, I discovered that, within each time period, a piece of advice proffered by one author was usually offered by at least one other author. This is hardly surprising when we consider that the self-help print industry is a type of mass media whose messages are often "'manufactured,' standard-ized, [and] always 'multiplied' in some way" (McQuail 1984, 34). Read-ers themselves acknowledge this standardization, but continue to read self-help books in search of a "nugget" of inspiration (Lichterman 1992, 430). It is the very repetition of ideas in these texts that enables me to treat the advice they offer as "commonsense" knowledge that reflects, reproduces, or challenges taken-for-granted power arrangements in society.

Time Periods

Throughout the book, I use decade labels (e.g., "the 1970s") to refer to the time periods under consideration; however, it is important to remember that social periodization does not necessarily correspond to the decimal system—that is, what we think of as the 1970s may actually span the years 1968 to 1984 (see Schulman 2001). When I use decade labels to generalize about a decade's social, cultural, and political events, I do so with the understanding that there is a loose fit between decades and their labels, and with the assumption that the decade labels provide a useful, if rough, guide to the spirit of a particular age.

In choosing my sample of advice texts, I clearly took a more literal approach to the notion of a particular decade, since I limited my focus to those books published in three eleven-year periods. Although this suggests that I might be artificially truncating a particular decade, two of my measures of popularity were fluid enough to ensure that this was not necessarily the case. Books with multiple publication dates were often published in the years immediately preceding or following the eleven-year period under consideration. Likewise, books that I sampled based on their placement on best-seller lists were sometimes best-sellers in the years preceding or following the time period of interest. Thus, while the books in my sample literally were published in the 1950s, 1970s, or mid-1980s to mid-1990s, their reach may not always be strictly limited to each eleven-year period.

Appendix B

Sampled Self-Help Books,
Child-Rearing Manuals, and Magazine Articles

1950–1960

Albert, Dora. 1957. *You're Better Than You Think*. Englewood Cliffs, NJ: Prentice Hall.

Allen, Betty, and Mitchell Pirie Brigs. 1950. *Behave Yourself: Etiquette for American Youth*. New York: J. P. Lippincott.

Ballard, Virginia, and Ruth Strang. [1951] 1965. *Ways to Improve Your Personality*. New York: McGraw-Hill.

Beecher, Marguerite, and Willard Beecher. 1955. *Parents on the Run: A Common Sense Book for Today's Parents*. New York: Julian Press.

Beery, Mary. 1954. *Manners Made Easy*. New York: McGraw-Hill.

———. 1957. *Young Teens Talk It Over*. New York: McGraw-Hill.

Brown, Charlotte Hawkins. [1941] 1995. "The Correct Thing To Do— To Say—To Wear." Pp. 39–109 in *"Mammy": An Appeal to the Heart of the South* (1919); *The Correct Thing To Do—To Say—To Wear* (1941), edited by Henry Louis Gates, Jr., Jennifer Burton, and Carolyn C. Denard. New York: G. K. Hall.

Bryant, Bernice Morgan. 1960. *Miss Behavior: Popularity, Poise, and Personality for the Teenage Girl*. Indianapolis: Bobbs-Merrill.

Cerami, Charles A. 1958. *Living the Business Life: Putting New Meaning and Purpose in Your Career*. Englewood Cliffs, NJ: Prentice Hall.

Claxton, Philander Priestley. 1953. *Some Rights of Children and Youth*. New York: Exposition Press.

Colton, Jennifer. 1953. *What to Do When.* New York: Harper and Brothers.

Crounse, Helen Louise. 1952. *Joyce Jackson Goes on a Date: Teen-Age Dating Etiquette for Girls.* New Haven, CT: College and University Press.

Cutts, Norma E., Ph.D., and Nicholas Moseley, Ph.D. 1954. *The Only Child: A Guide for Parents and Only Children of All Ages.* New York: G. P. Putnam's Sons.

Davies, Daniel R., and Robert T. Livingston. 1958. *You and Management.* New York: Harper and Brothers.

Dodds, Robert C. 1959. *Two Together: A Handbook for Your Marriage.* New York: Thomas Y. Cromwell.

Duvall, Evelyn Mills, Ph.D. 1958. *The Art of Dating.* New York: Association Press.

Duvall, Sylvanus M., Ph.D. [1949] 1959. *101 Questions to Ask Yourself before You Marry.* New York: Association Press.

Editors of Esquire Magazine. [1953] 1969. *Esquire Etiquette: A Guide to Business, Sport, and Social Conduct.* New York: J. B. Lippincott.

Ellenwood, James Lee. 1953. *One Generation after Another.* New York: Charles Scribner's Sons.

Fetter, Elizabeth. 1957. *Help Your Husband Stay Alive.* New York: Appleton-Century Crofts.

Fromme, Allan, Ph.D. 1956. *The Parents Handbook.* New York: Simon and Schuster.

Giblin, Les. 1956. *How to Have Confidence and Power in Dealing with People.* Englewood Cliffs, NJ: Prentice Hall.

Gilmer, B. Von Haller. 1951. *How to Help Your Child Develop Successfully.* New York: Prentice Hall.

Goodman, Dr. David. [1959] 1969. *A Parents' Guide to the Emotional Needs of Children.* New York: Hawthorn Books.

Gruenberg, Sidonie Matsner. 1958. *The Parents' Guide to Everyday Problems of Boys and Girls: Helping Your Child from Five to Twelve.* New York: Random House.

Huston, Alfred D., and Robert A. Sandberg. 1955. *Effective Speaking in Business.* New York: Prentice Hall.

Jones, Eve, Ph.D. 1959. *Natural Child Rearing.* Glencoe, IL: Free Press.

Katz, Barney, Ph.D. 1953. *How to Be a Better Parent.* New York: Ronald Press Company.

Kellogg, Rhoda. 1954. *Babies Need Fathers, Too.* New York: Comet Press Books.

Knox, James, Alice H. Horner, and Ruth Wade Ray. 1953. *Personality in Action*. Oak Park, IL: Knox Business Book Company.

Laird, Dr. Donald A., and Eleanor C. Laird. 1951. *Sizing Up People*. New York: McGraw-Hill.

Loeb, Robert. 1954. *He-Manners*. New York: Association Press.

———. 1959. *She-Manners*. New York: Association Press.

MacGibbon, Elizabeth Gregg. 1954. *Manners in Business*. New York: Macmillan.

Mitchell, Lucy Sprague, et al. 1954. *Know Your Children in School*. New York: Macmillan.

Moak, Helen. [1958] 1959. *The Troubled Child*. New York: Henry Holt.

Newton, Ray, and F. G. Nichols. 1954. *How to Improve Your Personality*. New York: McGraw-Hill.

Peale, Norman Vincent. 1955. *The Power of Positive Thinking*. Englewood Cliffs, NJ: Prentice Hall.

Post, Emily. [1940] 1959. *Children Are People: How to Understand and Guide Your Children*. New York: Funk and Wagnalls.

Prevette, Earl. 1953. *How to Turn Your Ability into Cash*. New York: Prentice Hall.

Prochnow, Herbert V. 1952. *1001 Ways to Improve Your Conversation and Speeches*. New York: Harper and Brothers.

Reid, Lillian N. 1950. *Personality and Etiquette*. Boston: D. C. Heath.

Reynolds, Martha May. [1939] 1951. *Children from Seed to Saplings*. New York: McGraw-Hill.

Roosevelt, Eleanor. 1960. *You Learn by Living*. New York: Harper and Brothers.

Saunders, Alta Gwinn. 1951. *How to Become a More Interesting Talker.* Indianapolis: Droke House Publishers.

Schwartz, David Joseph. 1959. *The Magic of Thinking Big*. Englewood Cliffs, NJ: Prentice Hall.

Schwarz, Berthold Eric, and Bartholomew A. Ruggieri. 1958. *Parent-Child Tensions*. Philadelphia: J. B. Lippincott.

Scott, Judith Unger. 1957. *Memo for Marriage*. Philadelphia: Macrae Smith.

Seipt, Irene Schumo. 1955. *Your Child's Happiness: A Guide for Parents*. Cleveland and New York: World Publishing.

Simmons, Harry. 1953. *How to Get Ahead in Modern Business*. New York: Prentice Hall.

Sinick, Daniel. 1960. *Your Personality and Your Job.* Chicago: Science Research Associates.

Stern, Catherine, and Toni S. Gould. 1955. *The Early Years of Childhood: Education through Insight.* New York: Harper and Brothers.

Strain, Frances Bruce. 1952. *Love at the Threshold: A Book on Social Dating, Romance, and Marriage.* New York: Appleton Century Crofts.

Stratton, Dorothy C., and Helen B. Schleman. 1955. *Your Best Foot Forward: Social Usage for Young Moderns.* New York: McGraw- Hill.

Wolf, Anna W. M., and Suzanne Szasz. [1950, 1952, 1953] 1954. *Helping Your Child's Emotional Growth.* Garden City, NY: Doubleday.

ZuTavern, A. B., and Elmer J. Erickson. 1950. *The Business of Life.* New York: University Publishing.

1970–1980

Adams, Linda (with Elinor Lenz). 1979. *Effectiveness Training for Women (E.T.W.).* New York: Simon and Schuster.

Andelin, Helen. 1970. *The Fascinating Girl.* Santa Barbara, CA: Pacific Press.

Beck, Joan. 1976. *Effective Parenting: A Practical and Loving Guide to Making Child Care Easier and Happier for Today's Parents.* New York: Simon and Schuster.

Bloom, Lynn Z., Karen Coburn, and Joan Pearlman. 1975. *The New Assertive Woman.* New York: Delacorte Press.

Bolton, Robert. 1979. *People Skills: How to Assert Yourself, Listen to Others, and Resolve Conflicts.* New York: Simon and Schuster.

Bottel, Helen. 1979. *Parents' Survival Kit: A Reassuring Guide to Living through Your Child's Teenage Years.* New York: Doubleday.

Braga, Laurie, and Joseph Braga. 1975. *Learning and Growing: A Guide to Child Development.* Englewood Cliffs, NJ: Prentice Hall.

Brazelton, T. Berry, M.D. 1974. *Toddlers and Parents: A Declaration of Independence.* New York: Delacorte.

Brothers, Dr. Joyce. 1978. *How to Get Whatever You Want Out of Life.* New York: Simon and Schuster.

Brown, Helen Gurley. 1970. *Sex and the Single Girl.* New York: Bernard Geis Associates.

Burton, Dee, Ph.D. 1980. *Rainbow: Finding the Better Person inside You.* New York: Macmillan.

Butler, Pamela. 1976. *Self-Assertion for Women: A Guide to Becoming Androgynous*. San Francisco: Canfield Press.

Coleman, Emily, and Betty Edwards. 1976. *Brief Encounters*. Garden City, NY: Doubleday.

Comer, James P., M.D., and Alvin F. Poussaint, M.D. 1975. *Black Child Care: How to Bring up a Healthy Black Child in America*. New York: Simon and Schuster.

DeVille, Jard. 1979. *Nice Guys Finish First: How to Get People to Do What You Want . . . and Thank You for It*. New York: William Morrow.

Dobson, Dr. James C. 1975. *What Wives Wish Their Husbands Knew about Women*. Weaton, IL: Tyndale House.

Drakeford, John W. 1970. *Games Husbands and Wives Play*. Nashville, TN: Broadman Press.

Dubrin, Andrew J. 1977. *Survival in the Office: How to Move Ahead or Hang on*. New York: Mason Charter.

Dyer, Dr. Wayne W. 1978. *Pulling Your Own Strings*. New York: Thomas Y. Crowell.

Eisenberg, Abne M. 1979. *Job Talk: Communicating Effectively on the Job*. New York: Macmillan.

Ellis, Albert. 1979. *The Intelligent Woman's Guide to Dating*. Secaucus, NJ: Lyle Stuart.

Fisher, Seymour, and Rhoda L. Fisher. 1976. *What We Really Know about Child Rearing: Science in Support of Effective Parenting*. New York: Basic Books.

Ford, Charlotte. 1980. *Charlotte Ford's Book of Modern Manners*. New York: Simon and Schuster.

Gardner, William I. 1974. *Children with Learning and Behavior Problems: A Behavior Management Approach*. Boston: Allyn and Bacon.

Girard, Joe (with Robert Casemore). 1979. *How to Sell Yourself*. New York: Simon and Schuster.

Golde, Roger A. 1979. *What You Say Is What You Get*. New York: Hawthorn Books.

Graubard, Paul S. 1977. *Positive Parenthood: Solving Parent-Child Conflicts through Behavior Modification*. Indianapolis and New York: Bobbs-Merrill.

Green, Robert L. 1978. *Robert L. Green's Live with Style*. New York: Coward, McCann, and Geoghegan.

Greenberg, Selma. 1978. *Right from the Start: A Guide to Non-Sexist Child Rearing*. Boston: Houghton Mifflin.

Greenwald, Dorothy, and Bob Greenwald. 1979. *Learning to Live with the Love of Your Life*. New York and London: Harcourt, Brace, Jovanovich.

Haupt, Enid. 1970. *The New Seventeen Book of Etiquette and Young Living*. New York: David McKay.

Higginson, Margaret V., and Thomas L. Quick. 1980. *The Ambitious Woman's Guide to a Successful Career*. New York: Amacom.

Homan, William E., M.D. 1977. *Child Sense: A Guide to Loving, Level-Heading Parenthood*. New York: Basic Books.

Hood, Sherry McKee. 1977. "Relationship Quiz." *Essence*, February, 38+.

Hyatt, Carole. 1979. *The Woman's Selling Game: How to Sell Yourself . . . and Anything Else*. New York: M. Evans.

Kappelman, Murray, M.D. 1975. *Raising the Only Child*. New York: E. P. Dutton.

Katz, Mort, M.S.S.W. [1974] 1975. *Marriage Survival Kit: A Daily Guide to Happier Marriage*. Rockville Center, NY: Farnsworth.

Keyes, Ken. 1975. *Handbook to Higher Consciousness*. Berkeley, CA: Living Love Center.

Korda, Michael. 1977. *Success!* New York: Random House.

Krumboltz, John D., and Helen Brandhorst Krumboltz. 1972. *Changing Children's Behavior*. Englewood Cliffs, NJ: Prentice Hall.

Landis, Paul H. 1971. *Your Dating Days: Looking Forward to Successful Marriage*. New York: McGraw-Hill.

Lang, Doe. 1980. *The Charisma Book: What It Is and How to Get It*. New York: Wyden Books.

Lasswell, Marcia E., and Norman M. Lobsenz. [1976, 1977] 1983. *No Fault Marriage: The New Technique of Self-Counseling and What It Can Help You to Do*. Garden City, NY: Doubleday.

Lazarus, Arnold, Ph.D., and Allen Fay, M.D. 1975. *I Can If I Want To*. New York: William Morrow.

Linkletter, Art. 1979. *Yes You Can! How to Succeed in Business and Life*. New York: Simon and Schuster.

Morgan, Marabel. 1973. *The Total Woman*. Old Tappan, NJ: Fleming H. Revell.

Mornell, Pierre, M.D. 1979. *Passive Men, Wild Women*. New York: Simon and Schuster.

Naylor, Phyllis Reynolds. 1972. *How to Find Your Wonderful Someone: How to Keep Him/Her If You Do, How to Survive If You Don't*. Philadelphia: Fortress Press.

Nightingale, Earl. 1970. *This Is Earl Nightingale.* Garden City, NY: Doubleday.

O'Neill, Nena, and George O'Neill. 1972. *Open Marriage: A New Lifestyle for Couples.* New York: M. Evans.

Osmond, Marie (with Julie Davis). 1980. *Marie Osmond's Guide to Beauty, Health, and Style.* New York: Simon and Schuster.

Palmer, James O., Ph.D. 1980. *The Battered Parent and How Not to Be One.* Englewood Cliffs, NJ: Prentice Hall.

Parker, Roland S. 1973. *Emotional Common Sense: How to Avoid Self-Destructiveness.* New York: Harper and Row.

Parrish, Milton. 1974. "Black Woman's Guide to the Black Man, Part 2." *Essence,* May, 64+.

Patterson, Gerald R., Ph.D., and M. Elizabeth Gullion, M.S. 1971. *Living with Children: New Methods for Parents and Teachers.* Champaign, IL: Research Press.

Peck, Ellen. 1971. *The Baby Trap.* New York: Bernard Geis Associates.

Powell, Barbara. 1979. *Overcoming Shyness: Practical Scripts for Everyday Encounters.* New York: McGraw-Hill.

Reid, Inez, and Frantz Reid. 1973. "Black Man, Black Woman at the Controversial Gate." *Essence,* October, 74+.

Richards, Arlene Kramer, and Irene Willis. 1979. *Boy Friends, Girl Friends, Just Friends.* New York: Atheneum.

Rutter, Michael. 1975. *Helping Troubled Children.* New York and London: Plenum Press.

Salk, Dr. Lee. 1979. *Dear Dr. Salk: Answers to Your Questions about Your Family.* New York: Harper and Row.

Sarnoff, Dorothy. 1970. *Speech Can Change Your Life: Tips on Speech, Conversation, and Speechmaking.* New York: Doubleday.

Schimel, John, M.D. [1963] 1970. *Your Future as a Wife.* New York: Richards Rosen Press.

Seaman, Dr. Florence, and Anne Lorimer. 1979. *Winning at Work: A Book for Women.* Philadelphia: Running Press.

Shain, Merle. 1973. *Some Men Are More Perfect Than Others.* New York: Charterhouse.

Sharp, Billy B. (with Claire Cox). 1970. *Choose Success: How to Set and Achieve Your Goals.* New York: Hawthorn Books.

Shedd, Charlie W. 1975. *Talk to Me!* New York: Doubleday.

Spock, Dr. Benjamin. 1974. *Raising Children in a Difficult Time: A Philosophy of Parental Leadership and High Ideals.* New York: W. W. Norton.

Stevens, Anita, M.D., and Lucy Freeman. 1970. *"I Hate My Parents!" The Real and Unreal Reasons Why Youth Is Angry.* New York: Cowles Book Company.

Stewart, Marjabelle Young, and Marian Faux. 1979. *Executive Etiquette: How to Make Your Way to the Top with Grace and Style.* New York: St. Martin's Press.

Taetzsch, Lyn, and Ellen Benson. 1978. *Taking Charge on the Job: Techniques for Assertive Management.* New York: Executive Enterprises.

Tanner, Tracy. 1978. *How to Find a Man . . . and Make Him Keep You.* New York: A and W Publications.

Tucker, Leota M., Ph.D., and Robert C. Tucker, Ph.D. 1979. "Working It Out." *Essence*, February, 11+.

———. 1980a. "Message to Men." *Essence*, Februrary, 62+.

———. 1980b. "Message to Women." *Essence*, February, 63+.

Tucker, Robert C., Ph.D. 1977. "Why Black Men Hide Their Feelings." *Essence*, August, 44.

Vanderbilt, Amy. 1978. *The Amy Vanderbilt Complete Book of Etiquette* (Revised and Expanded by Letitia Baldrige). New York: Doubleday.

Wagenvoord, James. 1978. *The Man's Book: A Complete Manual of Style.* New York: Avon Books.

Walker, Joseph A. 1973. "Dealin' with Ourselves." *Essence*, October, 39+.

Walters, Barbara. 1970. *How to Talk to Practically Anybody about Practically Anything.* New York: Doubleday.

Wassmer, Arthur C. [1978] 1990. *Making Contact: A Guide to Overcoming Shyness.* New York: Henry Holt.

Whitcomb, Helen, and Rosalind Lang. 1976. *Today's Woman.* New York: McGraw-Hill.

Williams, Dee. 1974. *How to Get and Keep Your Black Man in Spite of Women's Lib.* Washington, DC: Nuclassics and Science.

Williams, Robert L., and James D. Long. 1979. *Toward a Self-Managed Life Style.* Boston: Houghton Mifflin.

Willis, Jerry W., Ph.D., Jeanne Crowder, Ph.D., and Joan Willis, M.S.W. 1976. *Guiding the Psychological and Educational Growth of Children.* Springfield, IL: Charles C. Thomas.

1985–1995

Abell, Jason C. 1993. *Start Now: The Young Adult's Passport to Success and Well-Being Written by a Kid Who Wants You to Make It.* Hyattsville, MD: YJ Enterprises.

Adams, Jane. 1990. *Wake Up, Sleeping Beauty: How to Live Happily Ever After, Starting Right Now.* New York: William Morrow.

Adams, Junius. 1987. "Have You Declared Your Independence?" *Essence,* September, 95+.

Adams, Zelda, and Judy Simmons. 1987. "A New Light on Love." *Essence,* May, 83+.

Ali, Shaharazad. 1989. *The Blackman's Guide to Understanding the Blackwoman.* Philadelphia: Civilized Publications.

Ames, Louise Bates, Ph.D. 1988. *Questions Parents Ask: Straight Answers.* New York: Clarkson N. Potter.

Arond, Miriam, and Samuel Pauker, M.D. 1987 [1988]. *The First Year of Marriage: What to Expect, What to Accept, and What You Can Change.* New York: Warner Books.

Baber, Anne, and Lynne Waymon. 1992. *Great Connections: Small Talk and Networking for Businesspeople.* Manassas Park, VA: Impact.

Baldridge, Letitia. 1987. *Letitia Baldridge's Complete Guide to a Great Social Life.* New York: Rawson Associates.

———. 1990. *Letitia Baldridge's Complete Guide to the New Manners for the Nineties.* New York: Rawson Associates.

———. 1993. *Letitia Baldridge's New Complete Guide to Executive Manners.* New York: Rawson Associates.

Baldwin, Bruce A., Ph.D. 1988. *Beyond the Cornucopia Kids.* Wilmington, NC: Direction Dynamics.

Barak, Yoshua. 1992. *Blackmen Say Goodbye to Misery, Say Hello to Love: The Black Man's Alternative to the American Black Woman.* Brooklyn: A and B Books.

Barnes, Robert, and Rosemary Barnes. 1994. *We Need to Talk: Opening Doors of Communication with Your Mate.* Grand Rapids, MI: Zondervan.

Baye, Betty Winston. 1985. "You Men Want It Both Ways!" *Essence,* July, 66+.

Beattie, Melody. 1987. *Codependent No More: How to Stop Controlling Others and Start Caring for Yourself.* New York: HarperCollins.

Beck, Aaron T. 1988. *Love Is Never Enough: How Couples Can Overcome Misunderstanding, Resolve Conflicts, and Solve Relationship Problems through Cognitive Therapy.* New York: Harper and Row.

Billac, Pete. 1990. *How Not to Be Lonely Tonight.* Austin, TX: Eakin Press.

Booher, Diana. 1994. *Communicate with Confidence: How to Say It Right the First Time.* New York: McGraw-Hill.

Botwin, Carol. 1985. "16 Things Women Do Wrong in Relationships." *Essence*, August, 65+.

Brazelton, T. Berry, M.D. 1987. *What Every Baby Knows.* Reading, MA: Addison-Wesley.

Brodie, Richard. 1993. *Getting Past OK: A Straightforward Guide to Having a Fantastic Life.* Seattle, WA: Integral Press.

Brown, Elaine C. 1988. "10 Ways to Boost Your Self-Confidence." *Essence*, May, 89.

Browne, D. Anne. 1995. *You Can Get There from Here: Life Lessons on Growth and Self-Discovery for the Black Woman.* Orange, NJ: Bryant and Dillon.

Browne, Joy. 1988. *Nobody's Perfect: Advice for Blame-Free Living.* New York: Simon and Schuster.

Burns, Monique. 1990. "Ten Steps to Self-Esteem." *Essence*, August, 57+.

Butler, Pamela. 1991. *Self-Assertion for Women.* San Francisco: Harper.

Campbell, Bebe Moore. 1995. "Do You Love Me?" *Essence*, May, 214+.

Cheek, Jonathan M. (with Bronwen Cheek and Larry Rothstein). 1989. *Conquering Shyness: The Battle Anyone Can Win.* New York: Putnam.

Clinard, Helen Hall. 1985. *Winning Ways to Succeed with People.* Houston: Gulf.

Corbett, Corynne I. 1995. "The Winner Within." *Essence*, June, 65+.

Covey, Stephen R. 1989. *The Seven Habits of Highly Effective People.* New York: Simon and Schuster.

Cowan, Dr. Connell, and Dr. Melvyn Kinder. 1985. *Smart Women, Foolish Choices: Finding the Right Men and Avoiding the Wrong Ones.* New York: Clarkson N. Potter.

———. 1987. *Women Men Love, Women Men Leave: Why Men Are Drawn to Women, What Makes Them Want to Stay.* New York: Clarkson N. Potter.

Crawford, Vernon. 1992. *Elephants Don't Bite: How Doing the Little Things Right Can Make a Big Difference in Your Career—and Your Life.* New York: Donald Fine.

Davis, George. 1986. "How Men Feel." *Essence*, July, 54+.

De Angelis, Barbara, Ph.D. 1990. *Secrets about Men Every Woman Should Know.* New York: Delacorte Press.

———. 1995. *Real Moments for Lovers.* New York: Delacorte Press.

Dishy, Victor. 1990. *Inner Fitness: The Six-Step Program to Achieve a Fit Mind for Fast Decisions.* New York: Doubleday.

Dodson, Fitzhugh, Ph.D., and Ann Alexander, Ph.D. 1986. *Your Child: Birth to Age 6.* New York: Simon and Schuster.

Domash, Leanne, Ph.D. (with Judith Sachs). 1994. *"Wanna Be My Friend?" How to Strengthen Your Child's Social Skills.* New York: Hearst Books.

Dreikurs, Rudolph, M.D. (with Vicki Soltz, R.N.). 1992. *Children: The Challenge.* New York: Plume.

Eisenberg, Arlene, Heidi E. Murkoff, and Sandee E. Hathaway, B.S.N. 1989. *What to Expect the First Year.* New York: Workman Publishing.

———. 1994. *What to Expect: The Toddler Years.* New York: Workman Publishing.

Eyre, Linda, and Richard Eyre. 1987. *Teaching Your Children Sensitivity.* New York: Simon and Schuster.

Eysenck, Hans J., and Betty Nichols Kelly. [1983] 1985. *"I Do!" How to Choose Your Mate and Have a Happy Marriage.* New York: World Almanac Press.

Farber, Barry. 1987. *Making People Talk.* New York: William Morrow.

Fast, Julius. 1991. *Subtext: Making Body Language Work in the Workplace.* New York: Viking.

Fein, Ellen, and Sherrie Schneider. 1995. *The Rules: Time-Tested Secrets for Capturing the Heart of Mr. Right.* New York: Warner Books.

Finley, K. Thomas. 1991. *Mental Dynamics: Power Thinking for Personal Success.* Englewood Cliffs, NJ: Prentice Hall.

Fisher, Milton. 1992. *Haven't You Been Single Long Enough? A Practical Guide for Men or Women Who Want to Get Married.* Green Farms, CT: Wildcat Publishing.

Franck, Irene, and David Brownstone. 1991. *The Parent's Desk Reference.* New York: Prentice Hall.

Fraser, C. Gerald, and Craig Polite. 1988a. "Man Talk, Part One." *Essence*, July, 64+.

———. 1988b. "Man Talk, Part Two." *Essence*, August, 51+.

Friedman, Sonya. 1985. *Smart Cookies Don't Crumble: A Modern Woman's Guide to Living and Loving Her Own Life.* New York: G. P. Putnam's Sons.

Galinksy, Ellen, and Judy David. 1988. *The Preschool Years.* New York: Times Books.

Garber, Stephen W., Ph.D., Marianne Daniels Garber, Ph.D., and Robyn Freedman Spizman. 1993. *Monsters under the Bed and Other Childhood Fears: Helping Your Child Overcome Anxieties, Fears, and Phobias.* New York: Villard Books.

Garner, Alan. 1991. *Conversationally Speaking: Tested New Ways to Increase Your Personal and Social Effectiveness.* Los Angeles: Lowell House.

George, Nelson. 1995. "Do You Love Me?" *Essence*, May, 215+.

Glass, Lillian, Ph.D. 1991. *Say It Right: How to Talk in Any Social or Business Situation.* New York: G. P. Putnam's Sons.

Goldstein, Robin (with Janet Gallant). 1991. *More Everyday Parenting: The Six- to Nine-Year-Old.* New York: Penguin Books.

———. 1994. *"Stop Treating Me Like a Kid!" Everyday Parenting: The 10- to 13-Year-Old.* New York: Penguin Books.

Goodman, Gerald, and Glenn Esterly. 1989. *The Talk Book: The Intimate Science of Communicating in Relationships.* Emmaus, PA: Rodale Press.

Grant, Gwendolyn. 1985. "Keeping Your Balance in Love." *Essence*, October, 58+.

Grant, Gwendolyn Goldsby, Ed.D. 1995. "The Best Kind of Loving." *Essence*, February, 77+.

Gray, John. 1992. *Men Are from Mars, Women Are from Venus: A Practical Guide for Improving Communication and Getting What You Want in Your Relationships.* New York: HarperCollins.

———. 1994. *What Your Mother Couldn't Tell You and Your Father Didn't Know: Advanced Relationship Skills for Better Communication and Lasting Intimacy.* New York: HarperCollins.

Greenspan, Stanley I., M.D. (with Jacqueline Salmon). 1995. *The Challenging Child: Understanding, Raising, and Enjoying the Five "Difficult" Types of Children.* Reading, MA: Addison-Wesley.

Grice, Julia. 1985. *How to Find Romance after 40.* New York: M. Evans.

Harayda, Janice. 1987. "How to Be Happily Single." *Essence*, October, 61+.

Harley, William F., Jr. 1986. *His Needs, Her Needs: Building an Affair-Proof Marriage.* Grand Rapids, MI: Fleming H. Revell.

Hopson, Darlene Powell, Ph.D., and Derek S. Hopson, Ph.D. 1990. *Different and Wonderful: Raising Black Children in a Race-Conscious Society.* New York: Prentice Hall.

Hopson, Derek S., Ph.D., and Darlene Powell Hopson, Ph.D. 1994. *Friends, Lovers, and Soul Mates: A Guide to Better Relationships between Black Men and Women.* New York: Simon and Schuster.

Johnson, Pamela. 1994. "Jump Start Your Love Life." *Essence*, April, 71+.

Joseph, Joanne M. 1994. *The Resilient Child: Preparing Today's Youth for Tomorrow's World.* New York and London: Plenum.

Joslin, Karen Renshaw. 1994. *Positive Parenting from A to Z.* New York: Fawcett and Columbine.

Kaplan, Robert E. 1991. *Beyond Ambition: How Driven Managers Can Lead Better and Live Better.* San Francisco: Josey Bass.

Kassorla, Dr. Irene C. 1984. *Go for It: How to Win at Love, Work, and Play.* New York: Delacorte Press.

Kavanaugh, James. 1985. *Search: A Guide for Those Who Dare to Ask of Life Everything Good and Beautiful.* San Francisco: Harper and Row.

Kelly, Marguerite. 1989. *The Mother's Almanac II: Your Child from 6 to 12.* New York: Doubleday.

Kent, Margaret. 1987. *How to Marry the Man of Your Choice.* New York: Warner Books.

Kinder, Dr. Melvyn. 1994. *Mastering Your Moods: Recognizing Your Emotional Style and Making It Work for You.* New York: Simon and Schuster.

King, Norman. 1987. *The First Five Minutes: The Successful Opening Moves in Business, Sales, and Interviews.* New York: Prentice Hall.

Kramer, Johnathan, and Diane Dunaway. 1990. *Why Men Don't Get Enough Sex and Women Don't Get Enough Love.* New York: Pocket Books.

Kramer, Peter D. 1993. *Listening to Prozac.* New York: Viking.

Lerner, Harriet Goldhor, Ph.D. 1985. *The Dance of Anger: A Woman's Guide to Changing the Patterns of Intimate Relationships.* New York: Harper and Row.

Lovenheim, Barbara. 1990. *Beating the Marriage Odds: When You Are Smart, Single, and Over 35.* New York: William Morrow.

Mandell, Terry. 1992. *Power Schmoozing: The New Rules for Business and Social Success.* Los Angeles: First House Press.

Mason, LaDonna. 1993. "Laying Down the Weapons." *Essence*, April, 81+.

Mazel, Judy. 1985. *The Beverly Hills Style: How to Be the Star in Your Own Life.* New York: Stein and Day.

McAllister, Linda, Ph.D. 1992. *I Wish I'd Said That! How to Talk Your Way out of Trouble and into Success*. New York: John Wiley and Sons.

Milligan, Dr. Rosie. 1994. *Satisfying the Black Man Sexually Made Simple*. Los Angeles: Professional Business Consultants.

Murphy, Jim. 1994. *Managing Conflict at Work*. Burr Ridge, IL: Mirror Press.

Myers, David G., Ph.D. 1992. *The Pursuit of Happiness: Who Is Happy and Why*. New York: William Morrow.

Nelson, Jill. 1986. "How Women Feel." *Essence*, July, 55+.

———. 1992. "Taking It in Stride." *Essence*, October, 85+.

———. 1987. "A New Light on Love." *Essence*, May, 56+.

New York Hospital-Cornell Medical Center (with Mark Rubinstein, M.D.). 1987. *The Growing Years: A Guide to Your Child's Emotional Development from Birth to Adolescence*. New York: Atheneum.

Nichols, Michael P. 1995. *The Lost Art of Listening*. New York and London: Guilford Press.

Page, Susan. 1988. *If I'm So Wonderful, Why Am I Still Single?* New York: Bantam Books.

Palmer, Helen. 1988. *The Enneagram: Understanding Yourself and Others in Your Life*. San Francisco: Harper and Row.

Phillips, Dr. Debora (with Fred A. Bernstein). 1989. *How to Give Your Child a Great Self-Image*. New York: Random House.

Phillips, Gerald M. 1986. *Help for Shy People (and Anyone Else Who Ever Felt Ill at Ease on Entering a Room Full of Strangers)*. New York: Dorset Press.

Polland, Barbara Kay, Ph.D. 1994. *The Parenting Challenge: Practical Answers to Childrearing Questions*. Berkeley, CA: Tricycle Press.

Porter, Evette. 1990. "Can We Work It Out?" *Essence*, February, 57+.

Ray, Elaine C. 1986. "Staying Married: What It Takes." *Essence*, February, 85+.

Reuben, Steven Carr, Ph.D. 1994. *Raising Ethical Children: 10 Keys to Helping Your Children Become Moral and Caring*. Rocklin, CA: Prima.

Richardson, Jerry. 1987. *The Magic of Rapport: How You Can Gain Personal Power in Any Situation*. Cupertino, CA: Meta.

Righteous Mother. 1995. *Black Women: It's Time for You to Get on Top (and Stay There!) A Sister's Guide to Life, Love, and the Biggest Difficulty . . . the Black Man*. New York: Swing Street.

Rimm, Sylvia. 1992. *On Raising Kids: Practical, Commonsense Answers by a Leading National Psychologist, Author, and Radio Host*. Watertwon, WI: Apple.

Roane, Susan. 1988. *How to Work a Room: A Guide to Successfully Managing the Mingling.* New York: Shapelsky.

Robbins, Anthony. 1991. *Awaken the Giant Within.* New York: Summit Books.

Robinson, Everett T. 1994. *Why Aren't You More Like Me? Styles and Skills for Leading and Living with Credibility.* Amherst, MA: HRD Press.

Robinson, Rita. 1992. *When Women Choose to Be Single.* N. Hollywood, CA: Newcastle.

Rogers, Elizabeth Jen. 1994. *Create Your Own Joy: A Guide for Transforming Your Life.* St. Paul, MN: Llewellyn.

Rubin, Theodore Isaac, M.D. 1990. *Child Potential: Fulfilling Your Child's Intellectual, Emotional, and Creative Promise.* New York: Continuum.

Sanford, Linda T., and Mary Ellen Donovan. 1986. "Are You a Man Junkie?" *Essence,* February, 83+.

Scalia, Tonia. 1985. *Bitches and Abdicators.* New York: M. Evans.

Scarf, Maggie. 1987 [1988]. *Intimate Partners: Patterns in Love and Marriage.* New York: Random House.

Schachter, Dr. Robert, and Carole Spearin McCauley. 1988. *When Your Child Is Afraid.* New York: Simon and Schuster.

Schlesinger, Dr. Laura C. 1994. *10 Stupid Things Women Do to Mess Up Their Lives.* New York: Villard Books.

Schnebly, Lee. [1988] 1994. *I Do? Being Happy Being Married.* Tuscon, AZ: Fisher Books.

Schulman, Michael, Ph.D., and Eva Mekler. [1985] 1994. *Bringing Up a Moral Child: Teaching Your Child to Be Kind, Just, and Responsible.* New York: Doubleday.

Sears, William, M.D. 1985. *The Fussy Baby: How to Bring Out the Best in Your High-Need Child.* New York and Scarborough, Ontario: New American Library.

Segal, Dr. Julius. 1986. *Winning Life's Toughest Battles: Roots of Human Resilience.* New York: McGraw-Hill.

Shaffer, Judith, and Judith Lindstrom. 1989. *How to Raise an Adopted Child: A Guide to Help Your Child Flourish from Infancy through Adolescence.* New York: Copestone Press.

Shapiro, Nicole. 1993. *Negotiating for Your Life: New Success Strategies.* New York: Henry Holt.

Shure, Myrna B., Ph.D. (with Theresa Foy DiGeronimo, M.Ed.). 1994. *Raising a Thinking Child: Help Your Young Child to Resolve Everyday Conflicts and Get Along with Others.* New York: Henry Holt.

Sills, Judith. 1987. *A Fine Romance: The Psychology of Successful Courtship: Making It Work for You.* New York: St. Martin's Press.

Silverstein, Olga, and Beth Rashbaum. 1994. *The Courage to Raise Good Men.* New York: Viking.

Simmons, Judy D. 1988. "Take Charge." *Essence*, October, 87.

Sims, Claudette. 1989. *Don't Weep for Me.* Houston: Impressions.

Singletary, Donald. 1985a. "Why Men Don't Open Up." *Essence*, November, 68+.

———. 1985b. "You New Women Want It All!" *Essence*, July, 67+.

Smith, Dian G. 1991. *Parents' Guide to Raising Kids in a Changing World: Preschool through Teen Years.* New York: Prentice Hall.

Smith, Lucinda Irwin. 1987. *Growing Up Female: New Challenges, New Choices.* New York: Julian Messner.

Spock, Benjamin, M.D., and Michael B. Rothenberg, M.D. 1985. *Baby and Child Care.* New York: E. P. Dutton.

———. 1992. *Dr. Spock's Baby and Child Care.* New York: Pocket Books.

Stewart, Doug. 1986. *The Power of People Skills: A Manager's Guide to Assessing and Developing Your Organization's Greatest Resource.* New York: Wiley.

Stewart, Marjabelle Young, and Marian Faux. 1994. *Executive Etiquette in the New Workplace.* New York: St. Martin's Press.

Stoppard, Dr. Miriam. 1995. *Complete Baby and Child Care.* New York: Dorling Kindersley.

Syndor, Rebecca. 1989. *Making Love Happen: The Smart Approach to Romance Management in the 90s.* Latham, NY: British-American Publishing.

Tannen, Deborah, Ph.D. 1986. *That's Not What I Meant: How Conversational Style Makes or Breaks Your Relationship.* New York: William Morrow.

Templeton, John Marks. 1994. *Discovering the Laws of Life.* New York: Continuum.

Tracy, Brian. 1993. *Maximum Achievement: The Proven System of Strategies and Skills That Will Unlock Your Hidden Powers to Succeed.* New York: Simon and Schuster.

Tucker, Dorothy. 1987. "Guess Who's Coming to Dinner Now?" *Essence*, April, 45+.

Turecki, Stanley, M.D. (with Sarah Wernick, Ph.D.). 1994. *The Emotional Problems of Normal Children: How Parents Can Understand and Help.* New York: Bantam Books.

Turecki, Stanley, M.D., and Leslie Tonner. 1985. *The Difficult Child.* New York: Bantam Books.

Warschaw, Tess Albert, Ph.D. 1988. *Winning with Kids: How to Negotiate with Your Baby Bully, Kid Tyrant, Loner, Saint, Underdog or Winner So They Love Themselves and You, Too.* New York: Bantam Books.

Wassmer, Arthur C. [1978] 1990. *Making Contact: A Guide to Overcoming Shyness.* New York: Henry Holt.

Weathers, Diane. 1990. "White Boys." *Essence*, April, 65+.

Welch, Martha G., M.D. 1988. *Holding Time: How to Eliminate Conflict, Temper Tantrums, and Sibling Rivalry and Raise Happy, Loving Successful Children.* New York: Simon and Schuster.

Weston, Carol. 1985. *Girltalk: All the Stuff Your Sister Never Told You.* New York: Harper and Row.

———. 1987. "10 Ways to Keep Your Marriage Strong." *Essence*, November, 65+.

Wheeler, Bern. 1990. *The One and Only Law of Winning.* New York: Shapolsky.

Wheeler, Marilyn. 1995. *Problem People at Work: The Essential Survival Guide to Dealing with Bosses, Co-Workers, Employers, and Outside Clients.* New York: St. Martin's Press.

White, Burton L. 1994. *Raising a Happy, Unspoiled Child.* New York: Simon and Schuster.

White, Kate. 1995. *Why Good Girls Don't Get Ahead . . . But Gutsy Girls Do: Nine Secrets Every Career Woman Must Know.* New York: Warner.

Whyte, David. 1994. *The Heart Aroused: Poetry and the Preservation of the Soul in Corporate America.* New York: Currency Doubleday.

Williams, Kim. 1986. *Kim Williams' Book of Uncommon Sense: A Practical Guide with Ten Rules for Nearly Everything.* Tuscon, AZ: HP Books.

Wolf, Sharon. 1993. *Guerrilla Dating Tactics: Strategies, Tips, and Secrets for Finding Romance.* New York: Dutton.

Yoder, Jean, M.D., and William Proctor. 1988. *The Self-Confident Child.* New York and Oxford: Facts on File.

Zey, Michael G., Ph.D. 1990. *Winning with People: Building Lifelong Professional and Personal Success through the Supporting Cast Principle.* Los Angeles: Jeremy P. Tarcher.

Zimbardo, Philip G. [1977] 1995. *Shyness: What It Is, What to Do about It.* Reading, MA: Addison-Wesley.

Notes

1. For historical treatments of emotions such as anger, jealousy, and love, see Cancian (1987); Cancian and Gordon (1988); Lystra (1989); Seidman (1991); Stearns (1989, 1994); Stearns and Stearns (1986).

2. Zimbardo [1977] (1995).

3. I obtained this information by searching the PsycInfo database. PsycInfo indexes over 1,300 journals, as well as dissertations, book chapters, and books related to psychology, medicine, psychiatry, education, pharmacology, physiology, and linguistics. It excludes popular literature. I limited the search to articles, dissertations, book chapters, and books published in English that concerned a human population.

4. As the numbers in figures 1.1 and 1.2 suggest, there are many more authors whom I could cite here. Rather than provide the reader with an exhaustive list, I have chosen to cite one or two authors who discuss each type of shyness.

5. See also Lee, Zimbardo, and Bertholf (1977).

6. It is important to note that this was not the first appearance of shyness in the DSM. The 1952 and 1968 editions of the manual contain the malady "inadequate personality," defined as "inadaptability, ineptness, poor judgment, lack of physical and emotional stamina, and social incompatibility" (American Psychiatric Association 1952, 35) (the definition remained unchanged in the 1968 edition). "Social incompatibility" could be considered a code word for shyness. The 1980 edition of the DSM contained "avoidant personality disorder," which could also be considered a form of shyness. It was defined as "hypersensitivity to potential rejection, humiliation or shame; . . . social withdrawal in spite of a desire for affection and acceptance; and low self-esteem (American Psychiatric Association 1980). But none of these terms generated the attention that social phobia did.

7. While social constructionist views of emotion vary, particularly regarding the intermediary role that cognition plays in emotion (e.g., Coulter 1989), they do agree that emotions are primarily social, public phenomena.

8. Although Gordon (1989, 133 n. 1) argues that the term "emotional culture" is broader than the Stearns's term "emotionology," I regard them as interchangeable.

9. Hochschild (1983, 7) distinguishes between emotion work, performed in private, and emotional labor, performed for pay. I use the terms interchangeably.

10. For example, Powell (1979), Wassmer ([1978] 1990), and Zimbardo ([1977] 1995).

11. According to this definition, subordinated ideologies such as feminism are not ideologies at all, but "contestatory, disrupting interventions" (Thompson 1990, 68).

12. See Stearns (1994, 193–95, 221) for other sources of change in emotional cultures.

13. In 1956, the median age of marriage in the United States was at its lowest point in the twentieth century: 20.1 years for women, and 22.5 years for men (Jones 1980, 23–24).

14. During the 1950s, a million more children were born each year in the United States than during the 1930s (Mintz and Kellogg 1988, 180).

15. White women's labor force participation rate grew steadily from 24.1 percent in 1940 to 28.1 percent in 1950 to 33.6 percent in 1960 (U.S. Bureau of the Census 1953; U.S. Bureau of the Census 1963).

16. See also Harvey (1993, 17).

17. Fifty percent of white men admitted to erotic responses to other men, 37 percent had had at least one postadolescent homosexual experience culminating in orgasm, and 4 percent were exclusively homosexual (Kinsey, Pomeroy, and Martin 1948).

18. In 1950, the rate of black male unemployment was 6.4 percent, versus 3.4 percent for white men (Smith and Horton 1995, 1100). In 1959, black men earned 71 percent of what white men with similar characteristics, such as age and education, earned (Smith and Horton 1995, 1000–1001).

19. In 1940, 18 percent of all families were headed by black women; in 1960, this figure was 22 percent (Smith and Horton 1995, 781).

20. Between the late 1950s and late 1960s, the percentage of boys dating by age 15 declined from 78 to 59 percent; the percentage of girls dating by age 15 declined from 82 to 65 percent (Modell 1989, 292).

21. In 1991, 62.4 percent of white women and 54.1 percent of black women were in the civilian labor force (Horton and Smith 1993, 590). In 1970, among whites, there were 88 divorced persons per 1,000 married persons. In 1985, the comparable figure was 240. Among blacks, there were 166 divorced persons per 1,000 married persons in 1970, and 505 in 1985 (Chadwick and Heaton 1992, 87).

22. The debate over family values was most evident in Vice President Dan Quayle's controversial critique of the television character Murphy Brown's decision to bear a child out of wedlock (Nolan 1996, 158).

23. Democrats and Republicans squared off over women's role in society in the persons of Hillary Clinton, a working mother proud of not "staying home and baking cookies" and Barbara Bush, a stay-at-home mom (Nolan 1996, 159).

24. Bill Clinton was the first presidential candidate to openly appeal to homosexuals as a voting bloc; Republican Pat Buchanan warned that, if elected, Clinton would "impose 'homosexual rights' on all Americans" (Nolan 1996, 160).

NOTES TO CHAPTER 2

1. Mason (1935, 4) defines courtesy literature as books that set forth a "code of ethics, esthetics, or peculiar information for any class-conscious groups." Typically, courtesy books expounded upon "ideals of character, accomplishments, habits, manners, and morals—in short, the art of living in society" (Curtin 1985, 395).

2. Western Europe is obviously not homogeneous, but some scholars argue that it is possible to occasionally treat it as such. I used the term "Europe" following the lead of the historians I consulted; when they differentiated, I did as well.

3. The primary distinctions between women that medieval preachers and moralists recognized were between virgins, wives, and widows (Casagrande 1992, 82–83).

4. Herlihy (1995, 52) labels the two types of kinship "ego focused" and "ancestor focused." Ego-focused kinship centered on a particular individual and was redefined every generation, while ancestor-focused kinship traced its line to a specific ancestor, inspiring a family name, coat of arms, etc.

5. These fears are ably illustrated by the fact that the female version of "courtier," "courtesan," meant "prostitute" (Jones 1987, 44).

6. Ingram (1994, 68) argues that the legal charge of scold did not result from just *any* form of verbal assertiveness on the part of women, but instead was usually the result of "indiscriminate slander, tale-bearing, the stirring up of strife, the deliberate sowing of discord between neighbours, and sometimes also the pursuit of quarrels through needless lawsuits and legal chicanery."

7. Also known as the "ducking" stool.

8. This punishment could be meted out in both mild and violent forms. First offenders were sometimes merely carried home from court on the stool, or had the stool placed against their door (Ingram 1994, 62). Others were not so lucky: Thomas (1971, 533) reported that "at Calne, Wiltshire, in 1618 a party of three or four hundred men, sounding horns and bells, and led by a drummer, broke into Thomas Wells's house, and seized his wife Agnes, handling her violently, and intending to place her in the cucking-stool."

9. Men who wished to protest publicly frequently took advantage of women's greater freedom to create disorder by dressing in female clothing in a number of peasant riots throughout the seventeenth century (Davis 1975, 147, 150).

10. Salons first appeared in England in the eighteenth century (Dulong 1993, 400).

11. In the 1660s, Virginia and Maryland ordered every county to build and maintain a ducking stool (Spruill 1938, 331).

12. New Jersey women were granted suffrage two days after the signing of the Declaration of Independence (Coontz 1988, 146).

13. I focus here and in the following section on black men and women, but other races were also viewed in a similar light. Espiritu (1998, 244) points out that in the nineteenth century, Asian men, who often worked as domestic servants, were stereotyped by whites as "feminine."

14. Not all white men were captured under this label: during this period, Irish men and women were considered, like blacks, to be racially inferior to native-born whites. It was not until the late nineteenth century that the Irish were considered to be white; see Ignatiev (1995); Roediger (1991, 137); Takaki (1993, 149–51).

15. Hansen (1992) also finds evidence of romantic friendship between working-class men in the nineteenth century.

16. Although violence is usually characterized as a failure of self-control, whites claimed that lynching was a "quiet and quick" act of retribution (Bederman 1995, 415).

NOTES TO CHAPTER 3

1. See Breines (1992, 127–66); Douglas (1994, 49–51); Press (1991, 29–30).

2. Women wrote 47 percent of the books in the 1950s sample, but 64 percent of the text that was devoted to dating.

3. Emphasis added, Strain (1952, 75). Given the young age of marriage in the 1950s, texts on dating were directed primarily at teenage girls and boys. In later decades, as the age of first marriage increased, as well as the divorce rate, authors directed their advice to women and men of all ages.

4. Bryant (1960, 33).

5. Duvall (1958, 11). Self-help authors' views of the negative effects of aloofness were shared by most high-school girls. A study relying on a national sample of 2,005 girls in grades six through twelve conducted in the mid-1950s found that the majority of those aged 14 and over rated "snobbishness" as the primary source of unpopularity in girls (Douvan and Adelson 1966, 402).

6. Beery (1957, 98); Duvall (1958, 11).

7. Duvall (1958, 11).

8. Reid (1950, 224).

9. Beery (1954, 195); Crounse (1952, 4); Duvall (1958, 11).

10. Scott (1957, 132).

11. Crounse (1952, 4).

12. Duvall (1958, 12).

13. Beery (1954, 194).

14. Loeb (1959, 71).

15. Allen and Brigs (1950, 90); Newton and Nichols (1954, 89).

16. Loeb (1959, 123) (emphasis in original).

17. These "mannish" qualities included sports prowess, male attire (i.e., anything other than a dress or skirt), physical strength, swearing, and a lack of grace (Allen and Brigs 1950, 90; Beery 1954, 194; Bryant 1960, 30–31; Newton and Nichols 1954, 89).

18. Fewer than one American in ten believed that an unmarried person could be happy (Mintz and Kellogg 1988, 180).

19. See D'Emilio (1983, 49).

20. This was a replication of Komarovsky's (1946, 187) study of 153 women college seniors (with data collected in 1942 and 1943) which found that 40 percent occasionally "played dumb" on dates "in obedience to the unwritten law that men must possess [intellectual] skills to a superior degree."

21. Bryant (1960, 33).

22. Beery (1954, 194).

23. Reid (1950, 250).

24. Loeb (1959, 26). Younger boys who suffered from shyness were not let off the hook quite so easily. Authors of child-rearing manuals were nearly unanimous in agreeing that shyness and timidity posed a serious threat to a young boy's (and girl's) social and emotional development (Beecher and Beecher 1955, 129; Cutts and Moseley 1954, 72; Gilmer 1951, 156, 166; Goodman [1959] 1969, 178; Katz 1953, 177; Kellogg 1954, 127; Mitchell et al. 1954, 32; Moak [1958] 1959, 43–44; Stern and Gould 1955, 134–39). They urged mothers to do all that they could to help their children overcome it; one important step mothers could take was to encourage independence by "cutting the apron strings" that they tied to their children (Goodman [1959] 1969, 173; Stern and Gould 1955, 134). This was particularly important in the case of timid boys, who were apt to become "weaklings" if allowed to "hang onto . . . mother's skirt" (Stern and Gould 1955, 134). However, once the young boy established his independence from his mother and developed a healthy group-oriented, social personality, he was free to feel bashful around girls on occasion when he got older, as most of his peers would be experiencing the same feelings of fear, and girls would be responsible for alleviating them.

25. Although I focus here on the impact of the women's movement on conceptions of white femininity, women of color were also involved in the women's movement, participating with white women both in large, mainstream feminist organizations like the National Organization for Women, and in smaller ones (Giddings 1984, 303–4). Women of color also founded their own feminist organizations, such as the National Black Feminist Organization and the Combahee River Collective (Chafe 1977, 125; Combahee River Collective 1979).

26. Walters (1970, 144).

27. Andelin (1970, 152–53).

28. Andelin (1970, 77).

29. Andelin (1970, 203).

30. Andelin (1970, 161–62, 165).

31. Andelin (1970, 263).

32. Bloom, Coburn, and Pearlman (1975, 152); Butler (1976, 4); Powell (1979, 1).

33. Coleman and Edwards (1976, 68); Ellis (1979, 111); Williams and Long (1979, 80).

34. Ellis (1979, 39); Wassmer ([1978] 1990, 153).

35. Wassmer ([1978] 1990, 38, 181); Zimbardo ([1977] 1995, 127, 130).

36. Ellis (1979, 29).

37. Bloom, Coburn, and Pearlman (1975, 13); Butler (1976, 4–5).

38. Powell (1979, 102); Wassmer ([1978] 1990, 3); Zimbardo ([1977] 1995, 95–96); Ellis (1979, 112).

39. Zimbardo ([1977] 1995, 128–29, 135–39).

40. Drakeford (1970, 73); Lazarus and Fay (1975, 38); Shedd (1975, 47); Wagenvoord (1978, 284); Wassmer ([1978] 1990, 119); Zimbardo ([1977] 1995, 113).

41. O'Neill and O'Neill (1972, 115); Wagenvoord (1978, 283).

42. Lasswell and Lobsenz (1976, 146).

43. Dodds (1959, 89–90); Fetter (1957, 212). This finding is consistent with Cancian and Gordon's (1988) historical analysis of representations of love and anger in American women's magazines, which found that, prior to the 1960s, wives were advised that the repression of anger was the epitome of love for their husbands.

44. Fetter (1957, 45).

45. Dodds (1959, 60); Giblin (1956, 92).

46. O'Neill and O'Neill (1972, 113); Shedd (1975, 5).

47. See Brothers (1978, 208); Lasswell and Lobsenz ([1976, 1977] 1983, 142); Mornell (1979, 19); Peck (1971, 224); Sarnoff (1970, 121); Shedd (1975, ix). Although it seems unlikely that the phenomenon of male silence was unheard of in the 1950s, self-help texts devoted little space to the topic; wives were not counseled on how to cope with or overcome it, suggesting that it was either considered normal, and hence unremarkable, or it was indeed not a widespread problem. In fact, Thomson's (1992, 506) analysis of best-selling 1950s self-help manuals suggests that authors were simply not likely to address any kind of difficulty in love relationships, an omission she attributes to the low divorce rate.

48. Teenage boys, too, seemed to be suffering from the same problem. Garner, Sterk, and Adams's (1998, 67) analysis of sexual advice in teen magazines found that in 1974, young men were represented as "unable to express themselves verbally or emotionally."

49. Andelin (1970, 61).

50. Andelin (1970, 61). Indeed, Kimmel (1994, 133) cites a study by Noble (1992, 105–6) which found that men reported being most afraid of being laughed at, while women were most afraid of being raped or murdered.

51. Zimbardo ([1977] 1995, 163); Wassmer ([1978] 1990, 3).

52. Morgan (1973, 49); Shedd (1975, 41–43).

53. Andelin (1970, 62–63); Brothers (1978, 209); Dobson (1975, 83); Ellis (1979, 99); Morgan (1973, 50, 180); Peck (1971, 224); Shedd (1975, 50).

54. Cowan and Kinder (1985, 187; 1987, 38); Grice (1985, 71); Lovenheim (1990, 60).

55. Lovenheim (1990, 58).
56. Glass (1991, 199); Baldridge (1987, 307); Grice (1985, 87, 221).
57. Cowan and Kinder (1985, 158); Grice (1985, 195).
58. Cowan and Kinder (1987, 243).
59. Weston (1985, 67).
60. Cowan and Kinder (1985, 158).
61. Authors may have been willing to portray some men as emotional and nonaggressive given critiques of masculinity emerging from various wings of the "men's movement" during the late 1970s and early 1980s (see Connell 1995, 78 and Messner 1997, 41–44).
62. Fein and Schneider (1995, 9). Although the authors never explicitly say so, their reliance on biological arguments also suggests that they regard homosexual relationships as "unnatural."
63. Fein and Schneider (1995, 27).
64. Fein and Schneider (1995, 24).
65. Fein and Schneider (1995, 7, 45).
66. Biology also began to play a prominent role in some (18 percent) child-rearing experts' discussions of children's shyness in the 1980s and 1990s. As one group of authors explained, "Shyness, like a knack for figures or a flair for writing, is an inherited trait" (Eisenberg, Murkoff, and Hathaway 1989, 368; see also Galinsky and David (1988, 129); Garber, Garber, and Spizman (1993, 55); Joseph (1994, 48); Rimm (1992, 59). In contrast to the view of nature offered by the authors of *The Rules*, however, authors of child-rearing manuals argued that both boys and girls could inherit this trait. Shy boys (and, for that matter, girls) might still be able to acquire the necessary "ambition and animal drive" despite their genetic handicap, however. Most authors who claimed that shyness was largely inherited still maintained that shy children could learn to be less inhibited, more confident, and even gregarious with proper parental guidance and support (Eisenberg, Murkoff, and Hathaway 1989, 368; 1994, 405; Galinsky and David 1988, 129; Joseph 1994, 19–20; Rimm 1992, 59). Fein and Schneider would no doubt caution parents not to take this support too far in the case of shy girls, as certain shy characteristics, such as silence, would serve them well as adults engaged in the search for "Mr. Right."
67. Cowan and Kinder (1987, 9); DeAngelis (1990, 7); Gray (1992, 1994); Tracy (1993, 295).
68. Kramer and Dunaway (1990, 125); Gray (1992, 1994).
69. Gray (1994, 204).
70. Gray (1994, 202).
71. Tracy (1993, 295).
72. Gray (1994, 157).

NOTES TO CHAPTER 4

1. "Sambo," the name given to the second son in certain African societies, was a popular name among male slaves (Williamson 1986, 15).

2. As I explain in appendix A, I focus solely on African Americans here due to a lack of available data for other groups, such as Hispanics or Asian Americans.

3. Brown's statement "Acquire manners . . ." is taken from the *Pittsburgh Courier*, April 20, 1940, cited in Smith and West (1982, 205).

4. Brown ([1941] 1995, 108).

5. Brown ([1941] 1995, 88, 93).

6. Brown ([1941] 1995, 93).

7. Brown ([1941] 1995, 132).

8. Brown ([1941] 1995, 94).

9. In 1950, the rate of black male unemployment was 6.4 percent, versus 3.4 percent for white men; in 1960, the black male unemployment rate was 7.8 percent, versus 3.7 percent for white men (Smith and Horton 1995, 1100). In 1959, black men with the same characteristics as white men (i.e., occupational prestige, age, education, weeks worked, hours worked last week, and state of residence) earned 71 percent of what white men earned (Smith and Horton 1995, 1000–1001).

10. In 1950, 36.7 percent of non-white women worked, compared to 28.1 percent of white women; in 1960, the figures were 41.8 percent and 33.6 percent for non-white and white women respectively (U.S. Bureau of the Census 1963). In addition, between 1940 and 1960, black mothers of school-aged children were more likely than white mothers to work outside the home (Jones 1985, 269).

11. In 1950, 17.6 percent of all black and "other" (i.e., non-white) families were headed by women, including women who were widowed, divorced, separated, and women whose husbands were in the Armed Forces or in jail; 8.5 percent of all white families were headed by women. In 1960, the comparable figures were 21.7 percent for black families and 8.1 percent for white families (Smith and Horton 1995, 780).

12. "We are tired of our men being emasculated" is taken from a speech by Martin Luther King, Jr., at the Mason Temple in Memphis, March 18, 1968, cited in Estes (2000, 160).

13. A Labor Department document that came to be known as *The Moynihan Report*.

14. Moynihan (p. 78) cites figures from a 1964 report by the President's Committee of Equal Employment Opportunity which showed that black women represented 3.1 percent of the total female white-collar workforce and 6 percent of all female professionals, while black men made up 1.2 percent of the total male white-collar workforce and 1.1 percent of all male professionals.

15. Moynihan (p. 77) cites unpublished Bureau of Labor Statistics data which show that as of March 1964, "non-white" women's median years of school completed were 10.0, while non-white men's were 9.2.

16. The study was by Robert O. Blood, Jr., and Donald M. Wolfe, *Husbands and Wives: The Dynamics of Married Living* (Illinois: Free Press of Glencoe, 1960).

17. Williams (1974, 193).

18. Williams (1974, 193).

19. Williams (1974, 193).

20. Williams (1974, 191–93).

21. Williams (1974, 192).
22. Williams (1974, 68).
23. Williams (1974, 68).
24. Williams (1974, 68; emphasis in original).
25. Crounse (1952, 4).
26. Williams (1974, 13–14, 39–42).
27. Williams (1974, 94).
28. Williams (1974, 171, 179, 181).
29. Williams (1974, 94).
30. Williams (1974, 97).
31. Williams (1974, 192).
32. Williams (1974, 191, 192).
33. Williams (1974, 192).
34. Parrish (1974, 65); Walker (1973, 39).
35. Walker (1973, 74).
36. Parrish (1974, 65).
37. Reid and Reid (1973, 74).
38. Walker (1973, 74).
39. Walker (1973, 74); Parrish (1974, 64).
40. Tucker (1977, 44); Tucker and Tucker (1979, 12); Tucker and Tucker (1980a, 80).
41. Tucker and Tucker (1980a, 81).
42. E.g., Hopson and Hopson (1994).
43. E.g., Milligan (1994); Sims (1989).
44. E.g., Ali (1989); Barak (1992). A group of African American writers alarmed by the misogynistic tone of Ali's book responded with *Confusion by Any Other Name: Exploring the Negative Impact of The Blackman's Guide to Understanding the Blackwoman* (see Madhubuti 1991).
45. Ali (1989); Barak (1992).
46. Ali (1989, 67); see also Barak (1992, 29).
47. Fraser and Polite (1988a, 66); Mason (1993, 81).
48. Davis (1986, 54).
49. Fraser and Polite (1988b, 52).
50. Botwin (1985, 66); Grant (1985, 58).
51. Nelson (1986, 58).
52. Baye (1985, 66); Adams and Simmons (1987, 83); Sims (1989, 50).
53. Weathers (1990, 107).
54. Botwin (1985, 66); Harayda (1987, 61); Sims (1989, 18, 64).
55. George (1995, 215); Singletary (1985a, 70).
56. Davis (1986, 54); Johnson (1994, 71); Nelson (1992, 86); Singletary (1985a, 68).
57. Nelson (1992, 85); Singletary (1985a, 69).
58. As of 1985, black women's divorce rate was 326 per 1,000 married persons, compared to 179 for black men, 142 for white women, and 98 for white men (Chadwick and Heaton 1992, 87). In 1989, 51.1 percent of black households with minor children had a mother only (Horton and Smith 1993, 359).

59. As of June 29, 1990, 43 percent of jail inmates were black males (Horton and Smith 1993, 147).

60. As of 1988, black men's death rate was 10.4 per 1,000, compared to 6.6 for white men, 5.9 for black women, and 3.8 for white women (Horton and Smith 1993, 874).

NOTES TO CHAPTER 5

1. The percentage of black women employed in white-collar jobs grew from 17 percent to 32 percent between 1960 and 1970, while the percentage of black men employed in such jobs grew from 11 percent to 17 percent (Horton and Smith 1993, 1088–99).

2. "The man with the smile . . ." (Simmons 1953, 93).

3. Albert (1957, 171); Cerami (1958, 124); Giblin (1956, 41); MacGibbon (1954, 51); Peale (1955, 243); Prochnow (1952, 19); Simmons (1953, 69); Schwartz (1959, 42).

4. Albert (1957, 40); Laird and Laird (1951, 230); MacGibbon (1954, 41, 150); Prochnow (1952, 17); Sinick (1960, 18). Self-help authors' representation of a gendered job hierarchy matched reality: in 1959, white women were more likely to be employed in sales, clerical, or kindred occupations than managerial or administrative ones, while white men were equally likely to be employed in either (Horton and Smith 1993, 1088–89).

5. If one was a man doing clerical work, a promotion was much more likely, however (see, for example, Cerami 1958, 10–11).

6. Davies and Livingston (1958, 74); Giblin (1956, 5, 41); Prevette (1953, 92); Simmons (1953, 67, 69).

7. Davies and Livingston (1958, 75); Huston and Sandberg (1955, 15); Simmons (1953, 67, 93); ZuTavern and Erickson (1950, 205); Knox, Horner, and Ray (1953, 3, 119).

8. Giblin (1956, 5); Huston and Sandberg (1955, 15); Knox, Horner, and Ray (1953, 3). Self-help authors appear to have been relatively successful in convincing Americans of the general if not relative importance of personality: in 1952, 59 percent of male Dartmouth undergraduates and 65 percent of male University of Michigan undergraduates ranked "having a pleasant personality" as nearly as important as hard work in achieving success (Hoge 1976, 159).

9. Davies and Livingston (1958, 74); Giblin (1956, 40); Huston and Sandberg (1955, 15); Prevette (1953, 113); Simmons (1953, 67, 89).

10. Huston and Sandberg (1955, 15); Simmons (1953, 91); ZuTavern and Erickson (1950, 256).

11. Newton and Nichols (1954, 22).

12. Beecher and Beecher (1955, 156); Gilmer (1951, 155); Goodman ([1959] 1969, 179); Katz (1953, 177); Schwarz and Ruggieri (1958, 82).

13. Knox, Horner, and Ray (1953, 113).

14. This advice was also in keeping with the "human relations approach" to management in the 1920s and 1930s (associated with Elton Mayo), which gave more attention to the feelings of workers and managers (Bendix 1974, 321).

15. Dale Carnegie's (1936) *How to Win Friends and Influence People* is the most well known example of the personality ethic of success (Carnegie 1982).

16. Davies and Livingston (1958, 20); Giblin (1956, 70); Knox, Horner, and Ray (1953, 119); Simmons (1953, 89).

17. Giblin (1956, 70).

18. Giblin (1956, 6); Knox, Horner, and Ray (1953, 4); Prevette (1953, 4); Newton and Nichols (1954, 10); ZuTavern and Erickson (1950, 202).

19. Caspar Milquetoast was a character in a comic strip created by H. T. Webster in 1935 called "The Timid Soul."

20. Simmons (1953, 89, 305).

21. Simmons (1953, 305); see also Giblin (1956, 72); Prevette (1953, 29).

22. Giblin (1956, 73).

23. Prevette (1953, 31).

24. Prevette (1953, 113–14); Giblin (1956, 74); Simmons (1953, 67).

25. Simmons (1953, 98).

26. Giblin (1956, 78); Simmons (1953, 90).

27. Giblin (1956, 97); see also Prevette (1953, 37–38).

28. See also Simmons (1953, 91).

29. MacGibbon (1954, 52); Simmons (1953, 67, 90).

30. "One may smile . . . ," *Hamlet*, Act I, Scene 5, 105.

31. Relevant legislation included (1) the Equal Pay Act of 1963, which specified that employers must pay men and women equal wages for jobs that require equal skill, effort, and responsibility, and that are performed under similar working conditions; (2) Title VII of the 1964 Civil Rights Act, which prohibited discrimination in all terms and conditions of employment based on race, sex, color, religion, and national origin. As amended by the Equal Employment Opportunity Act of 1972, Title VII forbade an employer to discriminate between men and women regarding hiring, discharge, and compensation, as well as any terms, conditions, and privileges of employment; (3) Executive Order 11246 (1965) (signed by President Johnson) prohibited race-based discrimination in employment; it was amended by Executive Order 11375 (1968) to include a ban on discrimination by sex. It applied to all federal contractors and subcontractors with contracts of $10,000 or more. Government contractors with fifty or more employees and contracts totaling $50,000 or more were also required to develop affirmative action plans to correct any inequities in employment, promotion, and training which existed. The penalty for noncompliance was the withholding or cancelation of government contracts (all of the preceding taken from Jongeward and Scott 1977, 45–65). In addition, the Equal Employment Opportunity Commission prohibited the practice of specifying the preferred sex of job applicants in classified ads (Lynch 1973, 161).

32. There were six success manuals devoted exclusively to women in the 1970s sample, compared to one in the 1950s sample.

33. Bolton (1979, 7); Brothers (1978, 132); Dubrin (1977, 159, 171); Eisenberg (1979, 5); Girard (1979, 105); Higginson and Quick (1980, 180, 202); Nightingale (1970, 93, 190); Powell (1979, 152); Stewart and Faux (1979, 79).

34. Bolton (1979, 118); Girard (1979, 96, 169); Korda (1977, 124); Linkletter (1979, 104); Seaman and Lorimer (1979, 139, 141); Taetzsch and Benson (1978, 17, 44, 50).

35. Gardner (1974, 6–7); Graubard (1977, 144); Patterson and Gullion (1971, 93); Willis, Crowder, and Willis (1976, 47).

36. Seaman and Lorimer (1979, 140–41).

37. Bolton (1979, 7, 65); DeVille (1979, 77); Nightingale (1970, 190); Powell (1979, 152); Seaman and Lorimer (1979, 141).

38. Fisher and Fisher (1976, 30–31); Gardner (1974, 300–302); Spock (1974, 43, 49); Willis, Crowder, and Willis (1976, 128).

39. Eisenberg (1979, 5); Korda (1977, 190); Parker (1973, 176); Seaman and Lorimer (1979, 140).

40. Powell (1979, 161); Wassmer ([1978] 1990, 150).

41. Dubrin (1977, 178); Eisenberg (1979, 130); Linkletter (1979, 104–5); Powell (1979, 7, 65, 118, 150, 160–63); Taetzsch and Benson (1978, 50); Wassmer ([1978] 1990, 7, 9, 35, 38, 50, 167); Zimbardo ([1977] 1995, 3, 29, 95, 187).

42. Powell (1979, 150, 152, 161); Wassmer ([1978] 1990, 167).

43. Bloom, Coburn, and Pearlman (1975, 11); Butler (1976, 4–5); Hyatt (1979, 11, 15); Seaman and Lorimer (1979, 159).

44. Adams (1979, 24); Bloom, Coburn, and Pearlman (1975, 138).

45. Adams (1979, 24); Bloom, Coburn, and Pearlman (1975, 153); Butler (1976, 298); Korda (1977, 187).

46. Seaman and Lorimer (1979, 134–36); see also Bloom, Coburn, and Pearlman (1975, 17); Butler (1976, 298); Korda (1977, 194–95).

47. "There's daggers . . . ," *Macbeth*, Act II, Scene 3, 146.

48. Dubrin (1977, 172); Taetzsch and Benson (1978, 17).

49. Eisenberg (1979, 5); Korda (1977, 190); Parker (1973, 176); Wassmer ([1978] 1990, 150).

50. Between 1970 and 1980, women's presence increased by ten or more points in 25.5 percent of 361 predominantly male occupations (60–100 percent male); between 1980 to 1990, women's presence increased by ten or more points in only 10.6 percent of 330 predominantly male occupations (Roos and McDaniel 1996).

51. The Reagan administration dramatically slashed the EEOC budget at a time when reports of sex discrimination and harassment were reaching record highs (Faludi 1991, 368–69).

52. Scalia (1985, 13); White (1995, 12).

53. Butler (1991, 12); Scalia (1985, 18–19); White (1995, 114).

54. Eagly, Makhijani, and Klonsky's (1992) meta-analysis of experimental research on the evaluation of women and men who occupy leadership roles found only a slight tendency for subjects to evaluate women leaders less favorably than men leaders. However, women leaders who behaved in a stereotypically "masculine" manner, including being assertive, were more likely to receive unfavorable evaluations.

55. "Damn the men . . . ," Sinclair Lewis, *Arrowsmith*, 1925.

56. Baber and Waymon (1992, 12); Cheek (1989, 168); Farber (1987, 11); Kassorla (1984, 177); King (1987, 19); Mandell (1992, 47); Phillips (1986, 6); Robinson (1994, 120).

57. Booher (1994, 11, 14, 70); Crawford (1992, 143); Dishy (1990, 153); Kassorla (1984, 183); King (1987, 39); Murphy (1994, 3, 6); Stewart (1986, 19, 21, 22).

58. Covey (1989, 240); see also Cheek (1989, 97); Clinard (1985, 32); King (1987, 42); Murphy (1994, 3); Nichols (1995, 15); Richardson (1987, 84); Stewart (1986, 33); Tracy (1993, 278).

59. Cheek (1989, 97); Clinard (1985, 32); King (1987, 44); Richardson (1987, 84); Tracy (1993, 278).

60. Cheek (1989, 67–68); Phillips (1986, 66); Stewart (1986, 32); Wassmer ([1978] 1990, 6–7); Zimbardo ([1977] 1995, 188).

61. Cheek (1989, 97); Covey (1989, 242); Stewart (1986, 31); Tracy (1993, 278).

62. Wheeler (1990, 124); see also Cheek (1989, 67–68); Phillips (1986, 66); Stewart (1986, 32); Wassmer ([1978] 1990, 6–7); Zimbardo ([1977] 1995, 188).

63. Eisenberg, Murkoff, and Hathaway (1989, 368); Galinsky and David (1988, 129); Garber, Garber, and Spizman (1993, 56); Joseph (1994, 48); Rimm (1992, 59).

64. Tracy (1993, 278).

NOTES TO CHAPTER 6

1. "Intimacy is a difficult art" from Virginia Woolf, "Geraldine and Jane," *The Common Reader*, 1932.

2. Gilmer (1951, 165).

3. See also Albert (1957, 171); Allen and Brigs (1950, 156); Beery (1954, 9); Knox, Horner, and Ray (1953, 120); Peale (1955, 243).

4. Albert (1957, 167); Allen and Brigs (1950, 159); Beery (1957, 72, 100); Knox, Horner, and Ray (1953, 122–23, 126–34); Peale (1955, 244); Reid (1950, 213, 216).

5. Albert (1957, 163); Allen and Brigs (1950, 156); Beery (1957, 71); Knox, Horner, and Ray (1953, 114); Peale (1955, 244).

6. Albert (1957, 168).

7. Beery (1954, 12); Reid (1950, 215).

8. Beery (1954, 13).

9. Albert (1957, 167); Knox, Horner, and Ray (1953, 130).

10. Peale (1955, 236).

11. Prochnow (1952, 3); Huston and Sandberg (1955, 44).

12. Knox, Horner, and Ray (1953, 384).

13. Allen and Brigs (1950, 156); Beery (1957, 71); Knox, Horner, and Ray (1953, 126); Newton and Nichols (1954, 64, 152).

14. Beery (1954, 134); Knox, Horner, and Ray (1953, 131).

15. Allen and Brigs (1950, 158); Beery (1954, 12; 1957, 70).

16. Reid (1950, 288); see also Newton and Nichols (1954, 62).

17. In 1957, 35 percent of respondents sought help of some kind from another person when they were worried, compared to 48 percent in 1976. During periods of unhappiness, 37 percent of 1957 respondents turned to others, versus 50 percent in 1976. Of those who sought help about their worries in 1957, only 12 percent turned to friends or neighbors, while 24 percent did so in 1976 (Veroff, Douvan, and Kulka 1981a, 482, 484).

18. "I get by . . . ," John Lennon and Paul McCartney, "With a Little Help from My Friends," EMI/Capital, 1967.

19. Golde (1979, 172–73); Keyes (1975, 32); Lazarus and Fay (1975, 39–40); Wassmer ([1978] 1990, 115); Zimbardo ([1977] 1995, 113–14).

20. Golde (1979, 174); Zimbardo ([1977] 1995, 113).

21. Keyes (1975, 33); Linkletter (1979, 95).

22. Keyes (1975, 33).

23. Golde (1979, 156); Lazarus and Fay (1975, 38); Walters (1970, 131); Williams and Long (1979, 78).

24. Wassmer ([1978] 1990, 115); Zimbardo ([1977] 1995, 113–14).

25. Fisher and Fisher (1976, 31); Gardner (1974, 302); Willis, Crowder, and Willis (1976, 126).

26. Keyes (1975, 32); Lazarus and Fay (1975, 38–39); Wassmer ([1978] 1990, 114).

27. Golde (1979, 150); Keyes (1975, 32); Lazarus and Fay (1975, 39); Wassmer ([1978] 1990, 119).

28. Green (1978, 25).

29. Zimbardo ([1977] 1995, 242).

30. Gardner (1974, 300, 302); Graubard (1977, 144–45); Spock (1974, 43, 49); Willis, Crowder, and Willis (1976, 126).

31. "The only way to have a friend is to be one," from Ralph Waldo Emerson's *Essays, First Series,* 1841. Booher (1994, 14); Browne (1988, 79); Cheek (1989, 132–33); Kassorla (1984, 194); Mandell (1992, 135); Myers (1992, 127); Nichols (1995, 11); Segal (1986, 26); Stewart (1986, 193); Wassmer ([1978] 1990, 115); Zimbardo ([1977] 1995, 113–14).

32. Goodman and Esterly (1989, 193); Stewart (1986, 193); Wassmer ([1978] 1990, 114).

33. Baldridge (1990, 62); Phillips (1986, 102); Tracy (1993, 280); Weston (1985, 48); Williams (1986, 110).

34. Tracy (1993, 280); see also Baldridge (1990, 62).

35. Booher (1994, 13); see also Baber and Waymon (1992, 21); Baldridge (1990, 62); Mazel (1985, 142); Myers (1992, 128); Tracy (1993, 261, 275, 284); Wassmer ([1978] 1990, 172–73); Weston (1985, 46).

36. Baldridge (1987, 13); Tracy (1993, 275); Weston (1985, 47).

37. Baldridge (1987, 287); Browne (1988, 80); Phillips (1986, 203); Weston (1985, 47).

38. See also Mandell (1992, 13); Phillips (1986, 205); Roane (1988, 45); Weston (1985, 145).

39. Mandell (1992, 47).

40. I use the term "vocal" because of the extreme popularity and ubiquity of author John Gray, whose book *Men Are from Mars, Women Are from Venus* had not only sold 6.5 million copies as of August 1998, but had also spawned audio and videotapes, a CD of love songs, a board game, and a "Mars-Venus Institute" to train professionals to lead relationship-saving workshops (Stevens 1998, 3).

41. Cowan and Kinder (1987, 182, 228, 233); De Angelis (1990, 267).

42. Beck (1988, 82); Cowan and Kinder (1987, 233); Kramer and Dunaway (1990, 218); Tannen (1986, 142–43).

43. Beck (1988, 82); Booher (1994, 336); Cowan and Kinder (1987, 233); Kramer and Dunaway (1990, 128–39); Tannen (1986, 142–43).

44. Cowan and Kinder (1987, 235).

45. Beck (1988, 82); De Angelis (1990, 267); Gray (1992, 69); Tannen (1986, 143).

NOTES TO CHAPTER 7

1. The Isaac Bashevis Singer quotation is taken from Charlotte K. Beyers, "Don't Worry If You're Shy," *Parade*, January 18, 1976, 12.

NOTES TO APPENDIX A

1. Parts of this appendix may strike the reader as overly detailed; however, I chose to err on the side of inclusiveness to spare other researchers some of the troubles I faced when trying to determine how, exactly, to locate and choose a representative sample of texts on a somewhat elusive topic.

2. I include etiquette books under the more general rubric of "self-help."

3. Didactic literature of this sort has been popular in the West since the Renaissance, when "courtesy" books (such as Castiglione's *The Courtier* and Della Casa's *Il Galateo* [1558]) acted as an important medium for the discussion of proper social behavior (including manners, morals, character, and accomplishments) among the upper classes (Curtin 1985, 395). Eventually, they were adopted by the aspiring middle classes as well, and their focus shifted to a greater emphasis on practicality, efficiency, and success (Carré 1994, 6). See Mason (1935) for a discussion of Renaissance English courtesy literature, and Newton (1994) on the tradition of advice literature in the United States before 1900.

4. In contrast to Kasson (1990) and Hemphill (1998, 34), Hart (1963, 19–20) argues that even less financially secure colonists purchased or borrowed self-help books.

5. Starker's (1989) random mail survey of Portland residents listed in the phone book is frequently cited as evidence that women are more frequent readers of self-help books, but the fact that the response rate was only 19 percent suggests that there is no solid evidence for this assertion.

6. In this sense, readers acted as the "active readers" postulated by reader response theory, which argues that the meaning of a text is not intrinsic to the text

itself, but is dependent upon the activities and experiences of the reader; see Fish (1980); Suleiman and Crosman (1980); and Tompkins (1980).

7. In addition to searching for published sources, I contacted a representative of the American Booksellers Association, who informed me that they, too, lacked sales information on individual titles.

8. For the 1944–1975 period, the authors based their lists on the yearly best-seller lists printed in *Publisher's Weekly* (in January or February) (see Löfroth 1983, 21, n. 34). These lists reflect publishers' sales to bookstores and libraries *before* returns; that is, they do not reflect sales to actual bookstore customers. The lists are limited to new trade books and exclude paperbacks, reprints, text-books, and books sold by mail, such as book-club selections (Hackett and Burke 1977, 3).

9. If one includes, as Hackett and Burke do, diet books, cookbooks, sex man-uals, and books on home repair or design under the rubric of "how-to" or "self-help," then the number of these books that appear on the yearly best-seller lists increases to five or six.

10. The list of best-selling hardcover advice books was limited to four or five, since, "beyond that point, sales in this category are not generally large enough to make a longer list statistically reliable" (*New York Times Book Review*, February 3, 1985, p. 32). The number of titles on the best-selling paperback list was larger, ranging from four to thirteen.

11. I found a total of eighty-three books on shyness in the Library of Con-gress's catalog. Many of these were books written for children or parents of shy children; others, written for adults, were published outside of the three time pe-riods in which I was interested. Within the three time periods, I found no advice books on adult shyness published in the 1950s, eight in the 1970s, and eight in the mid-1980s to mid-1990s.

12. Many of these inappropriate texts were easily identifiable by title or by my knowledge of English and American literature (i.e., I was aware that Edith Wharton's *Age of Innocence* was a work of fiction). For titles that were less obvi-ous, but about which I had my suspicions (i.e., a book published by a press that primarily published religious texts), I returned to the Library of Congress's on-line catalog to identify the book's complete list of subject classifications.

13. There is some debate about the precise definition of "edition." Unwin (1947, 120–21) argues that the term "impression" should be used for reprints "in which there are no alterations of any kind," and the term "edition" for "reprints containing revisions or additions or a change of format." In practice, publishers appear to use the term "edition" even for reprints issued without many changes, particularly if the second edition closely follows the first. I identified a second or third edition of a book that was not marked as such in the catalog by looking for the terms "new edition" or "revised and enlarged" or by looking at the date the book was published (in the United States only); if one book had multiple publica-tion dates (excluding the publication of a special "large type" book), I considered it to have multiple editions.

14. The publishers I contacted were HarperCollins, Simon and Schuster, Little, Brown, and Co., and Warner Books; I also spoke to a buyer for Borders Books in Ann Arbor, Michigan.

15. Most of the multiple editions were released within the eleven-year time span of each of the three time periods, but 16 percent (97) of the titles had editions that straddled two (or occasionally three) time periods (i.e., one edition appeared in 1979 and the second in 1995). These "straddlers" appear on the sampling frame only once, in the time period in which the first edition was released. Books with an edition released *prior to* the time period under consideration (i.e., a first edition published in 1943 and a second in 1951) were included in the sampling frame under the time period in which the subsequent edition was released (in this case, the 1950s).

16. *Booklist* began publication in 1905 (originally called *The American Library Association Booklist*), *Kirkus Reviews* in 1933 (originally called *Virginia Kirkus' Bookshop* Service), *Library Journal* in 1876 (originally called *The American Library Journal*), and *Publishers' Weekly* in 1873.

17. *Booklist* reviews rarely had symbols assigned to them by the *Digest*, so I read these reviews, including in the sampling frame books that were regarded positively (i.e., the reviews included statements like "will be popular," or "very informative," or some other accolade).

18. Seventeen of the twenty-six multiple-edition books that were reviewed received positive reviews.

19. From the *Library Journal*'s October 15, 1977 (p. 2155) review of Michael Korda's *Success!* (1977).

20. Fifty-four of the seventy-three multiple-edition books that were reviewed received positive reviews.

21. Forty-five of the fifty-two multiple edition books that were reviewed received positive reviews.

22. In 1985, the *New York Times Book Review* reported that paperback listings "are based on computer-processed sales figures from 2,000 bookstores and from representative wholesalers with more than 40,000 retail outlets, including newsstands, variety stores, supermarkets, and bookstores. These figures are statistically adjusted to represent sales in all such outlets across the U.S." Over the eleven-year period, the *Book Review* reported that the number of bookstores and wholesalers from which these paperback listings were drawn grew in size, to 3,985 bookstores and 60,000 wholesalers by 1995. For hardcovers, the list was drawn solely from (the same) bookstores (*New York Times Book Review*, February 3, 1985, 32, 34).

23. I identified the population of best-sellers first, so any best-sellers that reappeared on the lists of books with multiple editions or favorable reviews were already marked as part of the population.

24. The neglect of Latinas by the self-help industry may be changing: there was one self-help book explicitly addressed to Latinas published each year from 1996 to 1998.

25. I did find two Spanish-language magazines, *Buen Hogar* ("Good Home") and *Temas* ("Topics").

26. Of the shyness self-help books that met one of the three popularity criteria, three were published in the 1970–1980 period, and two in the 1985–1995 period. All are included in the final sample.

27. I also determined that these books were written for a middle-class audience, or an audience striving to reach the middle class. The class bias of self-help books in general is evident in their distinctly middle-class theme, the notion of self-improvement through individual striving (DeMott 1990, 43). Authors of these particular texts also signaled their class leanings in their choice of illustrative examples: characters in vignettes were consistently doctors, lawyers, teachers, academics, or college students.

28. For the 1950–1960 period, of the nineteen child-rearing manuals I found with references to shyness, five had more than one edition; for the 1970–1980 period, one of twenty child-rearing manuals with references to shyness was published in multiple editions; for the 1985–1995 period, four of the forty-one manuals had multiple editions.

29. For books with two or more authors, I examined the degree associated with the first author only.

30. I scanned each page of text into the computer before importing it into Q.S.R. NUD.IST.

Bibliography

Some of the works referred to in the text are listed in Appendix B.

Acocella, Joan. 2000. "The Empty Couch." *New Yorker*, May 8, 112–18.

Altheide, David L. 1996. *Qualitative Media Analysis*. Thousand Oaks, CA: Sage.

———. 1987. "Ethnographic Content Analysis." *Qualitative Sociology* 10(1): 65–77.

American Bar Association Commission on Women in the Profession. 1995. *Basic Facts from Women in the Law: A Look at the Numbers*. Chicago: American Bar Association. December.

American Psychiatric Association. 1952. *Diagnostic and Statistical Manual of Mental Disorders*. 1st ed. Washington, DC: APA.

———. 1980. *Diagnostic and Statistical Manual of Mental Disorders*. 3d ed. Washington DC: APA.

———. 1987. *Diagnostic and Statistical Manual of Mental Disorders*. 3d ed., rev. Washington, DC: APA.

———. 1994. *Diagnostic and Statistical Manual of Mental Disorders*. 4th ed. Washington, DC: APA.

Amussen, Susan Dwyer. 1988. *An Ordered Society: Gender and Class in Early Modern England*. Oxford, UK: Basil Blackwell.

Anglo, Sydney. 1977. "The Courtier: The Renaissance and Changing Ideals." Pp. 33–54 in *The Courts of Europe: Politics, Patronage, and Royalty, 1400–1800*, edited by A. G. Dickens. London: Thames and Hudson.

Arkin, Robert M., Elizabeth A. Lake, and Ann H. Baumgardner. 1986. "Shyness and Self-Presentation." Pp. 189–203 in *Shyness: Perspectives on Research and Treatment*, edited by Warren H. Jones, Jonathan M. Cheek, and Stephen R. Briggs. New York: Plenum Press.

Arkowitz, Hal. 1977. "Measurement and Modification of Minimal Dating Behavior." Pp. 1–61 in *Progress in Behavior Modification*, vol. 5, edited by Michael Hersen, Richard M. Eisler, and Peter M. Miller. New York: Academic Press.

189

Asendorpf, Jens. 1986. "Shyness in Middle and Late Childhood." Pp. 91–103 in *Shyness: Perspectives on Research and Treatment*, edited by Warren H. Jones, Jonathan M. Cheek, and Stephen R. Briggs. New York: Plenum Press.

———. 1989. "Shyness as a Final Common Pathway for Two Different Kinds of Inhibition." *Journal of Personality and Social Psychology* 57(3): 481–92.

Averill, James R. 1984. "The Acquisition of Emotions during Adulthood." Pp. 23–43 in *Emotion in Adult Development*, edited by Carol Zander Malatesta and Carroll E. Izard. Beverly Hills, CA: Sage.

Bailey, Beth A. 1988. *From Front Porch to Back Seat: Courtship in Twentieth Century America*. Baltimore and London: Johns Hopkins University Press.

Balswick, Jack O., and James Lincoln Collier. 1976. "Why Husbands Can't Say 'I Love You.'" Pp. 58–59 in *The Forty-Nine Percent Majority*, edited by Deborah S. David and Robert Brannon. Reading, MA: Addison-Wesley.

Banerjee, Neela. 2001. "Toughness Has Risks for Women Executives." *New York Times*, August 10.

Barber, Richard. 1970. *The Knight and Chivalry*. Ipswich, UK: Boydell Press.

Barnett, Bernice McNair. 1993. "Invisible Southern Black Women Leaders in the Civil Rights Movement: The Triple Constraints of Gender, Race, and Class." *Gender and Society* 7(2): 162–82.

Barstow, Anne Llewellyn. 1994. *Witchcraze: A New History of the European Witch Hunts*. San Francisco: HarperCollins.

Bartky, Sandra Lee. 1990. *Femininity and Domination: Studies in the Phenomenology of Oppression*. New York: Routledge.

Beatty, Michael J., and P. J. Beatty. 1976. "Interpersonal Communication Anxiety." *Theory into Practice* 15(5): 368–72.

Beck, Aaron T., et al. 1988. "An Inventory for Measuring Clinical Anxiety: Psychometric Properties." *Journal of Counseling and Clinical Psychology* 56: 893–97.

Bederman, Gail. 1995. "'Civilization,' the Decline of Middle-Class Manliness, and Ida B. Wells's Antilynching Campaign (1892–1894)." Pp. 407–32 in *We Specialize in the Wholly Impossible: A Reader in Black Women's History*, edited by Darlene Clark Hine, Wilma King and Linda Reed. Brooklyn, NY: Carlson.

Bell, Iris R., et al. 1995. "Trait Shyness in the Elderly: Evidence for an Association with Parkinson's Disease in Family Members and Biochemical Correlates." *Journal of Geriatric Psychiatry and Neurology* 8(1): 16–22.

Bell, Robert R., and Kathleen Coughey. 1980. "Premarital Sexual Experience among College Females, 1958, 1968, and 1978." *Family Relations* 29: 353–57.

Beller, Andrea H. 1984. "Trends in Occupational Segregation by Sex and Race, 1960–1981." Pp. 11–26 in *Sex Segregation in the Workplace: Trends, Explanations, Remedies*, edited by Barbara F. Reskin. Washington, DC: National Academy Press.

Bendix, Richard. 1974. *Work and Authority in Industry: Ideologies of Management in the Course of Industrialization*. Berkeley, Los Angeles, and London: University of California Press.

Biggart, Nicole Woolsey. 1983. "Rationality, Meaning, and Self-Management: Success Manuals, 1950–1980." *Social Problems* 30(3): 298–311.

Blount, Jackie M. 1996. "Manly Men and Womanly Women: Deviance, Gender

Role Polarization, and the Shift in Women's School Employment, 1900–1976." *Harvard Educational Review* 66(2): 318–38.

Blumstein, Philip, and Pepper Schwartz. 1983. *American Couples: Money, Work, and Sex.* New York: William Morrow.

Bondi, Victor, ed. 1995. *American Decades, 1970–1979.* Detroit, Washington, DC, and London: Gale Research.

———. 1996. *American Decades, 1980–89.* Detroit, Washington, DC, and London: Gale Research.

Boose, Lynda E. 1991. "Scolding Brides and Bridling Scolds: Taming the Woman's Unruly Member." *Shakespeare Quarterly* 42(2): 179–213.

Bornstein, Diane. 1983. *The Lady in the Tower: Medieval Courtesy Literature for Women.* Hamden, CT: Archon Books.

Breines, Wini. 1992. *Young, White, and Miserable: Growing Up Female in the Fifties.* Boston: Beacon Press.

Brooke-Rose, Christine. 1986. "Woman as a Semiotic Object." Pp. 305–16 in *The Female Body in Western Culture: Contemporary Perspectives,* edited by Suan Rubin Suleiman. Cambridge, MA, and London: Harvard University Press.

Brooks, N. R., and M. Groves. 1996. "Woman to Run House That Barbie Built." *Los Angeles Times,* August 23, A1.

Brown, Charlotte Hawkins. 1940. "The Negro and the Social Graces." Radio address, March 10. Moorland-Springarn Research Center, Howard University.

Buss, Arnold H. 1980. *Self-Consciousness and Social Anxiety.* San Francisco: Freeman Press.

———. 1984. "A Conception of Shyness." Pp. 39–49 in *Avoiding Communication: Shyness, Reticence, and Communication Apprehension,* edited by John A. Daly and James C. McCroskey. Beverly Hills, CA: Sage.

———. 1986. "A Theory of Shyness." Pp. 39–46 in *Shyness: Perspectives on Research and Treatment,* edited by Warren H. Jones, Jonathan M. Cheek, and Stephen R. Briggs. New York: Plenum Press.

Camarena, Phame M., Pamela A. Sarigiani, and Anne C. Peterson. 1990. "Gender-Specific Pathways to Intimacy in Early Adolescence." *Journal of Youth and Adolescence* 19(1): 19–32.

Cancian, Francesca M. 1987. *Love in America: Gender and Self-Development.* Cambridge, UK: Cambridge University Press.

Cancian, Francesca M., and Steven L. Gordon. 1988. "Changing Emotion Norms in Marriage: Love and Anger in U.S. Women's Magazines Since 1900." *Gender and Society* 2(3): 308–42.

Carby, Hazel. 1987. *Reconstructing Womanhood: The Emergence of the African-American Woman Novelist.* New York and Oxford: Oxford University Press.

Carlson, Shirley J. 1992. "Black Ideals of Womanhood in the Late Victorian Era." *Journal of Negro History* 77(2): 61–73.

Carnegie, Dale. 1982. *How to Win Friends and Influence People.* Rev. ed. New York: Pocket Books. First ed. originally published in 1936.

Carré, Jacques. 1994. "Introduction." Pp. 1–8 in *The Crisis in Courtesy: Studies in the Conduct Book in Britain, 1600–1700,* edited by Jacques Carré. Leiden, Netherlands: E. J. Brill.

Carson, Gerald. 1966. *The Polite Americans: A Wide-Angle View of Our More or Less Good Manners over 300 Years*. New York: William Morrow.

Casagrande, Carla. 1992. "The Protected Woman." Pp. 70–104 in *A History of Women in the West*, vol. 2: *Silences of the Middle Ages*, edited by Christiane Klapisch-Zuber. Cambridge, MA: Belknap Press of Harvard University Press.

Castara. 1640. *A Mistris*. London.

Cawelti, John G. 1965. *Apostles of the Self-Made Man*. Chicago and London: University of Chicago Press.

Chadwick, Bruce A., and Tim B. Heaton. 1992. *Statistical Handbook on the American Family*. Phoenix, AZ: Oryx Press.

Chafe, William H. 1972. *The American Woman: Her Changing Social, Economic, and Political Roles, 1920–1970*. New York: Oxford University Press.

———. 1977. *Women and Equality: Changing Patterns in American Culture*. New York: Oxford University Press.

———. 1995. *The Unfinished Journey: America since World War II*. New York and Oxford: Oxford University Press.

Cheek, Jonathan M., and Arnold H. Buss. 1981. "Shyness and Sociability." *Journal of Personality and Social Psychology* 41: 330–39.

Cheek, Jonathan M., and Arden K. Watson. 1989. "The Definition of Shyness: Psychological Imperialism or Construct Validity?" *Journal of Social Behavior and Personality* 4(1): 85–95.

"Circulation Leaders." 1993. *Folio: Special Sourcebook Issue*.

Cleland, J. 1607. *The Institution of a Young Nobleman*. London.

Cline, Sally, and Dale Spender. 1987. *Reflecting Men at Twice Their Natural Size*. New York: Henry Holt.

Cockburn, Cynthia. 1983. *Brothers: Male Dominance and Technological Change*. London: Pluto Press.

Cogan, Frances B. 1989. *All-American Girl: The Ideal of Real Womanhood in Mid-Nineteenth Century America*. Athens: University of Georgia Press.

Cohen, Sol. 1983. "The Mental Hygiene Movement, the Development of Personality and the School: The Medicalization of American Education." *History of Education Quarterly* 23(2): 123–49.

Combahee River Collective. 1979. "The Combahee River Collective Statement." Pp. 362–72 in *Capitalist Patriarchy and the Case for Socialist Feminism*, edited by Zillah R. Eisenstein. New York: Monthly Review Press.

Connell, R. W. 1987. *Gender and Power: Society, the Person, and Sexual Politics*. Stanford, CA: Stanford University Press.

———. 1995. *Masculinities*. Berkeley: University of California Press.

Coontz, Stephanie. 1988. *The Social Origins of Private Life: A History of American Families, 1600–1900*. London and New York: Verso.

Coser, Lewis A., Charles Kadushin, and Walter Powell. 1982. *Books: The Culture and Commerce of Publishing*. New York: Basic Books.

Cott, Nancy F. 1987. *The Grounding of Modern Feminism*. New Haven and London: Yale University Press.

———, ed. 1972. *Root of Bitterness: Documents of the Social History of American Women*. New York: E. P. Dutton.

Cottle, Michelle. 1999. "Selling Shyness." *New Republic*, August 2, 24–29.

Coulter, Jeff. 1989. "Cognitive 'Penetrability' and the Emotions." Pp. 33–50 in *The Sociology of Emotions: Original Essays and Research Papers*, edited by David D. Franks and E. Doyle McCarthy. Greenwich, CT: JAI Press.

Crichton, J. 1989. "Road to Recovery." *Publisher's Weekly*, November 3, 32–34.

Crozier, W. Ray. 1979. "Shyness as a Dimension of Personality." *British Journal of Social and Clinical Psychology* 18(1): 121–28.

———. 1986. "Individual Differences in Shyness." Pp. 133–45 in *Shyness: Perspectives on Research and Treatment*, edited by Warren H. Jones, Jonathan M. Cheek, and Stephen R. Briggs. New York: Plenum Press.

Curtin, Michael. 1985. "A Question of Manners: Status and Gender in Etiquette and Courtesy." *Journal of Modern History* 57: 395–423.

Cushman, Philip. 1995. *Constructing the Self, Constructing America: A Cultural History of Psychotherapy*. Reading, MA: Addison-Wesley.

Cutrona, Carolyn E. 1996. *Social Support in Couples: Marriage as a Resource in Times of Stress*. Thousand Oaks, CA: Sage.

Dabakis, Melissa. 1993. "Gendered Labor: Norman Rockwell's *Rosie the Riveter* and the Discourses of Wartime Womanhood." Pp. 182–204 in *Gender and American History since 1890*, edited by Barbara Melosh. London and New York: Routledge.

Daly, John A., and L. Stafford. 1984. "The Development of Communication Apprehension: A Retrospective Analysis and Contributing Correlates." Pp. 125–43 in *Avoiding Communication: Shyness, Reticence, and Communication Apprehension*, edited by John A. Daly and James C. McCroskey. Beverly Hills, CA: Sage.

Daly, Mary. 1978. *Gyn/Ecology*. Boston: Beacon.

Davidoff, Leonore, and Catherine Hall. 1987. *Family Fortunes: Men and Women of the English Middle Class, 1780–1850*. Chicago: University of Chicago Press.

Davis, Natalie Zemon. 1975. *Society and Culture in Early Modern France*. Stanford, CA: Stanford University Press.

Degler, Carl N. 1980. *At Odds: Women and the Family in America from the Revolution to the Present*. New York and Oxford: Oxford University Press.

Delaney, D. D. 2000. "Autumn of the Patriarch." *Port Folio Weekly*. http://www.portfolioweekly.com/htm./patriarch.html.

Della Casa, Giovanni. [1558] 1990. *Il Galateo*. Ottowa: Dovehouse Editions.

D'Emilio, John. 1983. *Sexual Politics, Sexual Communities: The Making of a Homosexual Minority in the United States, 1940–1970*. Chicago and London: University of Chicago Press.

D'Emilio, John, and Estelle B. Freedman. 1988. *Intimate Matters: A History of Sexuality in America*. New York: Harper and Row.

DeMott, Benjamin. 1990. *The Imperial Middle: Why Americans Can't Think Straight about Class*. New York: William Morrow.

Denard, Carolyn C. 1995. "Introduction." Pp. xv–xxxv in *Charlotte Hawkins Brown's "Mammy": An Appeal to the Heart of the South; The Correct Thing To Do—To Say—To Wear*. Reprint, edited by Henry Louis Gates, Jr., Jennifer Burton, and Carolyn C. Denard. New York: G. K. Hall.

Denzin, Norman. 1983. "A Note on Emotionality, Self, and Interaction." *American Journal of Sociology* 89: 402–9.

———. 1984. *On Understanding Emotion*. San Francisco: Jossey-Bass.

Dessauer, John P. 1989. *Book Publishing: A Basic Introduction*. New York: Continuum.

De Swaan, Abram. 1981. "The Politics of Agoraphobia." *Theory and Society* 10: 359–85.

DeVitis, Joseph L., and John Martin Rich. 1996. *The Success Ethic, Education, and the American Dream*. Albany: State University of New York Press.

Diamond, Sara. 1995. *Roads to Dominion: Right-Wing Movements and Political Power in the United States*. New York and London: Guilford Press.

Dindia, Kathryn, and Mike Allen. 1992. "Sex Differences in Self-Disclosure: A Meta-Analysis." *Psychological Bulletin* 112(1): 106–24.

Donnell, Susan M., and Jay Hall. 1980. "Male and Female Managers: A Significant Case of No Significant Difference." *Organizational Dynamics* 8: 60–77.

Doss, Erika. 1998. "Imaging the Panthers: Representing Black Power and Masculinity, 1960s–1990s." *Prospects: An Annual of American Cultural Studies* 23: 483–516.

Douglas, Ann. 1988. *The Feminization of American Culture*. New York: Anchor Press.

Douglas, Susan J. 1994. *Where the Girls Are: Growing Up Female with the Mass Media*. New York: Times Book.

Douvan, Elizabeth, and Joseph Adelson. 1966. *The Adolescent Experience*. New York: John Wiley and Sons.

Duby, Georges. 1983. *The Knight, the Lady, and the Priest: The Making of Modern Marriage in Medieval France*. New York: Pantheon Books.

———. 1992. "The Courtly Model." Pp. 250–66 in *A History of Women in the West*, vol. 2: *Silences of the Middle Ages*, edited by Christiane Klapisch-Zuber. Cambridge, MA: Belknap Press of Harvard University Press.

Dulong, Claude. 1993. "From Conversation to Creation." Pp. 395–418 in *A History of Women in the West*, vol. 3: *Renaissance and Enlightenment Paradoxes*, edited by Natalie Zemon Davis and Arlette Farge. Cambridge, MA: Belknap Press of Harvard University Press.

Duncombe, Jean, and Dennis Marsden. 1993. "Love and Intimacy: The Gender Division of Emotion and 'Emotion Work.'" *Sociology* 27: 221–41.

———. 1995. "'Workaholics' and 'Whingeing Women': Theorising Intimacy and Emotion Work—the Last Frontier of Gender Inequality?" *Sociological Review* 43: 150–69.

Eagly, Alice H., Mona G. Makhijani, and Bruce G. Klonsky. 1992. "Gender and the Evaluation of Leaders: A Meta-Analysis." *Psychological Bulletin* 111(1): 3–22.

Eastburg, Mark, and W. Brad Johnson. 1990. "Shyness and Perceptions of Parental Behavior." *Psychological Reports* 66(3): 915–21.

Echols, Alice. 1989. *Daring to Be Bad: Radical Feminism in America, 1967–1975*. Minneapolis: University of Minnesota Press.

Ehrenreich, Barbara. 1983. *The Hearts of Men: American Dreams and the Flight from Commitment.* Garden City, NY: Anchor Press/Doubleday.

Ekman, Paul. 1971. "Universals and Cultural Differences in Facial Expressions of Emotion." Pp. 207–83 in *Nebraska Symposium on Motivation,* edited by J. K. Cole. Lincoln: University of Nebraska Press.

Elias, Norbert. 1978. *The Civilizing Process: The Development of Manners. Changes in the Code of Conduct and Feeling in Early Modern Times.* New York: Urizen Books.

Encyclopedia of Contemporary American Culture. 2001. Edited by Gary W. McDonagh, Robert Gregg, and Cindy H. Wong. London and New York: Routledge.

England, Paula, and George Farkas. 1986. *Households, Employment, and Gender: A Social, Economic, and Demographic View.* New York: Aldine.

Espiritu, Yen Le. 1998. "All Men Are Not Created Equal: Asian Men in U.S. History." Pp. 243–52 in *Women, Culture and Society: A Reader,* edited by Barbara J. Balliet and Patricia McDaniel. Dubuque, IA: Kendall Hunt.

Estes, Steve. 2000. "'I *AM* A MAN!': Race, Masculinity, and the 1968 Memphis Sanitation Strike." *Labor History* 41(2): 153–70.

Faludi, Susan. 1991. *Backlash: The Undeclared War against American Women.* New York: Crown.

Farrell, Warren. 1974. *The Liberated Man.* New York: Bantam Books.

Fasteau, Marc Feigen. 1974. *The Male Machine.* New York: McGraw- Hill.

Ferguson, Ann. 1989. *Blood at the Root: Motherhood, Sexuality, and Male Dominance.* London: Pandora Press.

Fierman, Jacklyn. 1990. "Why Women Still Don't Hit the Top." *Fortune,* 30 July, 40–66.

Fish, Stanley. 1980. *Is There a Text in This Class? The Authority of Interpretive Communities.* Cambridge, MA: Harvard University Press.

Fiske, John. 1987. *Television Culture.* London and New York: Methuen.

Fletcher, Anthony. 1995. *Gender, Sex and Subordination in England, 1500–1800.* New Haven and London: Yale University Press.

Foster, George G. 1850. *New York by Gas-Light: With Here and There a Streak of Sunshine.* New York: Dewitt and Davenport.

Foucault, Michel. [1976] 1990. *The History of Sexuality,* vol. 1: *An Introduction.* New York: Random House.

Fox, Greer Litton. 1977. "'Nice Girl': Social Control of Women through a Value Construct." *Signs* 2(4): 805–17.

Frazier, E. Franklin. 1948. *The Negro Family in the United States.* 0Chicago and London: University of Chicago Press.

Fredrickson, George M. 1972. *The Black Image in the White Mind: The Debate on Afro-American Character and Destiny, 1817–1914.* New York: Harper and Row.

Fremouw, William J. 1984. "Cognitive-Behavioral Therapies for Modification of Communication Apprehension." Pp. 209–15 in *Avoiding Communication: Shyness, Reticence, and Communication Apprehension,* edited by John A. Daly and James C. McCroskey. Beverly Hills, CA: Sage.

Friedan, Betty. 1963. *The Feminine Mystique.* New York: Dell.

Friedrich, Gustav, and Blaine Goss. 1984. "Systematic Desensitization." Pp. 173–87 in *Avoiding Communication: Shyness, Reticence, and Communication Apprehension,* edited by John A. Daly and James C. McCroskey. Beverly Hills, CA: Sage.

Garner, Ana, Helen M. Sterk, and Shawn Adams. 1998. "Narrative Analysis of Sexual Etiquette in Teenage Magazines." *Journal of Communication* 48(4): 59–78.

Gates, Jr., Henry Louis. 1997. "The Naked Republic." *New Yorker,* August 25 and September 1, 123.

George, Margaret. 1973. "From 'Goodwife' to 'Mistress': The Transformation of the Female in Bourgeois Culture." *Science and Society* 37: 152–77.

Giddings, Paula. 1984. *When and Where I Enter: The Impact of Black Women on Race and Sex in America.* New York: William Morrow.

Giles of Rome. 1607. *De Regimine Principum Libri III.* Rome.

Gilkes, Cheryl Townsend. 1983. "From Slavery to Social Welfare: Racism and the Control of Black Women." Pp. 288–300 in *Class, Race and Sex: The Dynamics of Control,* edited by Amy Swerdlow and Hanna Lessinger. Boston: G. K. Hall.

Gilmartin, Brian G. 1985. "Some Family Antecedents of Severe Shyness." *Family Relations Journal of Applied Family and Child Studies* 34(3): 429–38.

Glass, Carol R., and Diane B. Arnkoff. 1989. "Behavioral Assessment of Social Anxiety and Social Phobia." *Clinical Psychology Review* 9(1): 75–90.

Glass, Carol R., and Cheryl A. Shea. 1986. "Cognitive Therapy for Shyness and Social Anxiety." Pp. 315–27 in *Shyness: Perspectives on Research and Treatment,* edited by Warren H. Jones, Jonathan M. Cheek, and Stephen R. Briggs. New York: Plenum Press.

Glenmullen, Joseph. 2000. *Prozac Backlash: Overcoming the Dangers of Prozac, Zoloft, Paxil, and Other Anti-Depressants with Safe, Effective Alternatives.* New York: Simon and Schuster.

Goeder, Robert, et al. 2000. "Association of Paroxetine with Suicide Attempt in Obsessive-Compulsive Disorder." *Pharmacopsychiatry* 33(3): 116–17.

Goldin, Claudia. 1990. *Understanding the Gender Gap: An Economic History of American Women.* New York and Oxford: Oxford University Press.

Gordon, Steven L. 1989. "Institutional and Impulsive Orientation in Selectively Appropriating Emotions to Self." Pp. 115–35 in *The Sociology of Emotions: Original Essays and Research Papers,* edited by David D. Franks and E. Doyle McCarthy. London: JAI Press.

Gorn, Elliott J. 1986. *The Manly Art: Bare-Knuckle Prize Fighting in America.* Ithaca and London: Cornell University Press.

Gould, Stephen Jay. 1981. *The Mismeasure of Man.* New York: W. W. Norton.

Graves, A. J. 1844. *Girlhood and Womanhood: Or, Sketches of My Schoolmates.* Boston.

Greenburg, David. 1988. *The Construction of Homosexuality.* Chicago and London: University of Chicago Press.

Gregory, J. 1774. *A Father's Legacy to His Daughters.* London.

Greist, J. H. 1995. "The Diagnosis of Social Phobia." *Journal of Clinical Psychiatry* 56(5): 5–12.

Grodin, Debra. 1991. "The Interpreting Audience: The Therapeutics of Self-Help Book Reading." *Critical Studies in Mass Communication* 8: 404–20.

Groopman, Jerome. 1999. "Pet Scan." *New Yorker,* May 10, 46–50.

Haag, Pamela S. 1992. "In Search of the 'Real Thing': Ideologies of Love, Modern Romance, and Women's Sexual Subjectivity in the United States, 1920–1940." *Journal of the History of Sexuality* 2(4): 547–77.

Hackett, Alice Payne, and James Henry Burke. 1977. *Eighty Years of Best Sellers, 1895–1975.* New York: R. R. Bowker.

Hall, Stuart. 1981. "Notes on Deconstructing 'the Popular.'" Pp. 227–40 in *People's History and Socialist Theory,* edited by Raphael Samuel. London: Kegan Paul.

Haller, John S., Jr. 1971. *Outcasts from Evolution: Scientific Attitudes of Racial Inferiority, 1859–1900.* Urbana: University of Illinois Press.

Hallissy, Margaret. 1993. *Clean Maids, True Wives, Steadfast Widows: Chaucer's Women and Medieval Codes of Conduct.* Westport, CT: Greenwood Press.

Hansen, Karen V. 1992. "'Our Eyes Behold Each Other': Masculinity and Intimate Friendship in Antebellum New England." Pp. 35–58 in *Men's Friendships,* edited by Peter M. Nardi. Newbury Park, CA: Sage.

Hart, James D. 1963. *The Popular Book: A History of America's Literary Taste.* Berkeley and Los Angeles: University of California Press.

Harvey, Brett. 1993. *The Fifties: A Women's Oral History.* New York: Harper-Collins.

Hays, R. B. 1985. "A Longitudinal Study of Friendship Development." *Journal of Personality and Social Psychology* 48: 909–24.

Heath, Shirley Brice. 1978. "Social History and Sociolinguistics." *American Sociologist* 13: 84–92.

Hemphill, C. Dallett. 1996. "Middle Class Rising in Revolutionary America." *Journal of Social History* 30(2): 317–44.

———. 1998. "Class, Gender, and the Regulation of Emotional Expression in Revolutionary-Era Conduct Literature." Pp. 33–51 in *An Emotional History of the United States,* edited by Peter N. Stearns and Jan Lewis. New York and London: New York University Press.

Henderson, Katherine Asher, and Barbara F. McManus. 1985. *Half Humankind: Contexts and Texts of the Controversy about Women in England, 1540–1640.* Urbana: University of Illinois Press.

Henley, Nancy M. 1979. "Assertiveness Training: Making the Political Personal." Society for the Study of Social Problems. Boston, August.

Herlihy, David. 1995. *Women, Family and Society in Medieval Europe: Historical Essays, 1978–1991.* Providence: Berghahn Books.

Herman, Didi. 1997. *The Antigay Agenda: Orthodox Vision and the Christian Right.* Chicago and London: University of Chicago Press.

Herman, Ellen. 1995. *The Romance of American Psychology: Political Culture in the Age of Experts.* Berkeley: University of California Press.

Hilkey, Judy. 1997. *Character Is Capital: Success Manuals and Manhood in Gilded Age America.* Chapel Hill and London: University of North Carolina Press.

Hochschild, Arlie Russell. 1979. "Emotion Work, Feeling Rules, and Social Structure." *American Journal of Sociology* 85: 551–75.

Hochschild, Arlie Russell. 1983. *The Managed Heart: Commercialization of Human Feeling.* Berkeley, Los Angeles, and London: University of California Press.

Hoge, Dean R. 1976. "Changes in College Students' Value Patterns in the 1950's, 1960's, and 1970's." *Sociology of Education* 49(2): 155–63.

Holsti, Ole R. 1969. *Content Analysis for the Social Sciences and Humanities.* Reading, MA: Addison-Wesley.

Hondagneu-Sotelo, Pierrette, and Michael A. Messner. 1994. "Gender Displays and Men's Power: The "New Man" and the Mexican Immigrant Man." Pp. 200–218 in *Theorizing Masculinities,* edited by Harry Brod and Michael Kaufman. Thousand Oaks, CA: Sage.

Horton, Carrell Peterson, and Jessie Carney Smith. 1993. *Statistical Record of Black America.* 2d ed. Detroit and London: Gale Research.

Ignatiev, Noel. 1995. *How the Irish Became White.* New York: Routledge.

Ingram, Martin. 1994. "'Scolding Women Cucked or Washed': A Crisis in Gender Relations in Early Modern England?" Pp. 48–80 in *Women, Crime, and the Courts in Early Modern England,* edited by Jenny Kermode and Garthine Walker. Chapel Hill and London: University of North Carolina Press.

Izard, Carroll E., and Marion C. Hyson. 1986. "Shyness as a Discrete Emotion." Pp. 147–60 in *Shyness: Perspectives on Research and Treatment,* edited by Warren H. Jones, Jonathan M. Cheek, and Stephen R. Briggs. New York: Plenum Press.

James, Nicky. 1989. "Emotional Labour: Skill and Work in the Social Regulation of Feelings." *Sociological Review* 37: 15–42.

Jardine, Lisa. 1983. *Still Harping on Daughters: Women and Drama in the Age of Shakespeare.* Sussex, UK: Harvester Press.

Jeffreys, Sheila. 1985. *The Spinster and Her Enemies: Feminism and Sexuality, 1880–1930.* London, Boston, and Henley: Pandora.

Jennings, Eugene Emerson. 1971. *Routes to the Executive Suite.* New York: McGraw-Hill.

Jewell, K. Sue. 1992. *From Mammy to Miss America and Beyond: Cultural Images and the Shaping of U.S. Social Policy.* London and New York: Routledge.

Jezer, Marty. 1982. *The Dark Ages: Life in the United States, 1945–1960.* Boston: South End Press.

Jones, Ann Rosalind. 1987. "Nets and Bridles: Early Modern Conduct Books and 16th Century Women's Lyrics." Pp. 39–72 in *The Ideology of Conduct: Essays on Literature and the History of Sexuality,* edited by Nancy Armstrong and Leonard Tennenhouse. New York: Methuen.

Jones, Jacqueline. 1985. *Labor of Love, Labor of Sorrow: Black Women, Work, and the Family from Slavery to the Present.* New York: Basic Books.

Jones, Kathleen W. 1999. *Taming the Troublesome Child: American Families, Child Guidance, and the Limits of Psychiatric Authority.* Cambridge, MA: Harvard University Press.

Jones, Landon Y. 1980. *Great Expectations: America and the Baby Boom Generation.* New York: Coward, McCann and Geoghegan.

Jones, Warren H., and Dan Russell. 1982. "The Social Reticence Scale: An Objective Instrument to Measure Shyness." *Journal of Personality Assessment* 46(6): 629–31.

Jongeward, Dorothy, and Dru Scott. 1977. *Affirmative Action for Women: A Practical Guide for Women and Management.* Reading, MA: Addison-Wesley.

Jourard, Sidney M. 1971. *Self-Disclosure: An Experimental Analysis of the Transparent Self.* New York: Wiley Interscience.

Kagan, Jerome. 1989. "The Concept of Behavioral Inhibition to the Unfamiliar." Pp. 1–23 in *Perspectives on Behavioral Inhibition*, edited by J. Steven Reznick. Chicago: University of Chicago Press.

Kagan, Jerome, J. Steven Reznick, and Nancy Snidman. 1988. "Biological Bases of Childhood Shyness." *Science* 240: 167–71.

Kamensky, Jane. 1997. *Governing the Tongue: The Politics of Speech in Early New England.* New York and Oxford: Oxford University Press.

———. 1998. "Talk Like a Man: Speech, Power, and Masculinity in Early New England." Pp. 19–50 in *A Shared Experience: Men, Women and the History of Gender*, edited by Laura McCall and Donald Yacovone. New York and London: New York University Press.

Karlsen, Carol F. 1987. *The Devil in the Shape of a Woman: Witchcraft in Colonial New England.* New York: W. W. Norton.

Kasson, John F. 1990. *Rudeness and Civility: Manners in Nineteenth-Century America.* New York: Hill and Wang.

Kelly, Lynne. 1982. "A Rose by Any Other Name Is Still a Rose: A Comparative Study of Reticence, Communication Apprehension, Unwillingness to Communicate, and Shyness." *Human Communication Research* 8(2): 99–113.

———. 1984. "Social Skills Training as a Mode of Treatment for Social Communication Problems." Pp. 189–207 in *Avoiding Communication: Shyness, Reticence, and Communication Apprehension*, edited by John A. Daly and James C. McCroskey. Beverly Hills, CA: Sage.

Kennedy, Sidney H., et al. 2000. "Antidepressant-Induced Sexual Dysfunction during Treatment with Moclobemide, Paroxetine, Sertraline, and Venlafaxine." *Journal of Clinical Psychiatry* 61(4): 276–81.

Kessler-Harris, Alice. 1983. *Out to Work: A History of Wage-Earning Women in the United States.* New York: Oxford University Press.

Kidd, Virginia. 1975. "Happily Ever After and Other Relationship Styles: Advice on Interpersonal Relations in Popular Magazines, 1971–1973." *Quarterly Journal of Speech* 61: 31–39.

Kimmel, Michael. 1994. "Masculinity as Homphobia: Fear, Shame, and Silence in the Construction of Gender Identity." Pp. 119–41 in *Theorizing Masculinities*, edited by Harry Brod and Michael Kaufman. Thousand Oaks, CA: Sage.

———. 1996. *Manhood in America: A Cultural History.* New York: Free Press.

Kinsey, Alfred. 1953. *Sexual Behavior in the Human Female.* Philadelphia: Saunders.

Kinsey, Alfred C., Wardell B. Pomeroy, and Clyde E. Martin. 1948. *Sexual Behavior in the Human Male.* Philadelphia: Saunders.

Klatch, Rebecca E. 1987. *Women of the New Right.* Philadelphia: Temple University Press.

Komarovsky, Mirra. 1946. "Cultural Contradictions and Sex Roles." *American Journal of Sociology* 3: 184–89.

Kramer, Peter D. 1993. *Listening to Prozac.* New York: Viking Press.

Langlieb, Dr. Kenneth R. 1995. Personal communication. Paramus, NJ, April 3.

Lasch, Christopher. 1978. *The Culture of Narcissism: American Life in an Age of Diminishing Expectations.* New York: W. W. Norton.

Laskaya, Anne. 1995. *Chaucer's Approach to Gender in the Canterbury Tales.* Cambridge, UK: D. S. Bower.

Lears, T. J. Jackson. 1985. "The Concept of Cultural Hegemony: Problems and Possibilities." *American Historical Review* 90: 567–93.

Leary, M. R., and R. M. Kowalski. 1993. "The Interaction Anxiousness Scale: Construct and Criterion-Related Validity." *Journal of Personality Assessment* 61(1): 136–46.

Leary, Mark R. 1983. "The Conceptual Distinctions Are Important: Another Look at Communication Apprehension and Related Constructs." *Human Communication Research* 10(2): 305–12.

———. 1986. "Affective and Behavioral Components of Shyness: Implications for Theory, Measurement, and Research." Pp. 27–38 in *Shyness: Perspectives on Research and Treatment,* edited by Warren H. Jones, Jonathan M. Cheek, and Stephen R. Briggs. New York: Plenum Press.

Leary, Mark R., and B. R. Schlenker. 1981. "The Social Psychology of Shyness: A Self-Presentational Model." Pp. 335–58 in *Impression Management Theory and Social Psychological Research,* edited by J. T. Tedeschi. New York: Academic Press.

Lee, Melvin, Philip G. Zimbardo, and Minerva Bertholf. 1977. "Shy Murderers." *Psychology Today,* November, 68–70.

Lehmann-Haupt, Helmut. 1951. *The Book in America: A History of the Making and Selling of Books in the United States.* New York: R. R. Bowker.

Leslie, Virginia Kent Anderson. 1988. "The Myth of the Southern Lady: Antebellum Proslavery Rhetoric and the Proper Place of Woman." Pp. 19–33 in *Southern Women,* edited by Caroline Matheny Dillman. New York: Hemisphere.

Library of Congress (lcweb@loc.gov). 1996. "Library of Congress Mission Statement." http://lcweb.loc.gov/ndl/mission.html.

——— (lcweb@loc.gov). 1998. "25 Most Frequently Asked Questions by Visitors of the Library of Congress." http://marvel.loc.gov/00/loc/facil/25.faqs.

Lichterman, Paul. 1992. "Self-Help Reading as a Thin Culture." *Media, Culture, and Society* 14: 421–47.

Link, Henry C., and Harry Arthur Hopf. 1946. *People and Books: A Study of Reading and Book-Buying Habits.* New York: Book Industry Committee.

Linstead, Stephen. 1995. "Averting the Gaze: Gender and Power on the Perfumed Picket Line." *Gender, Work and Organization* 2(4): 192–206.

Löfroth, Erik. 1983. *A World Made Safe: Values in American Best Sellers, 1895–1920.* Stockholm: Almqvist and Wiksell International.

Lougee, Carolyn C. 1976. *Le Paradis des Femmes: Women, Salons, and Social Stratification in Seventeenth-Century France.* Princeton, NJ: Princeton University Press.

Lutz, Catherine A. 1990. "Engendered Emotion: Gender, Power, and the Rhetoric of Emotional Control in American Discourse." Pp. 69–91 in *Language and the Politics of Emotion*, edited by Catherine A. Lutz and Lila Abu-Lughod. Cambridge, UK: Cambridge University Press.

Lynch, Edith M. 1973. *The Executive Suite, Feminine Style*. New York: Amacom.

Lynch, Owen M. 1990. "The Social Construction of Emotion in India." Pp. 3–34 in *Divine Passions: The Social Construction of Emotion in India*, edited by Owen M. Lynch. Berkeley: University of California Press.

Lynes, Russell. 1957. *The Domesticated Americans*. New York: Harper and Row.

Lystra, Karen. 1989. *Searching the Heart: Women, Men and Romantic Love in Nineteenth-Century America*. New York and Oxford: Oxford University Press.

Macfarlane, Alan. 1970. *Witchcraft in Tudor and Stuart England*. London: Routledge and Kegan Paul.

Macleod, David I. 1983. *Building Character in the American Boy: The Boy Scouts, YMCA, and Their Forerunners, 1870–1920*. Madison: University of Wisconsin Press.

Madhubuti, Haki R., ed. 1991. *Confusion by Any Other Name: Essays Exploring the Negative Impact of the Blackman's Guide to Understanding the Blackwoman*. 2d ed. Chicago: Third World Press.

Mansfield, P., and Jean Collard. 1988. *The Beginning of the Rest of Your Life?* London: Macmillan.

Mason, John E. 1935. *Gentlefolk in the Making: Studies in the History of English Courtesy Literature and Related Topics from 1531 to 1774*. Philadelphia: University of Pennsylvania Press.

May, Martha. 1982. "The Historical Problem of the Family Wage: The Ford Motor Company and the Five Dollar Day." Pp. 111–25 in *Families and Work*, edited by Naomi Gerstel and Harriet Engel Gross. Philadelphia: Temple University Press.

McCarthy, E. Doyle. 1989. "Emotions Are Social Things: An Essay in the Sociology of Emotions." Pp. 51–72 in *The Sociology of Emotions: Original Essays and Research Papers*, edited by David D. Franks and E. Doyle McCarthy. Greenwich, CT: JAI Press.

McCroskey, James C. 1984. "The Communication Apprehension Perspective." Pp. 13–38 in *Avoiding Communication: Shyness, Reticence, and Communication Apprehension*, edited by John A. Daly and James C. McCroskey. Beverly Hills, CA: Sage.

McCroskey, James C., and Michael J. Beatty. 1984. "Communication Apprehension and Accumulated Communication State Anxiety Experiences: A Research Note." *Communication Monographs* 51(1): 79–84.

McLoughlin, William G., Jr. 1955. *Billy Sunday Was His Real Name*. Chicago: University of Chicago Press.

McMillen, Neil R. 1989. *Dark Journey: Black Mississippians in the Age of Jim Crow*. Urbana and Chicago: University of Chicago Press.

McQuail, Denis. 1984. *Mass Communication Theory: An Introduction*. London: Sage.

Messner, Michael. 1997. *Politics of Masculinities: Men in Movements*. Thousand Oaks, CA: Sage.

Meyerowitz, Joanne. 1994. "Beyond the Feminine Mystique: A Reassessment of Postwar Mass Culture, 1946–1958." Pp. 229–62 in *Not June Cleaver: Women and Gender in Postwar America, 1945–1960*, edited by Joanne Meyerowitz. Philadelphia: Temple University Press.

Miller, Chris. 1998. "The Representation of the Black Male in Film." *Journal of African-American Men* 3(3): 19–30.

Mills, C. Wright. 1953. *White Collar: The American Middle Classes*. New York: Oxford University Press.

Mintz, Steven, and Susan Kellogg. 1988. *Domestic Revolutions: A Social History of American Family Life*. New York: Free Press.

Modell, John. 1989. *Into One's Own: From Youth to Adulthood in the United States, 1920–1975*. Berkeley, Los Angeles, and London: University of California Press.

Morton, Patricia. 1988. "'My Ol' Black Mammy' in American Historiography." Pp. 35–45 in *Southern Women*, edited by Caroline Matheny Dillman. New York: Hemisphere.

Moynihan, Daniel Patrick. 1967. "The Negro Family: The Case for National Action." Pp. 39–124 in *The Moynihan Report and the Politics of Controversy*, edited by Lee Rainwater and William L. Yancey. Cambridge, MA: MIT Press.

Mullings, Leith. 1996. *On Our Own Terms: Race, Class, and Gender in the Lives of African-American Women*. New York and London: Routledge.

Murray, Pauli. 1970. "The Liberation of Black Women." Pp. 87–102 in *Voices of the New Feminism*, edited by Mary Lou Thomspon. Boston: Beacon Press.

Nestle, Joan. 1981. "Butch-Fem Relationships: Sexual Courage in the 1950s." *Heresies* 12: 21–24.

Newton, Sarah E. 1994. *Learning to Behave: A Guide to American Conduct Books before 1900*. Westport, CT: Greenwood Press.

Noble, V. 1992. "A Helping Hand from the Guys." In *Women Respond to the Men's Movement*, edited by K. L. Hagan. San Francisco: HarperCollins.

Nolan, James L., Jr. 1996. "Contrasting Styles of Political Discourse in America's Past and Present Culture Wars." Pp. 135–88 in *The American Culture Wars*, edited by James L. Nolan, Jr. Charlottesville and London: University Press of Virginia.

Norton, Mary Beth. 1980. *Liberty's Daughters: The Revolutionary Experience of American Women, 1750–1800*. Boston and Toronto: Little, Brown.

O'Connor, Pat. 1998. "Women's Friendships in a Post-Modern World." Pp. 117–35 in *Placing Friendship in Context*, edited by Rebecca G. Adams and Graham Allan. Cambridge and New York: Cambridge University Press.

Oden, Mary E. 1993. "Sexual Behavior and Morality." Pp. 1961–80 in *Encyclopedia of American Social History*, Vol. 3, edited by Mary K. Cayton, Elliott J. Gorn, and Peter W. Williams. New York: Charles Scribner's Sons.

Oliker, Stacey J. 1989. *Best Friends and Marriage: Exchange among Women*. Berkeley: University of California Press.

Online Newshour. 1996. "Catalyst's Women in Corporate Leadership Study." http://www.pbs.org/newshour/forum/background/jan-jun96/catalyst.

Otto, Michael W., et al. 1992. "Alcohol Dependence in Panic Disorder Patients." *Journal of Psychiatric Research* 26(1): 29–38.

Packard, Vance. 1959. *The Status Seekers: An Exploration of Class Behavior in America and the Hidden Barriers That Affect You, Your Community, Your Future.* New York: D. McKay.

Page, Randy M. 1990. "Shyness and Sociability: A Dangerous Combination for Illicit Substance Abuse in Adolescent Males?" *Adolescence* 25(100): 803–6.

Penn, Donna. 1993. "The Meanings of Lesbianism in Postwar America." Pp. 106–24 in *Gender and American History since 1890*, edited by Barbara Melosh. New York and London: Routledge.

Peplau, Letitia A., and Steven L. Gordon. 1985. "Women and Men in Love: Gender Differences in Close Heterosexual Relationships." Pp. 257–91 in *Women, Gender, and Social Psychology*, edited by Virginia E. O'Leary, Rhoda Kesler Unger, and Barbara Strudler Wallston. Hillsdale, NJ: Erlbaum.

Perinbanayagam, R. S. 1989. "Signifying Emotions." Pp. 73–92 in *The Sociology of Emotions: Original Essays and Research Papers*, edited by David D. Franks and E. Doyle McCarthy. Greenwich, CT: JAI Press.

Pfaffenberger, Bryan. 1988. *Microcomputer Applications in Qualitative Research.* Newbury Park, CA: Sage.

Philbrook, Mary. 1939. "Woman's Suffrage in New Jersey prior to 1807." *New Jersey Historical Society Proceedings* 97: 96.

Phillips, Gerald M. 1984. "Reticence: A Perspective on Social Withdrawal." Pp. 51–66 in *Avoiding Communication: Shyness, Reticence, and Communication Apprehension*, edited by John A. Daly and James C. McCroskey. Beverly Hills, CA: Sage.

———. 1986. "Rhetoritherapy: The Principles of Rhetoric in Training Shy People in Speech Effectiveness." Pp. 357–74 in *Shyness: Perspectives on Research and Treatment*, edited by Warren H. Jones, Jonathan M. Cheek, and Stephen R. Briggs. New York: Plenum Press.

———. 1991. *Communication Incompetencies: A Theory of Training Oral Performance Behavior.* Carbondale and Edwardsville: Southern Illinois University Press.

Phillips, Gerald M., and Karen A. Sokoloff. 1979. "An End to Anxiety: Treating Speech Problems with Rhetoritherapy." *Journal of Communication Disorders* 12(3): 385–97.

Pilkonis, Paul. 1977. "The Behavioral Consequences of Shyness." *Journal of Personality* 45: 596–611.

Pilkonis, Paul A. 1986. "Short-Term Group Psychotherapy for Shyness." Pp. 375–85 in *Shyness: Perspectives on Research and Treatment*, edited by Warren H. Jones, Jonathan M. Cheek, and Stephen R. Briggs. New York: Plenum Press.

Pleck, Elizabeth H., and Joseph H. Pleck. 1980. "Introduction." Pp. 1–49 in *The American Man*, edited by Elizabeth H. Pleck and Joseph H. Pleck. Englewood Cliffs, NJ: Prentice Hall.

Pleck, Joseph H. and Jack Sawyer, eds. 1974. *Men and Masculinity.* Englewood Cliffs, NJ: Prentice Hall.

Plomin, Robert, and Clare Stocker. 1989. "Behavioral Genetics and Emotionality." In *Perspectives on Behavioral Inhibition,* edited by J. Steven Reznick. Chicago: University of Chicago Press.

Powell, Barbara. 1979. *Overcoming Shyness: Practical Scripts for Everyday Encounters.* New York: McGraw-Hill.

Press, Andrea L. 1991. *Women Watching Television: Gender, Class, and Generation in the American Television Experience.* Philadelphia: University of Pennsylvania Press.

Publisher's Weekly. 1976. *The Business of Publishing: A Publisher's Weekly Anthology.* New York: Bowker.

Puffer, J. Adams. 1912. *A Boy and His Gang.* Boston: Houghton Mifflin.

Pugh, David G. 1983. *Sons of Liberty: The Masculine Mind in Nineteenth-Century America.* Westport, CT: Greenwood Press.

Putney, Clifford. 2001. *Muscular Christianity: Manhood and Sports in Protestant America, 1880–1920.* Cambridge, MA, and London: Harvard University Press.

Quinlan, Maruice J. 1941. *Victorian Prelude: A History of English Manners, 1700–1830.* New York: Columbia University Press.

Raghunathan, Anuradha. 1999. "A Bold Rush to Sell Drugs to the Shy." *New York Times,* May 18, C1.

Research and Forecasts, Inc. 1984. *1983 Consumer Research Study on Reading and Book Purchasing.* New York: Book Industry Study Group.

Reskin, Barbara F., and Polly A. Phipps. 1988. "Women in Male-Dominated Professional and Managerial Occupations." Pp. 190–205 in *Women Working: Theories and Facts in Perspective,* edited by Ann Helton Stromberg and Shirley Harkess. Mountain View, CA: Mayfield.

Reskin, Barbara F., and Patricia A. Roos. 1990. *Job Queues, Gender Queues: Explaining Women's Inroads into Male Occupations.* Philadelphia: Temple University Press.

Reskin, Barbara, and Catherine E. Ross. 1995. "Jobs, Authority, and Earnings among Managers: The Continuing Significance of Sex." Pp. 127–51 in *Gender Inequality at Work,* edited by Jerry A. Jacobs. Thousand Oaks, CA: Sage.

Rich, Adrienne. 1977. *Of Woman Born.* New York: Bantam Books.

———. 1980. "Compulsory Heterosexuality and Lesbian Existence." *Signs: Journal of Women in Culture and Society* 5(4): 631–60.

Richards, Lyn, and Tom Richards. 1991. "The Transformation of Qualitative Method: Computational Paradigms and Research Processes." Pp. 38–53 in *Using Computers in Qualitative Research,* edited by Nigel G. Fielding and Raymond M. Lee. London: Sage.

Ridgeway, Cecilia L. 1997. "Interaction and the Conservation of Gender Inequality: Considering Employment." *American Sociological Review* 62(2): 218–35.

Riesman, David. 1950. *The Lonely Crowd: A Study of the Changing American Character.* New Haven, CT: Yale University Press.

Robnett, Belinda. 1997. *How Long? How Long? African-American Women in the Struggle for Civil Rights.* New York and Oxford: Oxford University Press.

Roediger, David. 1991. *The Wages of Whiteness: Race and the Making of the American Working Class.* London and New York: Verso.

Roman, Leslie G., and Linda K. Christian-Smith. 1988. "Introduction." Pp. 1–34 in *Becoming Feminine: The Politics of Popular Culture,* edited by Leslie G. Roman, Linda K. Christian-Smith, and Elizabeth Ellsworth. London, New York, and Philadelphia: Falmer Press.

Roos, Patricia, and Patricia McDaniel. 1996. "Are Occupations Gendered? Evidence from Census Microdata, 1970–1990." American Sociological Association Meetings, New York, August.

Rothman, Ellen K. 1984. *Hands and Hearts: A History of Courtship in America.* New York: Basic Books.

Rotundo, E. Anthony. 1983. "Body and Soul: Changing Ideals of American Middle-Class Manhood, 1770–1920." *Journal of Social History* 16: 23–38.

———. 1989. "Romantic Friendship: Male Intimacy and Middle-Class Youth in the Northern United States, 1800–1900." *Journal of Social History* 23: 1–25.

———. 1993. *American Manhood: Transformations in Masculinity from the Revolution to the Modern Era.* New York: Basic Books.

Rubin, Lillian. 1976. *Worlds of Pain: Life in the Working-Class Family.* New York: Basic Books.

Ryan, Mary P. 1975. *Womanhood in America: From Colonial Times to the Present.* New York: New Viewpoints.

Sacks, Karen Brodkin. 1994. "How the Jews Became White." Pp. 78–102 in *Race,* edited by Steven Gregory and Roger Sanjek. New Brunswick, NJ: Rutgers University Press.

Saint-Gabriel, le sieur de. 1655. *Merite des dames.* Paris.

Sattel, Jack. 1983. "Men, Inexpressiveness, and Power." Pp. 118–24 in *Language, Gender, and Society,* edited by Barrie Thorne, Chris Kramare, and Nancy Henley. Rowley, MA: Newbury House.

Scaglione, Aldo. 1991. *Knights at Court: Courtliness, Chivalry, and Courtesy from Ottonian Germany to the Italian Renaissance.* Berkeley: University of California Press.

Schein, Sylvia. 1994. "Used and Abused: Gossip in Medieval Society." Pp. 139–53 in *Good Gossip,* edited by Robert F. Goodman and Aaron Ben-Ze'ev. Lawrence: University Press of Kansas.

Schneier, Franklin, and Lawrence Welkowitz. 1996. *The Hidden Face of Shyness: Understanding and Overcoming Social Anxiety.* New York: Avon Books.

Schneier, F. R., J. Johnson, C. D. Hornig, M. R. Liebowitz, and M. M. Weissman. 1992. "Social Phobia: Comorbidity and Morbidity in an Epidemiologic Sample." *Archives of General Psychiatry* 49(4) 282–88.

Schneir, Miriam. 1994. *Feminism in Our Time: The Essential Writings, World War II to the Present.* New York: Vintage.

Schulman, Bruce J. 2001. *The Seventies: The Great Shift in American Culture, Society, and Politics.* New York: Free Press.

Schur, Edwin. 1976. *The Awareness Trap: Self-Absorption Instead of Social Change.* New York: New York Times Book Company.

Schwel, Peter. 1984. *Turning the Pages: An Insider's Story of Simon and Schuster, 1924–1984*. New York: Macmillan.

Scott, Anne Firor. 1970. *The Southern Lady: From Pedestal to Politics, 1830–1930*. Chicago and London: University of Chicago Press.

Segal, Shirley A., and Charles R. Figley. 1985. "Bulimia: Estimate of Incidence and Relationship to Shyness." *Journal of College Student Personnel* 26(3): 240–44.

Seiber, Kimberly O., and Lawrence S. Meyers. 1992. "Validation of the MMPI-2 Social Introversion Subscales." *Psychological Assessment* 4(2): 185–89.

Seidman, Steven. 1991. *Romantic Longings: Love in America, 1830–1980*. New York and London: Routledge.

Seifert, Catherine Mary. 1984. "Reactions to Leaders: Effects of Sex of Leader, Sex of Subordinate, Method of Leader Selection and Task Outcome." Ph.D. diss. Northern Illinois University.

Sennett, Richard. 1974. *The Fall of Public Man*. New York and London: W. W. Norton.

Shapiro, Judith. 1982. "'Women's Studies': A Note on the Perils of Markedness." *Signs* 7: 717–21.

Shott, Susan. 1979. "Emotions and Social Life: A Social Interactionist Perspective." *American Journal of Sociology* 84: 1317–34.

Simmons, Christina. 1989. "Modern Sexuality and the Myth of Victorian Repression." Pp. 157–77 in *Passion and Power: Sexuality and History*, edited by Kathy Peiss and Christina Simmons. Philadelphia: Temple University Press.

Simon, Gary. 1999. *How I Overcame Shyness: 100 Celebrities Share Their Secrets*. New York: Simon and Schuster.

Simonds, Wendy. 1992. *Women and Self-Help Culture: Reading between the Lines*. New Brunswick, NJ: Rutgers University Press.

Smith, Jessie Carney, and Carrell Peterson Horton. 1995. *Historical Statistics of Black America*. New York: Gale Research.

Smith, Sandra N., and Earle H. West. 1982. "Charlotte Hawkins Brown." *Journal of Negro Education* 51(3): 191–206.

Sommers, Shula. 1988. "Understanding Emotions: Some Interdisciplinary Considerations." Pp. 23–38 in *Emotion and Social Change: Toward a New Psychohistory*, edited by Carol Z. Stearns and Peter N. Stearns. New York and London: Holmes and Meier.

Soyinka, Wole. 1997. "How the World Sees Us. Interview with Wole Soyinka." *New York Times Magazine*, June 8, 49.

Spacks, Patricia Meyer. 1985. *Gossip*. Chicago and London: University of Chicago Press.

Spruill, Julia Cherry. 1938. *Women's Life and Work in the Southern Colonies*. Chapel Hill: University of North Carolina Press.

Stansell, Christine. 1982. *City of Women: Sex and Class in New York, 1789–1860*. Urbana and Chicago: University of Illinois Press.

Starker, Steven. 1989. *Oracle at the Supermarket: The American Preoccupation with Self-Help Books*. New Brunswick, NJ: Transaction.

Stearns, Carol Zisowitz, and Peter N. Stearns. 1986. *Anger: The Struggle for Emo-*

tional Control in America's History. Chicago and London: University of Chicago Press.

———. 1988. "Introduction." Pp. 1–21 in *Emotion and Social Change: Toward a New Psychohistory,* edited by Carol Z. Stearns and Peter N. Stearns. New York and London: Holmes and Meier.

Stearns, Peter N. 1989. *Jealousy: The Evolution of an Emotion in American History.* New York and London: New York University Press.

———. 1993. "Girls, Boys, and Emotions: Redefinitions and Historical Change." *Journal of American History* 80: 36–74.

———. 1994. *American Cool: Constructing a Twentieth-Century Emotional Style.* New York and London: New York University Press.

Stearns, Peter N., and Carol Z. Stearns. 1985. "Emotionology: Clarifying the History of Emotions and Emotional Standards." *American Historical Review* 90(4): 813–36.

Stein, Murry B., and John R. Walker. 2002. *Triumph over Shyness: Conquering Shyness and Social Anxiety.* New York and London: McGraw-Hill.

Stevens, Kimberly. 1998. "Celestial Harmony." *New York Times,* 2 August, 3.

Suleiman, Susan R., and Inge Crosman, eds. 1980. *The Reader in the Text: Essays on Audience Interpretation.* Princeton, NJ: Princeton University Press.

Susman, Warren I. 1984. *Culture as History: The Transformation of American Society in the Twentieth Century.* New York: Pantheon Books.

Swidler, Ann. 1986. "Culture in Action: Symbols and Strategies." *American Sociological Review* 51: 273–86.

Takaki, Ronald. 1993. *A Different Mirror: A History of Multicultural America.* Boston: Little, Brown.

Taylor, Gordon Rattray. 1958. *The Angel-Makers: A Study in the Psychological Origins of Historical Change, 1750–1850.* London, Melbourne, and Toronto: Heinemann.

Tebbel, John. 1975. *A History of Book Publishing in the United States,* vol. 2: *The Expansion of an Industry, 1865–1919.* New York and London: R. R. Bowker.

Tebbutt, Melanie. 1995. *Women's Talk? A Social History of 'Gossip' in Working-Class Neighbourhoods, 1880–1960.* Aldershot, UK: Scholar Press.

Therborn, Goran. 1980. *The Ideology of Power and the Power of Ideology.* London: Verso.

Thomas, David. 1995. "The American Battle of the Decades: The 1960s versus the 1980s." *Contemporary Review* 266(1548): 10–15.

Thomas, Keith. 1971. *Religion and the Decline of Magic.* New York: Charles Scribner's Sons.

Thompson, E. P. 1971. "The Moral Economy of the English Crowd in the Eighteenth Century." *Past and Present* 50: 81–120.

Thompson, John. 1990. *Ideology and Modern Culture: Critical Social Theory in the Era of Mass Communication.* Stanford, CA: Stanford University Press.

Thomson, Irene Taviss. 1992. "Individualism and Conformity in the 1950s versus the 1980s." *Sociological Forum* 7(3): 497–516.

Tompkins, Jane P., ed. 1980. *Reader Response Criticism: From Formalism to Post-Structuralism.* Baltimore and London: Johns Hopkins University Press.

Trenque, T., D. Piednoir, C. Frances, H. Millart, and M. L. Germain. 2002. "Reports of Withdrawal Syndrome with the Use of SSRIs: A Case/Non-Case Study in the French Pharmacovigilance Database." *Pharmacoepidemiology and Drug Safety* 11(4): 281–83.

Trower, M., B. M. Bryant, and P. Shaw. 1978. "The Treatment of Social Failure: A Comparison of Anxiety-Reduction and Skills-Acquisition Procedures on Two Social Problems." *Behavior Modification* 2: 41–60.

Turner, Samuel M., Deborah C. Beidel, and Ruth M. Townsley. 1990. "Social Phobia: Relationship to Shyness." *Behaviour Research and Therapy* 28(6): 497–505.

Twentyman, C. T., and R. M. McFall. 1975. "Behavioral Training of Social Skills in Shy Males." *Journal of Consulting and Clinical Psychology* 43: 384–95.

Ulrich, Laurel Thatcher. 1979. "Vertuous Women Found: New England Ministerial Literature, 1668–1735." Pp. 58–80 in *Heritage of Her Own: Toward a New Social History of American Women*, edited by Nancy F. Cott and Elizabeth H. Pleck. New York: Simon and Schuster.

Unwin, Stanley. 1947. *The Truth about Publishing.* London: George Allen and Unwin.

U.S. Bureau of the Census. 1953. *U.S. Census of Population, 1950: vol. 2: Characteristics of the Population*, Part 1, *U.S. Summary.* Washington, DC: U.S. Government Printing Office.

———. 1963. *U.S. Census of Population, 1960. Detailed Characteristics, U.S. Summary. Final Report PC(1)-1D.* Washington, DC: U.S. Government Printing Office.

Valian, Virginia. 1998. *Why So Slow? The Advancement of Women.* Cambridge, MA: MIT Press.

Veroff, Joseph, Elizabeth Douvan, and Richard A. Kulka. 1981a. *The Inner American: A Self-Portrait from 1957 to 1976.* New York: Basic Books.

———. 1981b. *Mental Health in America: Patterns of Help Seeking from 1957 to 1976.* New York: Basic Books.

Walker, Karen. 1994. "Men, Women and Friendship: What They Say, What They Do." *Gender and Society* 8(2): 246–65.

Waller, Willard. 1937. "The Rating and Dating Complex." *American Sociological Review* 2: 727–34.

Wallin, Paul. 1950. "Cultural Contradictions and Sex Roles: A Repeat Study." *American Sociological Review* 15(2): 288–83.

Wassmer, Arthur C. [1978] 1990. *Making Contact: A Guide to Overcoming Shyness.* New York: Henry Holt.

Weber, Eugen. 1995. *The Western Tradition*, vol. 2: *From the Renaissance to the Present.* 5th ed. Lexington, MA: D. C. Heath.

Weber, Robert Philip. 1990. *Basic Content Analysis.* Newbury Park, CA: Sage.

Welter, Barbara. 1966. "The Cult of True Womanhood: 1820–1860." *American Quarterly* 18: 151–74.

Wender, Paul, and Donald Klein. 1981. *Mind, Mood and Medicine.* New York: Farrar, Straus, and Giroux.

West, Candace, and Don H. Zimmerman. 1987. "Doing Gender." *Gender and Society* 1: 125–51.

White, Deborah Gray. 1985. *Ar'n't I a Woman? Female Slaves in the Plantation South.* New York and London: W. W. Norton.

White, Kevin. 1993. *The First Sexual Revolution: The Emergence of Male Heterosexuality in Modern America.* New York and London: New York University Press.

White, William Alanson. 1920. "Childhood: The Golden Period for Mental Hygiene." *Mental Hygiene* 4: 266–67.

Whyte, William H. 1957. *The Organization Man.* Garden City, NY: Doubleday.

Wickman, E. K. 1928. *Children's Behavior and Teacher's Attitudes.* New York: Commonwealth Fund.

Wilkinson, Rupert. 1986. *American Tough: The Tough-Guy Tradition and American Character.* New York: Harper and Row.

Williams, Raymond. 1977. *Marxism and Literature.* Oxford: Oxford University Press.

———. 1982. *Problems in Materialism and Culture.* London: Verso.

Williamson, Joel. 1986. *A Rage for Order: Black/White Relations in the American South since Emancipation.* New York and Oxford: Oxford University Press.

Winkler, Allan. 1993. "Modern America: The 1960s, 1970s, and 1980s." Pp. 219–34 in *Encyclopedia of American Social History,* edited by Mary K. Cayton, Elliott J. Gorn, and Peter W. Williams. New York: Scribner.

Wood, Leonard. 1988. "Self-Help Buying Trends." *Publisher's Weekly,* 14 October, 33.

Woodard, J. David. 1996. "Same Sex Politics: The Legal Struggle over Homosexuality." Pp. 133–52 in *The American Culture Wars: Current Contests and Future Prospects,* edited by James L. Nolan, Jr. Charlottesville, VA, and London: University Press of Virginia.

Wright, Louis B. 1935. *Middle-Class Culture in Elizabethan England.* Chapel Hill: University of North Carolina Press.

Wright, Paul H. 1982. "Men's Friendships, Women's Friendships, and the Alleged Inferiority of the Latter." *Sex Roles* 8(1): 1–20.

Wyatt-Brown, Bertram. 1975. "The Abolitionist Controversy: Men of Blood, Men of God." Pp. 215–33 in *Men, Women, and Issues in American History,* vol. 1, edited by Howard H. Quint and Milton Cantor. Homewood, IL: Dorsey Press.

Wylie, Philip. 1955. *Generation of Vipers.* New York: Rinehart.

Yankelovich, Skelly, and White, Inc. 1978. *Consumer Research Study on Reading and Book Purchasing.* New York: Book Industry Study Group.

Zimbardo, Philip G. 1986. "The Stanford Shyness Project." Pp. 17–25 in *Shyness: Perspectives on Research and Treatment,* edited by Warren H. Jones, Jonathan M. Cheek, and Stephen R. Briggs. New York: Plenum Press.

———. [1977] 1995. *Shyness: What It Is, What to Do about It.* Reading, MA: Addison-Wesley.

Zourkova, A., E. Hadasova, and M. Robes. 2000. "Sexual Functions in Treatment with Paroxetine." *Homeostasis in Health and Disease* 40(6): 249–51.

Index

About the Author

Patricia A. McDaniel is a postdoctoral fellow at the University of California, San Francisco.